Has AMERICAN CHRISTIANITY FAILED?

Bryan Wolfmueller

CONCORDIA PUBLISHING HOUSE · SAINT LOUIS

Published by Concordia Publishing House
3558 S. Jefferson Ave., St. Louis, MO 63118–3968
1-800-325-3040 • cph.org

Manufactured in the United States of America

Library of Congress Cataloging-in-Publication Data

Names: Wolfmueller, Bryan, author.
 Title: Has American Christianity failed? / Bryan Wolfmueller.
 Description: St. Louis : Concordia Publishing House, 2016. | Includes bibliographical references and index.

 Identifiers: LCCN 2016008215 (print) | LCCN 2016009123 (ebook) | ISBN 9780758649416 (alk. paper) | ISBN 9780758649423 ()
Subjects: LCSH: Lutheran Church—Doctrines. | Evangelicalism—United States.
Classification: LCC BX8065.3 .W65 2016 (print) | LCC BX8065.3 (ebook) | DDC 230/.41--dc23
 LC record available at http://lccn.loc.gov/2016008215

7 8 9 10 11 12 13 14 15 16 30 29 28 27 26 25 24 23 22 21

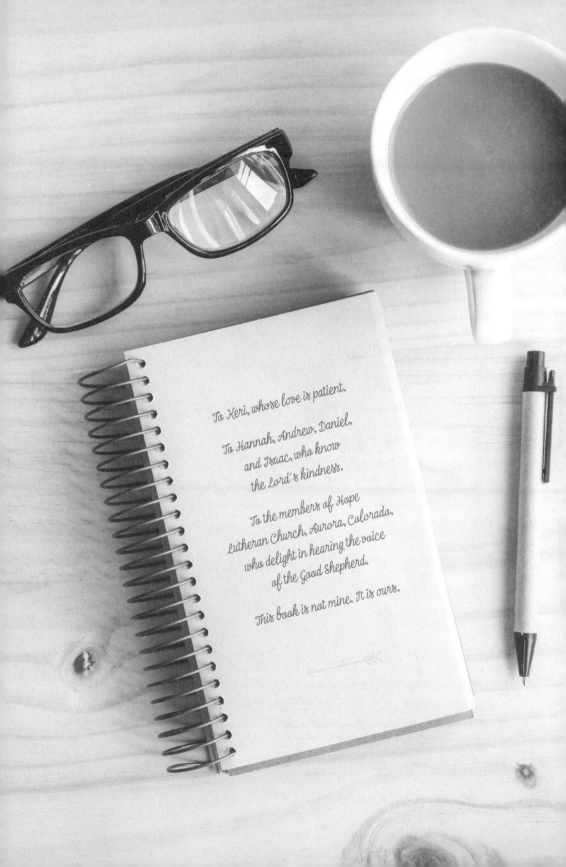

To Keri, whose love is patient.

To Hannah, Andrew, Daniel,
and Isaac, who know
the Lord's kindness.

To the members of Hope
Lutheran Church, Aurora, Colorado,
who delight in hearing the voice
of the Good Shepherd.

This book is not mine. It is ours.

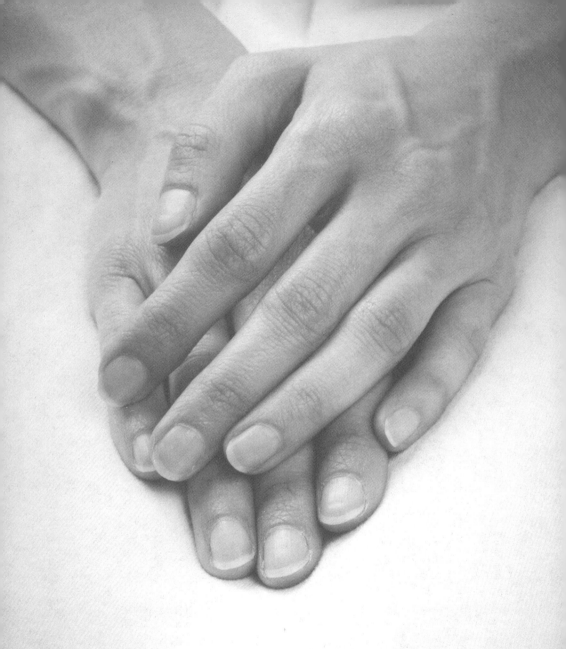

[Jesus said,] "Come to Me, all who labor and are heavy laden, and I will give you rest. Take My yoke upon you, and learn from Me, for I am gentle and lowly in heart, and you will find rest for your souls. For My yoke is easy, and My burden is light."

—Matthew 11:28–30

TABLE OF CONTENTS

ABBREVIATIONS

AC   Augsburg Confession

Ap   Apology of the Augsburg Confession

Ep   Epitome of the Formula of Concord

FC   Formula of Concord

LC   Large Catechism

LW   Luther's Works, American Edition

NKJV New King James Version

SA   Smalcald Articles

SC   Small Catechism

SD   Solid Declaration of the Formula of Concord

Tr   Treatise on the Power and Primacy of the Pope

WA   Weimar Edition of Luther's Works

NOSE-BLIND

When you are surrounded by a smell, you eventually go "nose-blind." You stop smelling what those outside your environment can smell. Your nose starts to ignore those common everyday smells. Nose-blindness is the reason you can't smell your house or yourself; it is the reason the pine-scented candle seems to lose strength as it gets closer to Christmas. Your brain has perceived the scent to be nonthreatening, which means there's little need to pay close attention to it. Our noses adapt to the familiar smells. Over time, we become less sensitive to the odor, and before long, we smell nothing.

The same phenomenon happens with our hearing. People who live in the city stop hearing the sounds of the street, at least until they are camping in the woods, and then they can't go to sleep because "it's too quiet." People who live by trains are so used to the sound that they rarely notice them passing by.

In a similar way, Christians in America have gone theologically nose-blind. There are theological thoughts and ideas that are always around us—so much so that we stop noticing them. We don't smell them. We don't hear them. They sink into the background and become an unnoticed part of the day-to-day environment we live in. But even when these theological ideas are unnoticed, they are still at work shaping the way we read and understand the Bible, shaping the way we pray and worship, informing our understanding of God and the world and our place in it.

AMERICAN CHRISTIANITY HAS A SMELL

American Christianity has a distinctive way of approaching the Scriptures, of thinking about our Christian life, of hearing the words of Jesus.

There are distinct ways of worshiping, praying, and talking about God. We are surrounded with American Christianity's unique theology, and without even noticing it, we begin to absorb this theology. We are theologically nose-blind. American Christianity teaches the centrality of the individual, my will, my experiences, my decision, my heart, my work and dedication—to the detriment of Christ and His saving and comforting work. American Christianity most often preaches the Christian instead of the Christ, and our senses are so dulled that we don't even notice He's missing.

We are thinking and praying and believing with a number of unexamined theological assumptions, and many of these assumptions, I'm convinced, are wrong. We don't know any different. We don't know there is an alternative way to read the Scriptures, an alternative that trusts the Bible is not only true, but it is the Word of God; an alternative that reads the Bible with comforting clarity.

COMBATING THEOLOGICAL NOSE-BLINDNESS

American Christianity has many strengths. It is earnest. It often takes the Bible seriously. It waits eagerly for the Lord Jesus to return. It strives to make the world a better place. But in the end, American Christianity and its teaching so often falls short of the Scriptures. It dilutes the Lord's Commandments and confuses the Lord's promises, resulting in churches full of confusion and Christians without the full comfort that Jesus intends for His people. In high school and college, I drank deeply from the well of American Christianity and spent seven years under its teaching. I lived its theology. There were times of great joy, but there were times of great sorrow, even despair. Altogether, it was a time of trouble and a teaching of burden. The teaching focused on my Christian life instead of on Christ, on my resolve instead of on God's mercy, on my decision instead of on the death of Jesus.

These years were spent in a theological wilderness. The life and joy of the Gospel dried up and was replaced with my efforts and experiences. The same teaching came from every direction: books, radio, journals, music, friends, small groups, all reinforcing the assumption that the Bible was, chiefly, about me. American Christianity is an echo chamber. The clamor destroys the ability to hear something else. This is especially dangerous when that something else is the Gospel.

Identifying American Christianity

American Christianity does not refer to a specific denomination or church body, nor does it refer to a specific person or teaching. This category is broader than Southern Baptist, this-or-that mainline denomination, or even American Evangelicalism. With "American Christianity," I intend to identify a few of the broad theological trends that reach into the American Church across denominations and, in one way or another, draw her attention away from Jesus and His words of comfort and life.

> "But when the fullness of time had come, God sent forth His Son, born of woman, born under the law, to redeem those who were under the law, so that we might receive adoption as sons."
>
> (Galatians 4:4–5)

American Christianity is a collection of theological trends that, while they define certain church bodies, touch all of them. The four characteristics of American Christianity are revivalism, pietism, mysticism, and enthusiasm.

Revivalism	teaches that the Christian life begins with a personal decision to accept Christ.
Pietism	teaches that the Christian life is chiefly marked by a growth in good works.
Mysticism	teaches that we can have direct, unmediated access to God.
Enthusiasm	teaches that the spiritual life happens inside of us.

Some of these trends exercise more influence in different places. Some are more obvious than others. But taken together, these characteristics describe the theological landscape of American Christianity. They shape the hearts and minds of America's Christians.

Revivalism, pietism, mysticism, and enthusiasm all, in their own way, assault the comfort of the Gospel and steal away the Christian's confidence in Christ's promise of mercy and kindness. Jesus wills that His Church would deliver the true comfort of the Gospel to sinners. But these four characteristics take the focus off of Christ and put it on the Christian.

Jesus says, "Come to Me, all who labor and are heavy laden, and I will give you rest. Take My yoke upon you, and learn from Me, for I am gentle and lowly in heart, and you will find rest for your souls. For My yoke is easy, and My burden is light" (Matthew 11:28–30). American Christianity fails because its yoke is wearisome. Its burden is heavy. Having taken its eyes off of Jesus as the Author and Perfecter of faith, American Christianity replaces the work of the Holy Spirit with the choice of the sinner. It replaces the comfort of the Gospel with the doubt of our resolve. It replaces the certainty of God's promise with the shakiness of our feelings. It puts burdens and doubts where the Lord would give us freedom and faith.

The alternative that Jesus has for us is light and easy. It is the yoke of the forgiveness of sins. It is the burden of His mercy and kindness. It is the comfort of His smile and the joy of His promises. It is His voice, full of grace and truth, calling us through the Scriptures. When we listen for that voice in the Scriptures, we hear it, and we rejoice.

This book intends to rouse us from our theological nose-blindness, to awaken our theological awareness. We sound the alarm against the false teaching and dangerous practices of American Christianity. We recognize the noxious stench of our theological assumptions, and we offer a beautiful alternative. The smelling salt of God's Law snaps us out of our self-satisfied complacency and pride. The sweet savor of the Gospel hands us over to the comfort, joy, peace, confidence, and sure hope of Christ. This is the "aroma of Christ" who is our life and salvation (2 Corinthians 2:15).

CHAPTER ONE

EXAMINING THE CHARACTERISTICS OF AMERICAN CHRISTIANITY

Revivalism, pietism, mysticism, and enthusiasm are the four rivers that water the errors of American Christianity. We will take a tour of each of these ideas, considering them in turn. Once you know them by name, you will see them everywhere—influencing churches, teachers, even your own thinking.

It Starts with Me: Revivalism

A typical service in a typical American Christian church is programmed to build to a climax. There are a few carefully selected songs, a performance or two, announcements, a sermon or Bible teaching, all with the purpose of driving the participants to the "time of decision," or the "altar call"—

A FINAL CALL TO ACTION: something that you're going to decide, or do, or pray. In the back of every Gideon Bible is a page that will walk you through the "Romans Road," explaining your sin, telling of the death of Jesus, and then inviting you to pray a prayer submitting your life to Him. At the end of almost every Christian concert or Christian event there is this call to commit yourself to Christ.

> **"You were dead in the trespasses and sins."**
> (Ephesians 2:1)

I remember attending a Christian sports camp where the director was going to shave his head at the end of the week if there were a certain number of "decisions for Christ." I've attended numerous concerts, rallies, and meetings that ended with "every head bowed, every eye closed" and an invitation to follow along as the leader led us praying the "Sinner's Prayer."

If we felt the Holy Spirit moving in our heart, we were to raise our hand or maybe come forward. And after we accepted Jesus into our heart, we were to talk to a trained usher. Numerous times I "accepted Christ into my heart," and numerous times I invited people to do the same.

I experienced this same theology in college as a member of Campus Crusade for Christ. They circulate a little pamphlet entitled *Have Your Heard of the Four Spiritual Laws?* to an enormous audience. Written in 1965 by Campus Crusade founder Bill Bright, the Four Spiritual Laws are perhaps the clearest encapsulation of American Christianity's theology of conversion:

LAW 1	God loves you and offers a wonderful plan for your life.
LAW 2	Man is sinful and separated from God. Therefore, he cannot know and experience God's love and plan for his life.
LAW 3	Jesus Christ is God's only provision for man's sin. Through Him you can know and experience God's love and plan for your life.
LAW 4	We must individually receive Jesus Christ as Savior and Lord; then we can know and experience God's love and plan for our lives.

We receive Christ through personal invitation. [Christ speaking] "Behold, I stand at the door and knock; if any one hears My voice and opens the door, I will come in to him" (Revelation 3:20).

Receiving Christ involves turning to God from self (repentance) and trusting Christ to come into our lives to forgive our sins and to make us what He wants us to be. Just to agree intellectually that Jesus Christ is the Son of God and that He died on the cross for our sins is not enough. Nor is it enough to have an emotional experience.[1]

---

1 From *Have You Heard of the Four Spiritual Laws?* written by Bill Bright, © 1965–2016 The Bright Media Foundation and Campus Crusade for Christ, Inc. All rights reserved. crustore.org/four-spiritual-laws-online/Included by permission.

For Bright, salvation is only a potential; something remains to be done. The Christian in America is led to "receive Jesus Christ by faith, as an act of the will." It is chiefly a relationship that will begin when the sinner receives Jesus through an individual, personal effort. Faith, we are taught, is "an act of the will."

This "MOMENT OF DECISION" is paramount to American Christianity. Before this act of the will, you are not a Christian, and after this act of the will, you are. This explains why the moment of decision is the end and goal of almost every event and conversation in American Christianity. It is the foundation and beginning of life as an American Christian.

Every Gideon Bible has a place to record your decision for Christ, the day you surrendered you heart. "When did you receive Christ?" is a common question. This individual moment of decision is what American Christianity understands as being "BORN AGAIN." Your "TESTIMONY" is basically the story of your moment of decision, including all the nasty sins that preceded it and the overflow of good works that followed. It is almost impossible to overemphasize the importance the moment of decision plays in the thinking of American Christianity.

My wife remembers with great clarity a conversation she had with friends. We were learning the Lutheran teaching that God alone saves us. Her friend asked, "If you don't know when you decided for Christ, how do you know you're a Christian?" In American Christianity, life and faith are built on the foundation of your decision. Comfort and confidence come forth the moment you exercise your faith as "an act of the will" to receive Christ.

After I became a Lutheran pastor, a Southern Baptist friend came to me and said, "I like your sermons, but when are you going to preach the Gospel?" I was stunned. Every sermon was a Gospel sermon: a sermon about Jesus, about His death for us, about the promise of the forgiveness of sins. I had been preaching the Gospel. But what he was asking was "When are you going to have an altar call? When are you going to invite people to make a commitment?"

For most of American Christianity, the decision for Christ is considered to be the Gospel itself—the moment of decision is the moment of salvation. The decision is key. Our will activates God's grace. It all begins with me.

We will consider the theology of these things later. It is enough here to give it a name: revivalism.

{ REVIVALISM teaches that the Christian life begins with a personal decision to accept Christ. }

Revivalism assumes the individual human will has some degree of spiritual freedom, and it also assumes that the will can be assisted on its way to making a decision. Thus the revivalist preachers aim to excite, move, and appeal to the will. Revivalism is built on the foundation of our decision, an act of the will, a moment of acceptance or decision.

The father of American revivalism is Charles Finney (1792–1875). Finney shaped the Second Great Awakening, crafting "new measures" that combined Scripture with techniques to manipulate emotions. His chief work, *Lectures on Revivals of Religion*, argues that our wills are involved in conversion, not only the will of the converted, but also the will of the preacher and evangelist. Finney is the inventor of the "anxious bench," the precursor of the altar call, and crafter of the tent revival. It is because of Finney's legacy that churches all around America are constantly praying for revival, looking for revival, and trying to incite a revival.

Finney's influence is everywhere in American Christianity, from the back page of every Gideon Bible to the invitation to accept Jesus that Joel Osteen offers at the end of each program, from the Billy Graham Crusades to the Four Spiritual Laws. Finney's fingerprints are on almost every American Christian worship service, every event, every book—and on almost every American Christian's conscience.

The first characteristic of American Christianity is revivalism. The decision for Christ is both the end and the beginning of everything. Jesus made salvation possible, but really, it all starts with me. Revivalism fails to see the big picture of the Scriptures: our gracious God and Savior comes after us, grabs us up, gives us the gift of repentance and faith, and calls us to be His own dear friends. Our salvation is His work from the very beginning, and we are the beneficiaries of His mercy.

I'm Getting Better: Pietism

If it starts with me, who would be surprised if it continued with me?

I kept a journal during my formative years in American Christianity. It is depressing. It is a chronicle of sadness, of failed attempts at a holy life. There is repentance, but page after page is full of resolve. "I will do better." "I will try harder." "I will make the change."

Resolve to keep God's Law is, of course, a godly sentiment, but on the pages of my journal (and in my own heart), this resolve overshadowed everything else. Most especially, it overshadowed Jesus. The purpose of my life and my daily goal was to keep God's Law, and a bit more: to make God happy by my obedience. Each day would begin with a rally to assault sin and overcome it. Each

> **"Are you so foolish? Having begun by the Spirit, are you now being perfected by the flesh?"**
>
> (Galatians 3:3)

day would end with defeat, sometimes despair. I was a loser in the battle to be holy. Like a worker with an overbearing boss, I assumed that the Lord was giving out daily evaluations, and most days were bad. Most days, I was sure God was frowning at me.

This is life on the treadmill of God's Law. I thought the Gospel made me a Christian, but the Law kept me a Christian. My decision made me a Christian, and my resolution kept me there. The Law had the central place in my conscience.

The only way to find certainty with the Law is through obedience. When Moses takes the place of Jesus, then obedience takes the place of forgiveness, earnest determination takes the place of hope, and despair takes the place of comfort. Really, the Law and its commands replace the Gospel and its promises. This is pietism.

> { **PIETISM teaches that the Christian life is chiefly marked by a growth in good works.** }

Pietism began in the German Lutheran Church in the seventeenth century, but its influence quickly spread in every direction. It is now so ubiquitous that we have difficulty seeing it.

Pietism is a theological move toward the centrality of works in the Christian life. Pietism understands that the order of salvation (sorrow over sin, faith in God's promise, and the spiritual fruit of repentance) occurs chronologically in a person's life. This means that after I've repented and accepted Jesus, then it's time to get after the serious business of keeping the Law and living a holy life. PIETISM MAKES GROWTH IN GOOD WORKS THE CHIEF AIM OF THE CHRISTIAN LIFE, and with this centrality comes the dislocation of comfort. Jesus says, "Where your treasure is, there your heart will be also" (Matthew 6:21), and this is a true diagnostic for our theology. If our treasure is our works, our obedience, or our keeping of God's Law, then our heart and our comfort and our confidence will be found in our works.

Some denominations take pietism to the extreme and teach that sinless perfection is attainable in this life. This was the teaching that distinguished the Methodists from the Anglicans, and subsequently the Nazarenes from the Methodists. These are the so-called "Holiness Bodies." Most Charismatic and Pentecostal teachers hold to this doctrine. Most of American Christianity does not go so far as to teach the doctrine of sinless perfection, yet it is there in practice. It is taught that the Christian life is, first and foremost, a life of obedience and works.

With pietism, the Gospel moves from the center to the side. At best, pietism makes the Gospel the motivation for our works. At worst, the Gospel is understood as a demand for us to do better.

"Jesus died for you; what will you do for Him?"

Have you heard that sermon? I am hard-pressed to find a more desperately horrendous, terrible, wicked, and nasty twisting of the grace of God. The cross is turned into a bribe, the grace of God is warped into compulsion. There are strings attached. God scratches your back, now you scratch His. The suffering of Jesus becomes a debt that we pay back! Lord, help us from such confusion! Lord, save us from the arrogance that presumes to earn God's grace, even if it's after our conversion! Lord, deliver us from the tyranny of such preaching that would steal away the grace of God as soon as we taste it, that would put us in debt to God, that would make us slaves instead of sons to our heavenly Father! But this is the heavy yoke of pietism. Grace is for the unbeliever. The Law is for the Christian. With pietism, "What are you doing for God?" replaces the preaching of what God has done for us in Christ.

Paul writes to the Galatians, "Are you so foolish? Having begun by the Spirit, are you now being perfected by the flesh?" (Galatians 3:3). Pietism does just this; the work begun in faith (or begun in my decision for Christ) is made perfect in obedience.

The centrality of works, the path of pietism, ends in one of two bad places. It must. If I determine what God thinks of me by my obedience, then either God is proud of me because of my goodness or disappointed in me because of my sin. Pietism ends either in the sin of pride or the sin of despair.

The second characteristic of American Christianity is pietism, an emphasis on our growth in good works. It might seem ironic to us that the pursuit of good works ends with sin, but this is how God designed the Law. "Through the law comes knowledge of sin" (Romans 3:20). When we try to achieve comfort, certainty, or confidence through our works, we are grasping for ourselves what only Christ can give. Pietism fails to teach the comfort of the Scriptures, that it is the Holy Spirit who keeps me in the faith through the Word, and that my life of love is a gift from God.

TOUCHING GOD: MYSTICISM

I remember a time before I was a Lutheran when, after attending a liturgical church service for the first time since I was a child, I walked out the door, saying, "I just didn't feel the Holy Spirit there." The Scriptures were read, the Gospel was preached, the faith was confessed

> "When you eat of it . . . you will be like God."
>
> (Genesis 3:5)

in creed and hymns, but still I wasn't moved. I had been worshiping with American Christians, so I had been trained to feel the Spirit, the wind blowing through my heart, the sensation that something is happening in the spiritual world around me, and I certainly didn't feel it in the Lutheran liturgy.

A few years ago, I interviewed Chris Tomlin, a prominent voice in the contemporary worship music world. He said the role of the worship leader is to bring people into the presence of God.

"How do you know when you've arrived in the presence of God?"

I asked.

"You just know it." [2]

This is about as accurate and precise as you can get. "You just know it." Some secret part of your insides lets you know when you are close to God.

This is mysticism.

> { MYSTICISM teaches that we can have direct, unmediated access to God. }

Mysticism is the religious practice that puts people in motion toward the internal and direct experience of the presence of God. The mystical experience is the immediate awareness that we are in contact with something much bigger than ourselves. Mysticism has been around from the beginning. The devil tempted Adam and Eve with mysticism: "You will be like God." He continues to tempt the world with the same dangerous teaching.

Mysticism, like a parasite, does not stand on its own. It comes alongside almost every theology and worldview. There is Jewish and Islamic mysticism, just as there is Christian mysticism. Mysticism describes the basic characteristics of the Eastern religions and philosophies. There is even a kind of secular mysticism with people who want to be "spiritual but not religious."

Mysticism assumes the capacity of the human soul to come into direct contact with divinity. The goal of mysticism is that mysterious direct contact: touching God.

In its pagan forms, mysticism talks about the "divine spark" in each person. Individuals are a spark thrown from the fire of the divine nature and returning to the same.

In its Christian forms, mysticism puts the emphasis on Christ in us, the unity of the Christian with the Holy Spirit, and especially the experience of direct contact with God. This direct contact takes different forms. Sometimes, it is direct communication, a word from God. Other times, God is "leading" or "prompting." Mostly, it is the impression that God is present on the inside. Our soul is tuned to sense the divine presence. God is touching us or we are touching God.

This impression, the experience of the internal and unmediated presence of God, is the goal of American Christian worship. A survey of contemporary praise

---

2   "Interview with Praise and Worship Songwriter Chris Tomlin" by Rev. Bryan Wolfmueller, *Table Talk Radio,* July 23, 2008, www.tabletalkradio.org/content/node/23. © Rev. Bryan Wolfmueller.

and worship songs shows all the marks of mystical worship. "Seeing God," "touching God," "feeling God," "losing ourselves," being "caught up" and "swept away" and "knowing God" in some sort of secret and direct way are all indications of what is happening: we are being trained to *feel* the presence of God.

This is why I left that liturgical service shaking my head. There was no excitement, no manipulation, no attempt to impart an ecstatic experience, no soft slow music as the preacher gave a heartfelt plea. For a mystic, the historic liturgy of the Church seems incredibly dry and void of spirituality. This is because the liturgy is interested in external and objective realities. The mystic is invested in internal and subjective experiences.

There is a dark, desperate, and despairing side to mysticism.

If you live by the experience, you will die by the experience. Trusting a secret part of your insides that says God is close also means trusting that secret part of your insides that says God is far away. There are times when worship isn't moving, when the Spirit isn't felt. There are times when you are not swept away, and these times are frightful. "I'm going through a drought." "I'm in the desert." "I've lost my passion." "I feel far from God." "I've come down off the mountaintop, and I'm in a valley." The highs are very high, and the lows are frightfully low.

The loss of the mystical experience, the drying up of the mystical well, sends the worshiper scrambling desperately to regain that lost feeling. The spark, the intensity, the fire and passion are brought back to life through a frenzy of praise songs, quiet times, and a resolve (always more resolve) to serve God. Sometimes the passion returns; sometimes it does not. The mystical fountain dries up.

This is a desperate time. Mysticism offers certainty and comfort through experience, and if the experience is not there, then neither is the comfort. Mysticism teaches me that God is there and that He loves me through my feelings. When the feelings are gone, I am left to conclude that God is not there or that He doesn't love me.

While pietism looks for comfort through growth in works, mysticism looks for comfort in the internal experience of the direct touch of God. Both are looking for comfort in the wrong place. Both are expecting from God things that He never promised.

Mysticism is the third theological mark of American Christianity, the movement toward an internal and direct experience of the presence of God, the confidence of our heart. It fails because it requires me to put my hope and my faith in my own internal experiences instead of in the Lord's promises. God has not promised the feeling of forgiveness. He promises forgiveness itself, if we feel it or not. God has not promised that we will experience His presence. He promises that He will never leave us or forsake us. The Lord delivers His comfort to us in the promise of the Gospel—which is true even if we don't feel it. Mysticism runs aground on the solid rock of the Scriptures. John writes, "Whenever our heart condemns us, God is greater than our heart" (1 John 3:20).

THE ACTION IS ON THE INSIDE: ENTHUSIASM

> "... so that we may no longer be children, tossed to and fro by the waves and carried about by every wind of doctrine, by human cunning, by craftiness in deceitful schemes. Rather, speaking the truth in love, we are to grow up in every way into Him who is the head, into Christ."
> (Ephesians 4:14–15)

Where does spiritual action occur? What is the realm in which God acts? While all Christians would recognize the work of God in creation (after all, God created the universe and continues to hold it together), American Christianity locates God's gracious and saving activity inside of us. All spiritual activity occurs in the heart.

American Christianity teaches that it is in my heart that God speaks; it is in my heart that the Lord gives gifts. It is with my heart that I make a decision for Christ. It is my heart that is charged with spiritual energy to motivate good works. It is with my heart that I know that God is close by. My heart is moved, changed, filled, assured, surrendered, and given over. God, according to American Christianity, is working on the inside.

By locating the activity of God on the inside, American Christianity has a great difficulty finding any gracious work outside of me. In fact, American Christianity assumes that anything outside of the heart, and especially anything physical, is a work that we do. It assumes that if something is physical, then it has nothing at all to do with salvation. If it is outside us, then it must be a work; if it is inside us, then it is probably grace. If something is outside of me, then it must have nothing to do with my salvation. This is enthusiasm.

{ **ENTHUSIASM teaches that the spiritual life happens inside of us.** }

We normally use the word *enthusiasm* to mean that we are really excited about something. "That guy has a lot of enthusiasm for the Broncos." But *enthusiasm* is also a technical theological word, and a very helpful one. Theological enthusiasm is the promotion of the internal testimony of "God" over the external testimony of the Scriptures. The enthusiast sees all the action on the inside.

The enthusiast might read the Scriptures and believe that they are true. But the Bible is a book, a physical thing, and therefore, according to the enthusiast, it cannot have any spiritual benefit unless the Spirit confirms it in my heart. When you ask the enthusiast how he or she hears the voice of God, the answer is not "In the pages of the Bible" or "In the preaching of God's Word," but "In my heart."

Enthusiasm is creeping around in the background of revivalism, pietism, and mysticism.

It is the internal tugging of the Holy Spirit on our heart that lets us know we need to walk up the aisle and receive Christ (revivalism). It is the internal voice of God that gives us direction in our daily living (pietism). It is the presence of God we feel in our heart that lets us know we are worshiping Him (mysticism). All of the gracious working of God is bottled up in our heart.

Now, it is true that God works in our heart. That is not the problem. Enthusiasm fails because it denies that God works *outside* our heart. The enthusiast denies the external work of God, specifically His promised work in the Word.

Here is an example: I remember studying Scripture's teaching on Baptism. (We will consider this topic in detail in the chapter "Go Play Outside.") Over and over, the Scriptures connect Baptism to the Lord's mercy and grace, to the promise of forgiveness and life in Christ. But Baptism is a *thing*, I thought. There is water and some guy standing there speaking, so it must be a work. It must not save." St. Peter said, "Baptism . . . saves you" (1 Peter 3:21). I said, "Baptism is a physical thing; it is not in my heart, so it can't save me." That is enthusiasm in action. It is the theological logic behind the rejection of the saving work of Baptism and the Lord's Supper. It is what makes American Christianity so individualistic. Enthusiasm is what drives the terrible swing between pride and despair that marks the life of most American Christians.

Enthusiasm looks for God, for His Word, for direction, for certainty, for truth, for comfort, for confidence, and for the Spirit on the inside. Everything is in my heart. This is the fourth and final mark of American Christianity. Enthusiasm fails to see that the Lord's gracious work is chiefly on the outside. Enthusiasm undercuts the Lord's promises and guts the Scriptures of their strength and comfort. Enthusiasm takes our eyes off of Christ and places them on our own heart. Yet the death of Jesus did not occur in our heart, but on a forsaken hill outside of Jerusalem. The Scriptures fix our eyes on Jesus, "the founder and perfecter of our faith" (Hebrews 12:2). His objective promise of the forgiveness of our sins is true long before we believe it. It is not our heart that confirms the truth of the Lord's Word, but the truth of the Lord's Word that comforts our heart.

The Pendulum of Pride and Despair

> "So then, there remains a Sabbath rest for the people of God."
>
> (Hebrews 4:9)

Revivalism, pietism, mysticism, and enthusiasm all direct our focus away from Jesus and toward ourselves. They are all different shapes of legalism, a theology of the Law. They all, in their own way, choke out the voice of the Gospel, the promise of the forgiveness of sins for the sake of Jesus. They are the fountains of the failure of American Christianity.

The most important thing in the Church is Christ and the preaching of His Gospel. If the promise of forgiveness is not heard, we lose everything good that Jesus has for us. Christians are marked by hearing the voice of Jesus (John 10:27), and that voice is the voice of mercy and forgiveness, the voice of the Gospel.

{ LEGALISM puts the Law above the Gospel by establishing requirements for salvation beyond repentance and faith in Jesus Christ. }

What happens when the Gospel is not heard, when the halls of the church echo with commands instead of promises, threats instead of grace, instruction instead of mercy? There are only two options: pride or despair.

PRIDE HEARS GOD'S LAW AND THINKS,

Yeah, I've done that. I've kept that. I've thought that. I got after it and accomplished it, and God must be proud of me.

The proud are the Pharisees, those who think they have measured up to God's standard and done what God expected. The proud are always measuring. They measure their own lives and works, and (really, they can't help it) they measure the works of the people around them. The proud keep score. This is a necessary part of their theology. If God is marking our accomplishments, then we should mark them as well. The proud can talk about grace and mercy and the death of Jesus, but the thing that really drives their theology is the cleanness of their life. Their works and efforts occupy their mind. They have managed, somehow, to make themselves pleasing to God.

The flip side of pride is despair. If the Pharisees are a picture of the proud, then Judas is the picture of despair. Judas knows his failure and sin, but he has no hope, no comfort. The despairing know that they have sinned. They know that they have broken God's Law. Like the proud, the despairing are always measuring, but they know that they do not measure up. They try and they fail, and try, and fail, and fail, and it seems like there is no hope, like God and the world are all against them. They are failures—doomed, lost, forsaken, and condemned.

This is the pendulum of pride and despair, the swing of the sinful flesh dangling on the Law. The Lutheran fathers knew about this danger:

> Concerning the revelation of sin, Moses' veil hangs [2 Corinthians 3:12–16] before the eyes of all people as long as they hear the bare preaching of the Law, and nothing about Christ. Therefore, they do not learn from the Law to see their sins correctly. They either become bold hypocrites ‹who swell with the opinion of

their own righteousness› like the Pharisees [Matthew 23], or they despair like Judas [Matthew 27:3–5]. (Ep V 8)

Pride or despair, Pharisees or Judas, self-justified or self-condemned—these are the two extremes between which a life without the Gospel flails.

Most American Christians are swinging back and forth on this pendulum of pride and despair. I know personally this pride-despair pendulum. One day I was sure that the Lord was pleased with me; the next day I was convinced that He was mad. One moment it seemed like heaven was smiling, and the next moment God and the universe turned against me. Now we are good enough to please God, and later our sins cry out for justice. When we swing on the pendulum of pride and despair, there is no certain answer to the question "What does God think of me?" Moment to moment it changes drastically, fearfully.

The Law doesn't help. It tells me what to do to please God, but I don't. I try and I fail. My failures mean the Law's commands are also accusations. It cannot instruct without also accusing, and with the Law, there is no help in sight. I only keep swinging higher and higher, faster and faster. Pride and despair settle in my heart and conscience. Joy is pushed out, then grace, then hope.

This is the path to hypocrisy. As the Law accuses and condemns, sin is magnified, and the temptation comes to cover it up. The Christian life is supposed to be filled with good works, but we are sinners through and through, so we simply *act* like Christians. We act as though we are good. We smile and carry huge Bibles and say the right-sounding "Christiany" words while our heart sinks deeper into the darkness of pride-colored despair. Where do we turn? We can certainly turn and run from indifference and unbelief; but there is no escaping the Law of God, not, at least, through our own efforts.

This is life with Law and no Gospel, with only commands and no promises. This pendulum of pride and despair is life without the Gospel. It is the life of most American Christians. It is not the life Jesus has for you.

The Law/Gospel Alternative

The Gospel is the alternative to the pendulum of pride and despair. The Law says "do," the Gospel says "done." The Law commands; the Gospel promises. The Law measures and judges, the Gospel forgives. The Law tells us how we ought to live, the Gospel tells us that Jesus died; and He died with a marvelous and gracious purpose: to save sinners. Both the Law and the Gospel are from God, but they have different purposes. The Law condemns. The Gospel saves.

THERE ARE THOSE WHO PREACH THE LAW INSTEAD OF THE GOSPEL.

Some think the Law is the Gospel, and some think the Gospel is the Law. Some modify them and preach neither the Law nor the Gospel. Those who hold these views rob Christians of the full comfort that is theirs in Christ.

There is no room for pride in the Gospel, no boasting, because there is no doing at all; everything is done. We who are dead in trespasses and sins (Ephesians 2:1), the enemies of God (Romans 5:10) and children of wrath (Ephesians 2:3), are raised, pardoned, and transferred into His gracious kingdom of life (Colossians 1:13).

> "For God did not send His Son into the world to condemn the world, but in order that the world might be saved through Him."
> (John 3:17)

There is no room for despair in the Gospel. The promise of the Gospel is the love of God poured out for us to save, rescue, and deliver sinners. God set His mind on your salvation, and He accomplished this salvation on the cross. He brings you this victory, this salvation, this mercy, this forgiveness in the promise of the Gospel. How can you despair? What will separate you from the love of God? Sin? Jesus died for your sins. Death? Jesus is raised from the dead. The devil? His authority is destroyed by the death of Jesus (Hebrews 2:14).

The Gospel replaces pride and despair with the humility and confidence of faith. The Gospel replaces our efforts with the work of Jesus. The Gospel replaces our confidence in ourselves with trust in Christ. The Gospel replaces the accusations of the Law with the tenderness and mercy of the Lord. And the Gospel is for Christians.

American Christianity teaches that the Gospel is for the unbeliever, not the believer. The unbeliever needs to hear about the cross, but the believer needs to hear the commands. The unbeliever needs the preaching of Jesus. The believer needs the preaching of the Commandments. The altar call and the sinner's prayer are for the unbeliever. Advice for being a better parent and strategies for a deeper prayer life are for the believer.

Holding back the Gospel from Christians is one of the greatest failures of American Christianity. If there is something like the Gospel and the grace of God, it is offered and given only to those who are not yet Christians. The Christians are fed a steady diet of commands and instructions without a shred of mercy and grace.

John says, "The law was given through Moses; grace and truth came through Jesus Christ" (John 1:17). I am desperately afraid that most American Christians have Moses living in their heart. They only hear God's Law. The Law's demands are preached, taught, and sung in the church. The Law's accusations echo in the conscience.

Make no mistake, the Law is good. But the Law does not save. It cannot comfort the sinner. It cannot comfort the *Christian* sinner. The Christian needs the Gospel just as surely as the unbeliever. The Scriptures teach and preach the Gospel for Christians. Forgiveness is also for Christians. Mercy and grace and the blood of Jesus are also for Christians. There is not a moment in this life when we do not need Jesus and His mercy, and there is not a moment when the Lord's mercy is not for us.

Paul wrote an epistle of warning to the Galatians. They had begun with the Gospel, but they wanted to stay Christian through the keeping of the Law. American Christianity has fallen into the same teaching. Paul knew the danger of this teaching. "Are you so foolish? Having begun by the Spirit, are you now being perfected by the flesh?" (Galatians 3:3). We never outgrow the Gospel. It is the beginning and the end. Jesus is the Alpha and the Omega, and His kindness and mercy are the start and finish of our Christian life. His mercy is the source and the goal of our life and our peace.

Dear Christian, the Gospel is for you. The forgiveness of sins is for you. Jesus, and His death and resurrection, His mercy and grace, His undeserved kindness are still for you, today and always. Your life is hidden with God in Christ, and it is His lavish love and kindness, not your obedience and commitment, that make a Christian life.

TRUSTING IN GOOD WORKS: MORALISM

If the Christian life is all about our obedience to the Law and our resolute determination to do better, then we fall victim to a bigger theological problem: the exaltation of our works. It is natural for fallen humanity to make more of ourselves than we ought. We think more highly of ourselves than we should. We are proud of ourselves and of our actions.

> "But now the righteousness of God has been manifested apart from the law, although the Law and the Prophets bear witness to it—the righteousness of God through faith in Jesus Christ for all who believe."
> (Romans 3:21–22)

This pride pushes itself into our theology. The logic goes like this: "If God is mad at me because of my sins, He will be happy with me because of my works." This is the foundation of every non-Christian religion, the creed of every social organization, and the motto of every sensitive conscience. Our fallen reason thinks the most important thing is to be good, to do good, and to try hard.

Each one of us is, according to our fallen nature, a moralist and a legalist. We all have a Pharisee living in our heart. We are all convinced by the logic of the flesh that obtaining salvation must somehow be connected to our works.

The ancient theologians called this the *opinio legis*, the opinion of the law, the most native and basic theology of our sinful flesh. It seems like we cannot help exalting our works as trophies. We demand judgment from God on the basis of the good things we've accomplished. We are convinced that we deserve heaven because of our works and efforts. When you ask people, "Will you go to heaven?" they most often say, "Yes." "Why?" We know what the answer will be. The creed of the sinful flesh: "I'm a good person."

This is the theology of the flesh. It is the theology of death.

{ Moralism teaches that the Gospel can be reduced to improvements in behavior. }

To be judged by God on the basis of works is to be condemned. "None is righteous, no, not one" (Romans 3:10). "We have all become like one who is unclean, and all our righteous deeds are like a polluted garment. We all fade like a leaf, and our iniquities, like the wind, take us away" (Isaiah 64:6).

We are tempted to place our trust in good works. We are tempted to look to our works for salvation. Our works tempt us to false confidence and idolatrous pride. This temptation puts us in great danger.

Trust in works is the foundational teaching of every non-Christian religion. This trust in works is also a constant temptation for the Christian. The first is salvation through works without Jesus. The second is salvation through works with the help of Jesus. Both are salvation through works. Both are wrong. This is the danger of trusting in our good works.

It seems strange to talk about the danger of good works, almost blasphemous. In fact, it is blasphemy to our flesh, the most fundamental heresy. Our flesh wants to trust in good works because it maintains the illusion of our own goodness and our strength to do good works. It trusts in this strength and finds comfort in these works.

The Scriptures warn us often of this dangerous trust in our goodness or our good works. "Do not let your left hand know what your right hand is doing" (Matthew 6:3). Our left hand would boast and be proud. Our left hand would hold up our right hand for all the world to see.

After Jesus called Matthew to be an apostle, He went to his house to eat. There were sinners and tax collectors gathered around, eating with Jesus. The Pharisees were offended, so Jesus told them a little one-verse parable: "Those who are well have no need of a physician, but those who are sick" (Matthew 9:12). If you think you are healthy, then you don't need a doctor. If you think you are well, then you don't take your medicine. There is a danger in not knowing if you are sick. The same thing is true spiritually. There is a danger in thinking that you are good. There is grave spiritual peril in trusting in your good works for your salvation. Just as the healthy do not need a doctor, so the good do not need a Savior.

The Pharisees did not think they were sinners, and therefore they had no need for Jesus. Matthew and the crowd of sinners around him knew their sin. They knew they needed help. They rejoiced when that help came. "For I came not to call the righteous, but sinners," Jesus says (Matthew 9:13).

See the danger of trusting in your own goodness and good works?

The Pharisees were sick. They were sinners, but they didn't know it. They thought they were righteous. They thought they were good. And the result is that they not only rejected Jesus, but they also sought to kill Him.

Imagine having a terrible disease but being completely unaware of it. You think you are healthy. The doctor prescribes medicine, insists on certain treatments, and you balk at this. You despise the doctor, and you die. The Pharisees were sinners unaware of their sin. They scoffed at Jesus' claims to be their Savior, and they died. When we trust in our goodness and our good works, we cannot hear the diagnosis of the Law. We balk at the cure. We reject the Savior and His saving work, or we think it is not for us.

GOOD WORKS CAN BE THE SUBTLEST, MOST COMMON, AND MOST DANGEROUS IDOLS.

This doesn't mean that good works are bad. (Those would be bad works.) Fire is good, but it is still dangerous. Our human reason is good, but also dangerous. Money is good, but likewise dangerous. All of these things have the potential to do great harm. In the same way, the temptation to trust in our good works destroys faith in Christ.

Paul, especially, talks of the danger of works: "For by works of the law no human being will be justified in His sight" (Romans 3:20). "And to the one who does not work but believes in Him who justifies the ungodly, his faith is counted as righteousness" (Romans 4:5). That last verse should not be missed. Justification is only for the one who does not work. Righteousness is only for the ungodly. Our works cannot save us. Our works cannot even help us to salvation. Our works, because we are tempted to trust them, can even stand in the way of salvation. When we confess this, we are renouncing the doctrine we were born with. When we put away the delusion of our own righteousness, we are, at last, ready for the righteousness of another. Faith begins when the trust in our works ends.

Faith is the anti-work, the un-work. Faith is not doing, but believing and trusting someone else. Our salvation, our justification, is by faith, and faith alone, apart from works.

If it is the instinct of our fallen flesh to trust in our works, we are not surprised that this theology finds its way into the Christian's mind and thinking, and even into the Church's theology. Works are like cockroaches, always sneaking into the Lord's house. Good works are wriggling into different Christian teachings of salvation. In one place, it is necessary for us to cooperate with the Lord's grace to do meritorious good works (Roman Catholicism). In another place, it is up to us to take the first step, to make a decision for Jesus (revivalism). Works are always coming alongside the Gospel, tagging along with Jesus. The result is a "Jesus and . . ." theology; a false theology of Jesus and my decision, Jesus and my cooperation, Jesus and my dedication, Jesus and my work, Jesus and my obedience. Whenever you have a "Jesus and . . ." theology, it is the "and" that matters. If our theology is "Jesus and our efforts," then the thing that matters is our efforts. The Gospel is diminished, and the Law is exalted. The forgiveness of sins is replaced with my earnest resolve.

The Scriptures stand against the invasion of works into our conscience and our confidence. The Gospel excludes boasting, all boasting. Jesus will not let you be your savior. Salvation belongs to Him alone.

The pendulum of pride and despair is, at last, destroyed when it swings into the cross of Jesus. He rescues us from this deadly roller coaster. He casts down the prideful and raises up the lowly. He brings to us, over and over, every day, with a ridiculous abundance, the relief of His mercy: the Gospel, the promise that our sins are forgiven and our shame is covered, the promise that by no work of our own, we are His and He is ours, our Brother, our Friend, our Savior.

"Christ is the end of the law for righteousness to everyone who believes" (Romans 10:4), the end of the striving, the strutting, the cowering; the end of pride that thinks it has done enough; the end of despair that knows it has not done enough. American Christianity has failed to teach that trusting in good works is harmful. It has failed to recognize that the center of the Christian life is the Gospel and the promise of forgiveness. It has failed to deliver to the Lord's people the comfort and peace that Jesus has for the Church. American Christianity has made people busy with the work of salvation. Jesus has given us rest. "There remains a Sabbath rest for the people of God" (Hebrews 4:9), and that rest is your Jesus. "For whoever has entered God's rest has also rested from his works as God did from His" (Hebrews 4:10).

God Wants Sons, Not Slaves

Our flesh is drawn to placing its trust in our goodness, in our good works. Our flesh is drawn to the Law, and so our flesh is drawn to slavery. All our natural theologies are slave theologies.

> "So you are no longer a slave, but a son, and if a son, then an heir through God."
> (Galatians 4:7)

Consider the parable of the prodigal son (Luke 15:11–32). The text would better be called the parable of the running, forgiving, sweeping-up-in-arms-of-mercy-and-killing-the-fatted-calf father.

A man has two sons. The younger comes to his father and asks for his inheritance. This is like saying, "I wish you were dead. I'd rather have your money than you." The father, instead of disinheriting the son, surprisingly gives him what he asks for. This son travels to a distant pagan place and uses his father's wealth in various and creative ways of breaking the Commandments. The money runs out. Famine sweeps the land. The boy is destitute. The Scriptures show him hitting rock bottom. He's feeding slop to the pigs (considered unclean animals) and is so famished that he wants to join them and eat the slop. And there, as he is coveting the pig food and drooling over their breakfast, he remembers his father's servants. "In my father's house, the servants had food and drink, house and clothing. I'll go back home and see if I can become my father's slave."

He plans his repentance as he travels home. "Father, I have sinned against heaven and before you. I am no longer worthy to be called your son. Treat me as one of your hired servants" (Luke 15:18–19). It is important to see this son rehearsing his speech as he walks along the road. He is crafting his repentance as an argument. He is convinced that he is unworthy of any honor from his father, and he only wants the place of a servant. He is a slave to despair, and he's going to apply to be a slave to his father.

Meanwhile, back home, the father has been scanning the horizon ever since his son left. At last, he sees his son in the distance. He grabs his robes and runs down the path. If we were surprised that the father handed the inheritance to the son, we are astonished to see him running, kicking up the dust, racing to his son. There is no holding back with this father, no concern for his dignity, no vengeance, no anger, no malice, no retaliation, no requirement, no waiting for a confession, no making a deal. There is only a father with a face bursting with joy, sprinting to his beloved son, wrapping his arms around him, and embracing him with a completely unexpected kindness.

Can you see it? The father hugging and kissing his son as the son tries to make his rehearsed confession? "Father, I'm not worthy . . . I've come to be your slave . . . " The father cuts him off. He'll have none of it. "Get the robe, the ring, the fattest calf. Today we feast, we laugh, we rejoice. My son was dead and is alive!" This boy wants to be a slave. This gracious father will have him only as his son, his blessed, loved, forgiven son. What a fantastic picture of the Gospel.

There is a second son, the older son. This son never asked for his inheritance; he never asked for anything. He stayed home, did his father's bidding, followed his father's commands. He honored and served his father, and he hated his brother. This is why he boycotts this feast of repentance. The father should shun his prodigal, the older brother thinks, not celebrate his return. Here is the third surprise of the parable. The father goes out to his older, pouting son to call him into the feast. We see, in his protest, the theology behind his anger: "Look, these many years I have served you, and I never disobeyed your command, yet you never gave me a young goat, that I might celebrate with my friends" (Luke 15:29). This oldest son also considered himself a slave of the father, a slave of obedience. "I served you. I obeyed you. I did everything right." The father won't have it. "Son," he says. "Son!" Do you see it? This father wants sons, not slaves. "All that is mine is yours" (Luke 15:31). "You are my son, I am your father, and I love you. We are bound up to one another. What is mine is yours." The father has the same love for this older son as well. The father wants, above all else, for his sons to be his sons.

THREE SLAVERIES

This is a theological truth. Jesus, with this parable, assaults the slave theology of our flesh. We see three slaveries in the text:

(1) THE HEDONISTIC SLAVERY TO PASSIONS AND SIN (THE PRODIGAL SON AND HIS DEBAUCHERY)

(2) THE SLAVERY OF DESPAIR OF GOD'S MERCY (THE PRODIGAL SON AND HIS REHEARSED REPENTANCE)

(3) THE SLAVERY OF OBEDIENCE TO GOD'S COMMANDMENTS (THE OLDER SON AND HIS POUTING PRIDE)

All of them are dangerous, but they are not equally obvious. We generally understand the first form of slavery: the bondage to the lusts of the flesh and the pride of life. The last two slaveries are subtler, yet just as dangerous.

The slavery of despair and the slavery of pride are really two sides of the same coin, the *opinio legis*, which measures our standing before God by our own works and efforts. "How have I measured up?" According to the *opinio legis*, the younger son was a miserable sinner and had, by his sin, exempted himself from the father's house. According to the *opinio legis*, the older son had earned a place in the father's house by his faithful and unswerving obedience to the father.

IT IS THE SWINGING PENDULUM OF PRIDE AND DESPAIR.

IT IS THE SWINGING PENDULUM OF PRIDE AND DESPAIR.

The younger son is despairing. "I am no longer worthy to be called your son. Treat me as one of your hired servants" (Luke 15:19). "Put me to work. I'll make up for my mistakes. I'll earn your respect, or at least a place in your home, if you just let me work hard enough. I can be good. I can be better than I was." Maybe the father would give him a chance to be a slave. Maybe not. He knows he certainly will never be a son to his father again. His best shot is being a slave.

The older son is proud. "Look, these many years I have served you, and I never disobeyed your command" (Luke 15:29). "I've done what you asked, checked all the boxes, been obedient. I was up early and I worked late. You should be impressed by me. Surely, I've done everything needed to earn your love." By all accounts, the father should reward this hardworking son, but he doesn't.

The *opinio legis* and the theology of our flesh insist on some interaction with God according to the Law and according to works. We insist on being God's slaves, but this results only in condemnation. The father in this parable refuses to pay out wages. He only gives gifts, undeserved gifts. The father refuses to have these sons as his slaves. This father operates only by mercy, by grace—shocking, even revolting to our flesh. Works do not count with this father.

American Christianity, with its insistence on our efforts and obedience, pushes the Christian toward slavery to God and away from the Father's joyful feast of repentance.

THE FATHER WANTS SONS, NOT SLAVES

It is only in being a *child* of God that we are saved from the wrath to come. "In Christ Jesus you are all sons of God, through faith" (Galatians 3:26). "The Spirit Himself bears witness with our spirit that we are children of God, and if children, then heirs—heirs of God and fellow heirs with Christ, provided we suffer with Him in order that we may also be glorified with Him" (Romans 8:16–17). Jesus does not come so that we might be His slaves, but that we might be His brothers and sisters and friends. "No longer do I call you servants, for the servant does not know what his master is doing; but I have called you friends, for all that I have heard from My Father I have made known to you" (John 15:15).

(Hebrews 4:10), no longer storming heaven or impressing God with our effort. We are no longer running from His wrath. We are forgiven, and this means we are free.

> "If the Son sets you free, you will be free indeed." (John 8:36)

> "For I am sure that neither death nor life, nor angels nor rulers, nor things present nor things to come, nor powers, nor height nor depth, nor anything else in all creation, will be able to separate us from the love of God in Christ Jesus our Lord." (Romans 8:38–39)

JESUS MADE A DECISION FOR YOU

Once while I was patiently waiting in line to return a movie, a little lady tottered up to me and asked abruptly, "What do you do?"

"I'm a Lutheran pastor."

"Oh," she said. "I'm a Baptist. What's the difference?"

What a surprise this conversation was!

"Well," I began, "I suppose in your church, they have a time of decision at the end of the service."

"Yes, an altar call."

"Right, an altar call, a time to receive Jesus into your life and pray the sinner's prayer."

"Yes," she said.

"Lutherans do things a bit differently. Instead of asking the sinner to receive Jesus, we ask if Jesus has received us. Instead of asking the sinner to dedicate his or her life to Christ, we ask if Christ has given His entire life and died for us. Instead of asking sinners to pray, we ask if Jesus prays for us. And the answer to this question is a sure and certain 'Yes'!"

She started crying. "That's the most wonderful thing I've ever heard."

For so many American Christians, their certainty is wobbly and their faith is unsure because it is built on the weak foundation of self: on their decision, their works, their experiences, their inner life, their resolve. These things are unsure. This chasing after certainty found in oneself is a failure of American Christianity. These things were never meant by God to give us certainty.

We were meant to be uncertain about ourselves, but sure of God. Our confidence is not in ourselves, in the things we decide, the things we do, or the things we feel. Our confidence is not in our goodness or the goodness of our works. Our confidence is in Christ. Faith in Jesus, His works, His words, and His love for sinners is our confidence. We are dubious. Jesus is sure.

Jesus is the one who died and was raised. He sits at the right hand of God. He intercedes for us. He sends the Holy Spirit with the Word of promise to give faith and impute righteousness.

THESE THINGS ARE SURE. When Jesus is the one saving and rescuing and delivering, then our salvation and rescue and deliverance are sure.

We are given the bold certainty of faith.

This is a certainty and a confidence outside us, a certainty more sure than we are. This is the certainty that the Lord Jesus wants for us. This is the certainty that made that woman cry while in line to return a video. This is the certainty that destroys doubt. Christ died for me!

John hands us over to that kind of certainty when he writes, "For whenever our heart condemns us, God is greater than our heart, and He knows everything" (1 John 3:20).

Paul expounds this certainty when he tells the Romans, "For I am sure that neither death nor life, nor angels nor rulers, nor things present nor things to come, nor powers, nor height nor depth, nor anything else in all creation, will be able to separate us from the love of God in Christ Jesus our Lord" (Romans 8:38–39).

Jesus plants this certainty into our heart with His cry "It is finished!" (John 19:30). The work is finished. The war is over. Our salvation is accomplished.

American Christianity seeks certainty in the Christian. American Christianity looks for certainty through the Law. American Christianity pursues certainty in my heart, my inner experiences.

American Christianity strives for certainty without the Gospel.

It tries to answer the most fundamental theological question, "What does God think of me?" with the Law.

If we were to determine what God thinks of us based on our works, we would all be in trouble. If our decision and sincere determination were the basis of God's acceptance, we could never know if we'd done it right. If we use our experience of feeling near or far from God as the way to answer this question, then it will never be settled. But God has settled this question; He answered it on the cross.

The cross stands as the unwavering, unmoving, unquestionable answer to the question "What does God think of me?" The answer is this: He loves you, and He forgives you all your sins. You can be sure of this. You cannot undo the cross. You cannot undo God's love for you. The love of God for you is certain and sure, as certain and sure as the death and resurrection of Jesus. This is the basis of our confidence and the source of our Christian comfort, and it is from this certainty that all our theology flows.

CHAPTER TWO

GOD SPEAKS

"God said . . ."
(Genesis 1:3)

"I'm spiritual, not religious." This anti-creed of American culture is as close as it gets to a universal doctrine of our age. No doubt you've heard someone say it, or you've seen it on a bumper sticker. Everybody, apparently, wants to be spiritual, but no one wants to be religious. WHAT IS THE DIFFERENCE? To be "spiritual, not religious" is to have a god that doesn't talk.

As soon as God opens His mouth, there is religion, doctrine, and assertions. As soon as God talks, there is truth, and the truth is always distinguished from error. The desire for spirituality without religion is the idolatrous longing of the sinful heart for a god that is mute. Conveniently for the spiritual-but-not-religious, if god is mute, then god doesn't say anything about what is right or wrong. The mute god of the spiritual-but-not-religious is very supportive, but it never tells me anything I don't know. It never tells me that something I am doing is wrong. It never tells me anything at all. The mute god makes no judgments, has no opinions, and its thoughts about right and wrong always match perfectly the judgments of the spiritual-but-not-religious person. The mute god will never interrupt my plans with its commands.

The mute god is nice, and apparently this god is what you find at the end of every "spiritual" path, no matter what kind of path it is. The mute god's chief concern is my happiness.

The mute god has no commands, but neither does it have any promises.

Spirituality without religion tries to free us from the Law and its condemnation, but in the end, it only mutes the Gospel. The Law cannot be silenced, but the Gospel can, and spirituality without religion silences the grace and kindness of God in Christ. It is impossible for sheep to hear a shepherd with no voice.

Christians have a God who speaks.

This is a fundamental Christian truth: God talks. In doing so, He not only gives us truth, but He also gives us life. God speaks, and there is light. God speaks, and there is life. God speaks, and the world is full of living things, and the world is good. God speaks, and sinners are forgiven. God speaks, and the dead are raised. God's speaking is our hope and our life, our confidence and our comfort.

Jesus says, "My sheep hear My voice, and I know them, and they follow Me" (John 10:27). There is a voice to be heard, a kind and forgiving voice. A voice that creates and re-creates. God speaks!

The Bible is this speaking of God. "All Scripture is breathed out by God" (2 Timothy 3:16). "Thus says the Lord" is the chief mark of the Scriptures, and it is what matters. The Bible alone is the fountain from which all saving truth flows.

In the Scriptures, God tells us things we don't know on our own, things we can't know on our own, and things we must know. And more than this—He accomplishes things with His Word. The Word of the Lord sounded in the nothingness before creation and brought forth the cosmos and the life that fills it. The Word of the Lord continues to sound forth in the ears of sinners, and it brings forth life and salvation.

American Christianity recognizes Scripture as the Word of God, but it fails to recognize the power and authority of God's Word. In American Christianity, God's Word teaches and informs, but it does not enliven or forgive. In this chapter, we will consider what it means to know that God speaks and that His speaking is in His Word.

A WORD FROM GOD

> **"All Scripture is breathed out by God."**
>
> (2 Timothy 3:16)

"Inspired." "Inerrant." "Infallible." These are the three attributes that American Christianity has for the Scriptures, and these attributes were hard-fought.

The twentieth century was marked, in American churches, with the "Battle for the Bible." Here's the story: In late-nineteenth-century Germany, a way of studying the Scriptures known as "higher criticism" was born. Higher criticism looked at the Scriptures with critical eyes. Instead of using our human reason as a servant of the text (the "ministerial" use of reason), reason became master over the text (the "magisterial" use of reason). The higher critics compared different ancient manuscripts and saw differences in the text—a different word here or a sentence missing there. For the higher critic, these differences confirmed their assumptions: the Scriptures are of human origin (or at least the result of a cooperation between God and humanity), and the Scriptures contain error.

{ While higher criticism admits that the Scriptures *contain* God's Word, it rejects the idea that the Scriptures *are* God's Word. Instead, it assumes that the Scriptures are of human origin, filled with human motives and agendas. }

For the higher critic, the goal of theology has changed. Rather than bringing truths out of the Scriptures, the critic is trying to determine which parts of the Bible are true and which are not.

Assuming the human origin of the Scriptures, higher critics are free to guess at the motives of the writers. It is no surprise they find the motives to be political. According to the higher critic, the writers of the Scriptures were writing propaganda to advance their own political-theological agenda. The higher critic looks past the words and finds the "true" meaning in the deceptive intent of the human author.

Is the Bible God's Word? Higher criticism might admit that the Scriptures *contain* God's Word, but it denies that the Scriptures *are* God's Word. Doubt is introduced into every page and promise of the Scriptures. If the Scriptures cannot be the standard of truth, higher critics need another standard with which to judge. They must have an abstract principle they can use to judge the Scriptures and determine if this or that passage is true. That principle might be an abstract idea of "the Gospel," or scientific thinking, or (most likely) the trends of popular or academic culture.

Higher criticism erodes the teaching of the Scriptures. The miracles of the Scriptures are the first to be questioned for being unscientific. Higher critics read Jonah like a fable and the story of Adam and Eve like a parable. They understand the creation account in Genesis 1 and 2 not as history, but mythology. Higher critics hear errors in the words of the prophets and apostles, especially when the teaching of the Bible conflicts with the norms of culture. Higher critics dismiss the teaching of Paul that women cannot be pastors as "sexist." They dismiss the teaching of Moses against homosexuality as "backwards." Scripture's teaching about the wrath of God is rejected as unenlightened. The Bible, in the hands of the higher critic, becomes a wax nose shaped to the image of the reader.

When higher criticism came to the United States, it found friends and foes. The old mainline denominations were very friendly to this teaching. Embracing higher criticism is the mark of the theologically liberal churches across all the different confessions. These denominations continue to listen for the voice of the Holy Spirit in culture. Under the sway of higher criticism, the Bible becomes a book of politically correct fables.

On the other hand, many of the churches in America stood opposed to higher criticism. They rejected the premise that the Scriptures were of human origin. They rejected the conclusion that the Scriptures contained error. They boldly stood against the ideology of the higher critic. The Southern Baptist congregations, Bible churches, and most nondenominational congregations have joyfully and clearly asserted against the higher critics that the Scriptures are inspired, inerrant, and infallible.

Inspired means "BREATHED BY GOD." Second Timothy 3:16–17 says, "All Scripture is *breathed out by God* and profitable for teaching, for reproof, for correction, and for training in righteousness, that the man of God may be complete, equipped for every good work" (emphasis added). God is the source of the Scriptures. Scripture "comes from the mouth of God" (Matthew 4:4). All of the other attributes of the Bible follow from the *inspiration* of the Scriptures.

Inerrant means "WITHOUT ERROR." When we speak of the inerrancy of the Scriptures, we are rejoicing that the Bible is true, that it is, in fact, the standard of truth. We measure the truth of any other claim against Scripture. The inerrancy of the Scriptures includes all the things that the Bible recounts, including historical facts. The Bible is both a theology book and a history book. This has profound implications, but here it is enough to note that the inerrancy of the Scriptures refers not only to the theology of the Bible but to its history as well.

Infallible means "UNABLE TO ERR." Infallibility is very close to inerrancy. The difference is subtle, but important. Inerrancy refers to the words written. Infallibility refers to the writer, in this case, God. It is possible for a human work to be inerrant, but it is impossible for a person to be infallible. Infallibility is more about the God who inspired the Scriptures than it is about the Scriptures He inspired. "It is impossible for God to lie" (Hebrews 6:18). The Scriptures, inspired by God, cannot lie.

These three attributes—
inspiration,
inerrancy,
and infallibility—
establish the trustworthiness of
the Scriptures.

The Scriptures are the only rule and norm for teaching and life. The Bible is the source and fountain of the teaching of the Church, "built on the foundation of the apostles and prophets" (Ephesians 2:20). Inspiration, inerrancy, and infallibility are only the beginning of the Lutheran doctrine of *Sola Scriptura*. There is much more to be said about the Scriptures that American Christianity does not say.

Here, though, we rejoice with American Christianity in confessing the foundational truthfulness of the Scriptures. From the very beginning, the devil raises the question "Did God really say . . . ?" The devil constantly works to undermine the commands and promises of God, as well as the life and joy that come from them. Being confident of the truth of the Scriptures, we fight the devil, saying, "Yes, the Lord did really say!"

More Than Instruction, More Than Information: Bonus Attributes of the Scriptures

The Scriptures are true. This is what is meant when we speak of their inspiration, inerrancy, and infallibility. The Church rejoices in this truth and, in fact, establishes all her teaching and doctrine on this truth. But is this all we can say about the Scriptures?

> "Lord, to whom shall we go? You have the words of eternal life."
> (John 6:68)

American Christianity confesses the truth of the Scriptures with tenacity. This is good. But its doctrine of the Scriptures stops there. There is more to say about the Bible—three more attributes to add to the list: clarity, sufficiency, and efficacy. American Christianity is weak on clarity and sufficiency, and it fails completely to confess the most important and comforting attribute, the efficacy of the Scriptures.

CLARITY

The Scriptures are clear.

The devil assaults the Word of God, and the first thing he attacks is the clarity of the Word. "Did God really say?" the devil asked Eve, and he has been asking that same question ever since. The devil wants the Bible to be unclear, the sound of the Scriptures muddled, and the light of God's Word dimmed. The devil asserts the "unclarity" of the Scriptures. He insists that something else is needed to understand the Bible.

Any church that needs someone or something to come alongside the Scriptures implicitly denies the clarity of God's Word. The Roman Catholic Church teaches the unclarity of the Scriptures when it insists that only the magisterium of the Church under the head of the pope can expound the Bible. The Roman Catholic Church puts tradition and the Church alongside the Scriptures, denying *Sola Scriptura*. Whatever stands alongside the Scriptures replaces the Scriptures. For Rome, what matters in the end is the teaching of the Church, which, in the end, is the teaching of the pope. Something similar happens in the Episcopalian confession. Tradition and reason are brought alongside the Scriptures. The Methodists add experience to the list. Whenever you have "Scripture and . . . ," the thing that matters is whatever comes after the "and."

When the clarity of Scripture is denied, an authoritative teacher is required to illuminate the text. In Roman Catholicism, this is the pope. In American Christianity, this is normally the "anointed" teacher and the visionary leader of the church. What they say from the stage is dangerously unquestioned.

The clarity of the Scriptures is also lost when an inner illumination of the Holy Spirit is needed to understand the text. It is true that the Holy Spirit gives us faith to believe the text, but in American Christianity, the Holy Spirit has to illuminate the text, teaching the individual believer the true meaning behind the words.

American Christianity finally denies the clarity of Scripture by denying theological certainty. It sounds like this: "I'm not Lutheran or Presbyterian; I'm Christian." This is saying, "I don't think we can know with certainty whose teaching is correct." The unclarity of the Scriptures abounds when small-group Bible studies are centered on the question "What does this text mean to you?" The unclarity of the Scriptures flourishes when theological assertions are labeled "opinions" or "the opinions of men." American Christianity is dogmatic on a few points, but it has a large and growing number of "open questions," that is, places where the Scriptures are not thought to speak with clarity. American Christianity is weak and growing weaker teaching the unclarity of the Scriptures.

Against anything that would cloud or muddy the text, we confess with King David the clarity of Scripture: "Your word is a lamp to my feet and a light to my path" (Psalm 119:105).

The Scriptures are sufficient.

The Lord has given us all that we need in the prophetic and apostolic Scriptures. The Bible is enough. Everything we need for life and salvation is found in Scripture; nothing more is necessary. The clarity and the sufficiency of the Scriptures go together. They stand together or they fall together.

The Roman Catholic Church denies the sufficiency of the Scriptures, teaching that the doctrine of the Church expands and grows. The liberal mainline denominations reject the sufficiency of the Scriptures, insisting that the Holy Spirit speaks through culture. The charismatic and Pentecostal churches negate the sufficiency of the Scriptures, looking for a "new work," a new word, or a new revelation from the Holy Spirit.

American Christianity has also failed in regards to the sufficiency of Scriptures. American Christianity teaches us to look for personal direction from God.

WE ARE PUT ON A CONSTANT SEARCH FOR GOD'S INDIVIDUAL WILL FOR OUR LIFE. American Christianity teaches that the Scriptures are not sufficient to answer the question "What is God's will for my life?"

According to American Christianity, if I have a "personal relationship with God," then I need a "personal revelation from God."

American Christianity expects God to let me know what job I should take, whom I should marry, what I should order for breakfast—all apart from Scripture. American Christianity fails by teaching that there is a word from God apart from the Word of God.

Jesus teaches the sufficiency of the Scriptures. Consider the story of Lazarus and the rich man (Luke 16:19–31). They both die. The rich man goes to hell. Lazarus is carried by the angels to paradise. The rich man somehow sees Lazarus in peace. He begs Abraham to send Lazarus back to his brothers so that they would see him raised from the dead and believe. The conversation unfolds like this:

> Abraham said, "They have Moses and the Prophets; let them hear them."
>
> And he said, "No, father Abraham, but if someone goes to them from the dead, they will repent."
>
> He said to him, "If they do not hear Moses and the Prophets, neither will they be convinced if someone should rise from the dead." (vv. 29–31)

Moses and the Prophets—that is enough. The Scriptures are sufficient. We rejoice that in the Lord's Word, we have all that we need for life and salvation.

EFFICACY

The Scriptures are efficacious.

This is the most important of all of the attributes of Scripture, and it is lost in American Christianity.

American Christianity understands Scripture as information, but it has no power unless we act upon it. This accounts for the great number of "ifs" in the preaching of American churches. "If you accept it . . . " "If you receive it . . . " "If you commit yourself . . . " The Scriptures tell us what to do; but it is up to us to make it count. For American Christianity, salvation is a potential. God gives you the information in the Bible. Now it is up to you if you will follow the instructions and be saved.

IF, HOWEVER, THE BIBLE IS THE VERY WORD OF GOD, THEN IT IS A DIFFERENT KIND OF WORD.

Most human talk is descriptive, but God's Word is creative. I can tell you if it is light or dark, but God says, "Let there be light," and the darkness becomes light. Pow! His Word creates. His Word declares. God's Word makes things happen.

This is the testimony of Scripture about itself: "I am not ashamed of the gospel, for it is the power of God for salvation to everyone who believes" (Romans 1:16).

"Faith comes from hearing, and hearing through the word of Christ" (Romans 10:17).

"For God, who said, 'Let light shine out of darkness,' has shone in our hearts to give the light of the knowledge of the glory of God in the face of Jesus Christ" (2 Corinthians 4:6).

"Come out," said Jesus to Lazarus (John 11:43), and he woke up from the dead. "Be still," said Jesus to the storm, and the waves went to sleep (Mark 4:39). "Believe," says Jesus to you, and you believe (Romans 1:16–17; Ephesians 2:8).

The power of the Word of God was not simply for the beginning, when the voice of God created the cosmos from nothing. This creation continues in His Word and the preaching of the Word today. Paul writes, "For since, in the wisdom of God, the world did not know God through wisdom, it pleased God through the folly of what we preach to save those who believe" (1 Corinthians 1:21).

The Word of God, and here Paul is talking about the preached Word of God, is the instrument the Holy Spirit uses to save. The Word of God is the means the Lord uses to work, to create and sustain faith, to deliver spiritual gifts, to convict us of our sin, and to comfort terrified consciences.

In the beginning, the Lord created everything *ex nihilo* ("out of nothing"). He continues to create out of nothing, and this includes our faith and our salvation.

THE EFFICACY OF THE SCRIPTURES IS THE TEACHING THAT God's Word has POWER and AUTHORITY.

The Bible is much more than information; the Scriptures themselves are active. God's Word is the sword that the Holy Spirit is wielding in the world.

The efficacy of the Scriptures is a foundational teaching. The loss of the efficacy of the Scriptures is at the root of many of the errors of American Christianity. When the efficacy of the Scriptures is lost, the result is great confusion with other doctrines, including conversion, the Sacraments, the Church, worship, evangelism, and our Christian living. If God's Word is not efficacious, creative, and powerful, then we are looking for strength and power in other places, most often in ourselves.

On the other hand, when we confess the clarity, sufficiency, and efficacy of the Scriptures, we know the Word of God is where and how the Holy Spirit works in the world and how He works on and in us. The location of spiritual activity shifts from inside to outside, from my heart to God's Word. This shift opens up the possibility of objectivity, the possibility of true certainty, and at last, true and lasting comfort.

WHERE'S THE COMFORT?

Basic

Instructions

Before

Leaving

Earth

American Christianity taught me that the Bible is an enormous instruction book. I cannot imagine a more terrible description. Who treasures instruction books? Who keeps instruction manuals on their shelf to read to their children at bedtime? Instructions can be helpful, but to call the Bible an instruction manual is to entirely miss the gifts that the Holy Spirit has for us in the Scriptures.

> "For whatever was written in former days was written for our instruction, that through endurance and through the encouragement of the Scriptures we might have hope."
>
> (Romans 15:4)

Our culture is obsessed with "self-help." We are all therapists, all on the hunt for the good life, all wanting things to be better, and we want the Bible to fit this template, to be the greatest self-help book ever. The Bible, though, decries self-help. "God helps those who help themselves" is not in the Scriptures. The prophets would call such sentiment idolatry. "The Lord is my helper" (Hebrews 13:6).

The Scriptures bring us to the end of ourselves. The Bible calls us sinners. Our help and our works are totally excluded from salvation. The Bible is not self-help. It is not therapy. It does offer us peace, but it is the peace of repentance, the peace that comes from the outside, peace accomplished before we were born in the bleeding and dying of Jesus.

Instruction books are all about what we do. Self-help is all Law. But the Scriptures are a Gospel book, full and overflowing with promises. If we read the Bible as an instruction book, then we find only Law. If we read the Bible like a self-help manual, then we totally miss the gifts, the promises, the kindness of God revealed in the Scriptures. If we treat the Bible like "Basic Instructions Before Leaving Earth," the central teaching of the Scriptures—the forgiving death of Jesus—is lost. THE PAGES OF THE BIBLE ARE DOUSED WITH THE FORGIVING BLOOD OF JESUS.

The Holy Spirit, the Comforter, inspires the words of Scripture. Those words bring comfort, hope, and peace, even as they create and sustain faith.

QUESTIONS TO BRING TO THE SCRIPTURES (OR, WHAT WE EXPECT TO FIND IN THE BIBLE)

In our reading, we often find what we are looking for. The questions we bring to the text determine what we take out of the text. If we look to the Scriptures only for instructions for daily living, we will find what we are looking for, but we will miss the promises. We will be blind to the comfort. I know this. For years I read my Bible asking, "What is God telling me to do today?" This is the question American Christianity teaches us to ask. It is really the only question American Christianity knows how to ask. The result of asking this question was a moral reading of the Bible. When I open up my old Bible, I find all the passages of instruction underlined. All the Law passages are highlighted. But none of the passages of forgiveness and promise are marked; it's as if they were skipped over. I didn't know what to do with them. My Christian life was always about me, my actions, my thoughts, my love for

God and neighbor, the strength of my faith, the depth of my sorrow. The Bible must be about the same things, right?

The Bible as an instruction book also makes the Bible into a measuring stick. How am I doing? Am I living a Christian life? Was God happy with me today? Did I disappoint Him or make Him proud? This is a Law-reductionism that reads only commands and completely misses the promises. The trouble is without the Gospel, there are no good answers to these questions.

If I think I've done well and accomplished all the things the Lord wanted, I am proud. If I see my own failures, I despair. A Gospel-less reading of the Scriptures puts us on the pendulum between pride and despair, swinging between the two devastating poles of success and failure.

American Christianity fails to teach the centrality of the Gospel in the Bible. When we read the Scriptures, we need to hear the

Lord's Law, but not only the Law. We need, above all, to hear the Gospel. "What is God telling me to do today?" although a good question, is not enough. We need another question.

So we next ask, "What is God teaching me about Himself?" This question gives us a theological reading of the Scriptures. This question helps bring out the truth of the Scriptures and helps us see theological errors. In many ways, the theological reading of the Scriptures needs to be recovered in the Church today. American Christianity has developed a distaste for theology, an aversion to careful distinctions. "Deeds, not creeds" is the rally cry, calling the Church away from theology and doctrine. This is absurd. The Bible gives us creeds and deeds, teaching and instruction, faith and life.

In fact, almost every book of the Bible was written to correct theological errors. We see this especially in Paul. He wrote his epistles because of the false teaching in the churches. He wrote to correct false doctrine (as well as bad practice). The true prophets preached and wrote against the false prophets. If God were not interested in correcting false doctrine, we wouldn't have a Bible. We search the Scriptures to know the truth, the truth about ourselves, and especially the truth about God. This truth is theology. When truth is set against error, we have doctrine.

Doctrine is a strange word for American Christianity, but it is nothing other than the answer to Jesus' questions: "Who do people say that the Son of Man is?" and "Who do you say that I am?" (Matthew 16:13, 15). The knowledge of the truth, the knowledge of Jesus, is more than trivia. It is life. Jesus prays, "This is eternal life, that they know You the only true God, and Jesus Christ whom You have sent" (John 17:3).

Our doctrine is our salvation.

This might sound outlandish to anti-theological and anti-doctrinal American Christianity, but it is true. Paul writes to Timothy, "Keep a close watch on yourself and on the teaching (doctrine). Persist in this, for by so doing you will save both yourself and your hearers" (1 Timothy 4:16).

The Scriptures warn us constantly about false teaching. In the Bible, the word *beware* is used only in regard to false doctrine. (See Matthew 7:15; 16:6–12; Philippians 3:2; Colossians 2:8; and 2 Peter 3:17.) The work of distinguishing truth from error, distasteful as it might seem to us, is a good work that Jesus has given to His Church. We read the Scriptures asking, "What does this teach me about God?" We read the Scriptures looking for teaching, looking for truth, looking for assertions and doctrine.

The theological question, though, is not the last question.

God gives the Scriptures to us so that we would have hope, life, and comfort. So we ask, at last, "WHERE IS THE COMFORT? Where is the forgiveness of my sins? Where is my Savior Jesus?" With these questions, the Gospel shines through. "For whatever was written in former days was written for our instruction, that through endurance and through the encouragement of the Scriptures we might have hope" (Romans 15:4). When we look for the comfort of the text, then we find the heart of the Scriptures and the purpose of God's Word: the forgiveness of our sins. The Bible, at last, is a revelation of God's work of salvation for us. The Scriptures give what we can obtain nowhere else: the life-winning, sin-forgiving death of Jesus brought into our ears and heart as the sure and certain promise of God's kindness for us.

"To Him all the prophets bear witness that everyone who believes in Him receives forgiveness of sins through His name" (Acts 10:43). The prophets, the apostles, and the evangelists all preach and write about Jesus and the forgiveness He brings to us. The Scriptures forgive. The Scriptures absolve. The Scriptures give hope. The Scriptures comfort us poor miserable sinners with the joy that Christ has died and risen for our salvation.

American Christianity fails when it teaches that the Bible is an instruction book. It is far more wonderful than that. The Bible is even more than a theology book. It is a promise book, swelling with God's grace and mercy, His comfort and peace. The Bible delivers to us the absolute certainty of His love and our salvation through Christ.

God's Word Is Awesome

> "I will delight in Your statues; I will not forget Your word."
> (Psalm 119:16)

"Inspired," "inerrant," "infallible," "clear," "sufficient," and "efficacious"—with these adjectives and attributes, we extol the Scriptures. The Bible has its origin in the mouth of God and its end in our salvation. It is altogether true and trustworthy to teach and to save. The Scriptures are our life.

Why, then, don't we study them? Why don't we delight in them? We have forgotten a last attribute of the Bible: it is awesome. The Bible is good. It is delightful. It is our treasure and our joy.

Consider Psalm 1. The psalmist gives two contrasting pictures. First, we see a tree planted by a river—its leaves always green, bearing fruit in its season. Then we see the chaff, the dusty and delicate husks of wheat blown away by the slightest breeze. "The wicked . . . are like chaff that the wind drives away" (v. 4). But who is this tree by the river? Is it the one who reads the Bible? Almost. "His delight is in the law of the Lord, and on His law he meditates day and night" (v. 2). The blessed man doesn't just read the Lord's Word and study the Lord's Word; the blessed man delights in the Word of the Lord. He loves it and considers it precious, the most precious thing he has.

A strange thing happens when we delight in the Scriptures. When we eat food, the more we eat, the more we are satisfied. We desire less. We all know that feeling of being "stuffed" after a big Thanksgiving meal. "I can't eat another bite." When we are satisfied with food, we do not want to eat another bite. Satisfaction ends desire. The Scriptures are the opposite. The more we hear, read, learn, and meditate on the Scriptures, the more we want to hear, read, learn, and meditate on them. With the Scriptures, satisfaction and desire belong together. Delighting and longing go together. When we delight in the Scriptures, we can't get enough. The Scriptures create in us a desire for more. "Behold, I long for Your precepts; in Your righteousness give me life!" (Psalm 119:40).

This is delighting in the Lord's Word, the longing of a thirsting soul for a drink, the cry of a sinful soul for forgiveness, the begging of an impoverished soul for the riches of the kingdom of heaven. In the Scriptures, these prayers are answered and these desires are fulfilled. The abundance of the Lord's kingdom tumbles down to us for the taking.

When it comes to desire, we think we are passive. We consider ourselves victims of our taste; we like something or we don't. And worse, we are often tempted by this world to think that our desires (our likes and wants) are inspired and infallible. "Whatever makes you happy," we say with godless abandon, as if our happiness is perfect or our desires can't be wrong. The Scriptures, on the other hand, teach that we can have sinful desires. We sin not only by what we do, say, and think, but also by what we want. Wanting the wrong thing is breaking God's Law.

We often use our desire as proof that our actions are good. "But I love him . . . " "Well," says God's Word, "you love the wrong thing." "This makes me happy . . . " "Your happiness is broken." God's Word judges even our wants and desires, our delight and our love. We hear this judgment in the last two commandments: "You shall not covet." It is entirely possible that we feel the wrong way, that we like the wrong things, and that our desires are wicked.

There is a war over our delight.

The devil puts before us every sort of thing we could want or desire. Our longing is pulled away from the things that are good and pushed toward things that destroy life and peace. We delight so easily in the things of this world. Our attention is swept away with the troubles and excitements of this life. These things are all passing away. Only the Lord's Word endures forever (Isaiah 40:8; 1 Peter 1:25). His Word is our delight, and when we delight in His Word, we have life and peace.

Delighting in Scripture is recognizing that Scripture is the voice of God our Father who loves us. That voice is not the booming condemnation of the Law, but the sweet promise of the Gospel. The delight of the Scriptures is that this Word marches out of the mouth of God, who loves me beyond comprehension. The delight of the Scriptures is that this Word comes from the mouth of Jesus, who did not come to condemn the world, but that the world through Him might be saved

(John 3:17). The delight of the Scriptures is that this Word is the sword of the Spirit by which I am given the gift of faith. The delight of the Scriptures is that in this Word, I am hearing the voice of the God who loves me, who has rescued me from sin, death, and hell. "My sheep hear My voice" (John 10:27). That is awesome. That is delighting in God's Word.

THE SURPRISE OF THE NEXT PAGE

> "And when Jesus finished these sayings, the crowds were astonished at His teaching."
> (Matthew 7:28)

We are rarely astonished about anything, especially when it comes to the things of the Scriptures.

The devil tempts us to desire things that are sinful. And there is an opposite and equally dangerous temptation: to not desire the things that we should. This is the sin of boredom. We rarely think of boredom as a sin, but the devil uses our lack of desire against us.

This often happens with married couples. The devil tempts them to be bored with each other. There is no liveliness in their conversation. Parents become bored with their children, and children with their parents. School becomes boring, work becomes boring, church becomes boring. The devil assaults us with boredom. Boredom is such a subtle sin that we don't even notice it. There is wisdom, though, in the Ancient Church. It recognized boredom as one of the seven deadly sins: *acedia*. Sometimes translated as "sloth," acedia is a flattening of desire. Acedia is a lack of desire for anything, especially the things of God.

Every Christian is tempted by the devil to become bored with the Scriptures. "I've read that before. I've heard it all. I know that." "The Bible is old hat, and I am looking for more exciting things."

This desire for something new and exciting runs through American Christianity. This desire for something new, exciting, and entertaining stands behind the adjective *contemporary*, which is stuck like a leech to the word *worship*. Buzzwords like *relevant* and *life-application* are indications that we seek excitement—most often an excitement apart from the Scriptures.

The excitement is in the text. The surprise is on the next page. The Bible has the most profoundly surprising words ever written. God never does what you expect. If you try to guess as you read the Bible, "What will happen next?" you will always be wrong.

Adam and Eve break God's design. What happens next? God comes and promises His own death to save them!

The entire world sinks into wickedness. What happens next? God has Noah build a boat and rescues him through the destroying flood.

Abram worships idols. What happens next? God calls him to be the father of the Messiah.

God's people are slaves in Egypt, and after four hundred years of things getting worse, they remember to pray and ask God for help. What happens next? God waits for eighty years and then sits in a flaming bush and tells Moses to go and argue with Pharaoh.

David wants to build a temple for God in Jerusalem. What happens next? God forbids it and promises to build David's house, promising the Messiah would be born of David.

Contrary to all the evidence, we are tempted to think of God like a machine (instead of a person, in fact, three persons). We think God will act according to a mathematical regression, that His actions will be precise and predictable. The Bible will not let this expectation stand.

While the Lord always keeps His promises, He never does what we expect. This is why reading the Bible is an adventure; it is about the three most astonishing and unpredictable characters there ever will be: the Father, the Son, and the Holy Spirit. Their conversation, their works, and their thoughts are all above ours. Every word and act of God is a surprise.

Every page of the Bible, every chapter, shows this. God never does what we expect of Him, and this delightful unexpectedness crescendos in the New Testament.

Jesus is the best at surprises. A man asks to be healed, and Jesus spits on his eyes. A woman prays that her daughter would be rescued from the demons, and Jesus acts like He can't hear her and then calls her a dog. He walks on water, sleeps through a storm, and pays taxes with a coin in a fish's mouth. Jesus blesses the children, drives out the money-changers with a whip, visits Samaritan towns, and talks to a Samaritan woman. In fact, we are always surprised to find Jesus in the company of sinners, tax collectors, and prostitutes. His teaching is always astonishing. His life is always shocking, and His death is the biggest surprise of all. "He opened not His mouth" (Isaiah 53:7) before His accusers. He is struck, whipped, mocked, spit on, falsely accused, nailed to a cross, dies, and is buried. That is not expected. The

Lord of Life, the Creator of the universe, in flesh and blood like mine, bearing my sin, suffering what I deserve. He was crucified. And all of this is for me!

We are awed, stunned, at the surprise of the Gospel. "My heart faints within me!" (Job 19:27).

The Gospel is always a surprise.

We, in some ways, expect the Law. God says, "You're a sinner." And we say, "Yeah, I thought You would say that. I figured You noticed." But then: "Your sins are forgiven." "Really?" "I died for you." "What!?" "I love you. I delight in you." "Can this be true?" The Gospel is always a surprise because it is never earned. It is never expected because it is never deserved.

American Christianity fails when it looks for something to spice up the Scriptures and when it seeks something more exciting than God's Word. The devil tempts us to be bored with the Scriptures, but we fight this temptation with the Scriptures themselves. The Bible is the antidote. God's Word creates faith, and God's Word creates delight and joy in His Word, in His Gospel.

The blood of Jesus is spilled on every page of the Scriptures.

This is the same blood that covers you and washes away your sins. And with this blood, your name is written in His Book of Life.

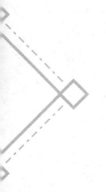

CHAPTER THREE

HOW BAD A BOY ARE YA?

"You were dead in the trespasses and sins."
(Ephesians 2:1)

All falls are not the same. Falling off your bike is quite different from falling off the top of a building.

Every theology has a doctrine of the fall. And every doctrine of the fall answers certain questions about the fall. The questions are How far was the fall? Was man wounded or killed? How much of man's original goodness and freedom is left, if anything? What is our true condition?

The latter is an especially important question. An error here will spread through our entire theological thinking. If we get the diagnosis wrong, then the cure will certainly be wrong as well. Woe to the man with a gunshot wound whom the doctor diagnoses with cancer!

We know we can't trust ourselves with the question of our true condition. If you ask the man on the street if he is a good person, the answer is almost always "Yes!" or at least, "I'm better than most." Everyone can't be "better than most." Paul reminds us that we are all bad, really bad. "None is righteous, no, not one; no one understands; no one seeks for God. All have turned aside; together they have become worthless; no one does good, not even one" (Romans 3:10–12).

The Scriptures teach that we are "dead in the trespasses and sins" (Ephesians 2:1). Our sinful flesh is incapable of knowing or understanding God's Word (1 Corinthians 2:14). We are, by nature, God's enemies (Romans 5:10), "children of wrath" (Ephesians 2:3). The diagnosis is bleak.

The Bible's teaching of original sin is the preface to the Gospel. If we are not the "children of wrath," then the wrath of God poured out on Jesus is ridiculous. If we are not "dead in the trespasses and sins," then the death of God for us is nonsense. In other words, the only way the death of Jesus makes sense is if we are broken beyond repair.

Unfortunately, many theologies soften the Bible's teaching on sin, and this is true of American Christianity.

> { American Christianity softens the Bible's teaching on sin. }

According to American Christianity, the fall made us sick and weak, but not dead. American Christianity teaches that we are depraved, but not totally. It assumes that there is some spark of good, some small amount of strength and power left in us after the fall, enough for us to cooperate in the work of salvation.

American Christianity teaches that we have a tendency to sin, but that this tendency is not itself sin, and that our free will to obey God was not destroyed in the fall. In fact, all of the theological tenets we have identified at the root of American Christianity require some manner of goodness to be preserved in us after the fall. This teaching is wrong and has disastrous results in the conscience.

Revivalism, which necessitates that the unbeliever make a decision for Christ, requires a free will. Pietism, which expects me to find comfort in my own good works, assumes my ability to accomplish good works. Mysticism assumes I can stand face-to-face with God, so there must be something good or noble left inside me that can withstand the holy presence of God.

How Original Is Sin? Or, How Did Things Get This Bad?

One of the worst sentences in the Bible is Genesis 3:8:

> "[We] were by nature children of wrath, like the rest of mankind."
> (Ephesians 2:3)

And they [Adam and Eve] heard the sound of the Lord God walking in the garden in the cool of the day, and the man and his wife hid themselves from the presence of the Lord God among the trees of the garden.

This is not how things should be. When Adam and Eve hear the sound of the Lord God in the garden, they should want to run to Him and fall at His feet, laughing like children who hear their father coming home from work. Adam and Eve should delight to be in God's presence, to talk with Him, to spend the day learning from Him, to rejoice in all the gifts of creation. There should have been peace and joy and love between Adam and Eve and God.

Adam and Eve were created by God and set in the Garden of Eden in order to rejoice in the Lord's gifts. They were to eat of every tree but one. They were to have dominion over all the living things. They were to see that the earth brought forth life. They were to rejoice in one another, to have a large family and fill the earth. Most of all, Adam and Eve were to rejoice in God. There should have been no greater joy than "the sound of the LORD God walking in the garden."

But Adam and Eve run and hide, scared for their lives. They are in the bushes holding their breath, hoping the Lord won't find them. They had eaten the fruit. They had broken the universe. They had undone the goodness of God's creation with their disobedience. The sound of Adam's teeth crunching into the fruit was the sound of a million deaths. So the sound of God walking in the garden was the most fearful thing Adam and Eve would ever know. They should be afraid. They are naked, ashamed, and doomed, and we are doomed with them.

This is the day they died, the day they listened to the voice of the devil, the day they doubted God's Word. Adam and Eve stood as judges over the Lord's command. Instead of believing God's Word that on the day they ate of the forbidden fruit, they would "surely die" (Genesis 2:17), they believed the words of the devil.

Unbelief came first, then death. By the time Adam and Eve ate the fruit, they were already dead.

AND SO WERE YOU.

The crunch of the fruit was the sound of the universe breaking; it was the song of the devil's coronation, the beginning of the reign of death.

This is original sin. Adam and Eve's disobedience affected more than this first couple. Their sin sent shock waves through the entire creation, even into the future. All the children born of Adam and Eve are born with their sin and their rebellion. We inherit their fall.

> Original sin does not refer to the origin of sin but to the guilt of Adam's sin imputed to his offspring. It also refers to the corruption of man's nature that occurred when sin entered and that inheres in the human will and inclinations. It is "the chief sin, which is a root and fountainhead of all actual sins." (FC SD I 5)

I remember teaching original sin to a group of youth. One of them thanked me; she always thought that "original sin" meant a sin that no one else had ever thought of! As it turns out, original sin is not that original at all.

There is a very important text in the opening chapters of Genesis:

> This is the book of the generations of Adam. When God created man, He made him in the likeness of God. Male and female He created them, and He blessed them and named them Man when they were created. When Adam had lived 130 years, he fathered a son in his own likeness, after his image, and named him Seth.
> (Genesis 5:1–3)

Adam and Eve were created in God's image and likeness. Now, after the fall, Seth was born in the image and likeness of his father, Adam. The image and likeness of God had been lost. Seth was born a sinner, born dying, born in a fallen world to fallen parents with a fallen sinful flesh. "In sin did my mother conceived me," said King David, generations later (Psalm 51:5). "In Adam all die" (1 Corinthians 15:22). We inherit Adam's sin. We inherit Adam's death.

This inherited death is more than physical death. In Romans 5:12–21, Paul explores the depth of the fall, comparing it with the height of Jesus' love. "Therefore, just as sin came into the world through one man, and death through sin, and so death spread to all men, because all sinned . . . " (Romans 5:12).

- Notice, first, the connection between death and sin. These three—sin, death, and the devil—are always bound up to one another. You cannot have one without the other.

- Second, no one is exempted from sin and death. "Death spread to all men." Sin and death are universal.

- Third, the fact that we inherited our sin does not excuse us from the guilt of sin. "All sinned" means everyone is guilty of sin and personally responsible for the consequences of sin: God's wrath in hell. When we inherit sin, we inherit everything that goes with it. We are born "children of wrath" (Ephesians 2:3). Our birthright is destruction. Our inheritance is hell.

This is not a particularly cheerful teaching, but it is true. We are guilty and condemned before we ever manage to commit a sin. From the moment of our conception, we are damnable. Sin has corrupted everything about us: our body and soul, our reason and all our senses, our conscience and our will.

There is an old theological chicken-and-egg question: Are we sinners because we sin, or do we sin because we are sinners? Which comes first: our sinful nature or our sinful acts?

Most theologies, including many in American Christianity, teach that we become sinners when we sin. Sinful actions come first, and when we sin, we become sinners.

The Scriptures teach the opposite. The bad tree produces bad fruit. Our sinful nature comes first, and then the fruit of actual sins. We sin because we are sinners. We are the bad tree that bears bad fruit. Before our sinful actions make us guilty, we are guilty because of our sinful flesh. We are, "by nature," children of wrath. This has profound implications. It is not primarily our sins that get us into trouble with God; they are the symptoms of a deeper problem. The root of our trouble is our sinful heart.

If it was our sinful actions that got us in trouble in the first place, then maybe, just maybe, our good works could get us out of it. But we were in trouble long before we managed to commit our first sin. We were conceived in sin and deserving of wrath from the very first moment of our existence. This means it is impossible for us to save ourselves. Our only hope for salvation is another, a Savior. We inherited sin and condemnation from our father Adam, so we must inherit life and new birth and find salvation in our adoption into a new family. Adam brought death. Christ brings life.

I'm Talking About the Man in the Mirror

Theologians speak of three uses (or functions) of the Law: the curb, the mirror, and the guide.

The curb of the Law keeps society in order. It keeps us from hurting and harming one another, dishonoring marriage, taking other people's stuff, and damaging the reputation of our neighbor. The Law as a curb is why we have government, military, police, courts and judges, and jails and stop signs.

Skipping ahead for a minute, the third use of the Law is the guide or map. According to this use, the Law gives shape to our Christian love and service to the neighbor. While the first use of the Law makes sure I don't hurt or harm my neighbors, the third use puts me alongside my neighbors to love them, to serve them, to lay down my life for them, to forgive them, to pray for them and bless them.

> "Through the law comes knowledge of sin."
> (Romans 3:20)

Because we are forgiven by Jesus, we are set free from the need to self-justify. There is no need to justify our existence or our actions, to ourselves, to God, or to our neighbor. You are already justified. The righteous One, the Son of God who sits at the right hand of the Father, declares you righteous through the spoils of His victorious death and resurrection. This means you have nothing to prove. Think of that! God loves you, and this gives you the freedom and courage to risk a good work, to suffer and die for the neighbors God has given you.

The second use of the Law is the mirror. The Law shows us our sin. It accuses us. This is the theological use of the Law, and it is the chief and most important function of the Law. As a mirror, the Law condemns us. The Law teaches us something that we can't know by our feelings and experiences, namely, that sin has corrupted us to the core. The Law teaches us that all of the wrong things we do, say, and think are the symptoms of an even deeper problem. I am a poor, miserable sinner.

Any honest person would confess that he makes mistakes. "I'm not perfect." We might even confess that those mistakes are sins. But if we are to know that our nature is corrupt and our heart is wicked, then God's Law must teach this to us.

The Law as a mirror not only shows me my sin, but it also shows me what that sin deserves: God's wrath. The mirror of the Law shows me that I deserve to be condemned to hell.

The prophet Jeremiah called the Law of God a hammer that smashes us to pieces (Jeremiah 23:29). The Law smashes us when it shows us how repulsive and offensive we are to the holiness of God. The cross and suffering of Jesus are the most severe preaching of the Law. His pain and shame and darkness should be ours. We should be the ones forsaken and smitten by God (see Psalm 22:1 and Isaiah 53:4).

When the Law is doing this mirror work of showing us our sin and accusing us, we are tempted to think that the Law is the problem, that the Law is bad. No, the Law is supremely good. The problem is our sin.

Have you seen those bathroom mirrors with lights and magnification? Every blemish, every spot, every wrinkle is magnified in those mirrors. They make mountains out of molehills and out of noses. The problem is not the mirror. The problem is the face. This is what the perfect Law of God does. It shines the light of God's holiness on our sin. It magnifies failures that we want to cover up.

If we compare ourselves to one another, we think we are okay, but as soon as the Lord's perfection comes into the picture, we see what failures we are. We are undone. The mirror of the Law undoes us; it brings us to the end of ourselves; it demolishes the delusion of our righteousness. This is exactly what Jesus wants. He wants us undone. He wants us to know our sin. He wants us to despair our own goodness. He wants us to come to the end of ourselves. "He has brought down the mighty from their thrones" (Luke 1:52). The mirror of the Law crushes our trust in ourselves to make room for faith in His promises.

I remember a time when my mom asked me to clean my room. I went in and turned off the lights. "Done!" My filthy room looked like a museum in the dark! (It looked like a dump in the light.) The mirror of the Law throws the lights on. It shows our sin. It contrasts our failure with the Lord's perfect righteousness.

This is what Paul teaches in Romans 3: "Through the Law comes knowledge of sin" (v. 20). The Law puts our lives, our actions, our motives, even ourselves in the light of God's holiness. There is no escaping the conclusion: we are poor, miserable sinners. The Law shows us how far we have fallen, how much was lost in Adam's rebellion, the righteousness we had when God created us in His image.

Only the Sick Need a Doctor, and You Are More Than Sick

> "Those who are well have no need of a physician, but those who are sick."
> (Matthew 9:12)

"Those who are well have no need of a physician, but those who are sick" (Matthew 9:12). With these words, Jesus condemns the Pharisees. The problem with the Pharisees was not that they were healthy and didn't need a doctor. The problem was that they did not know they were sick. If you don't know you are sick, you don't know that you need a doctor. If you don't know you are a sinner, you don't know that you need a Savior.

One of the indicators of the depth of our fall is that we don't know how bad we are. We are so broken that we can't feel our brokenness. Sin has corrupted us so profoundly that we don't know how sinful we are.

I remember a Sunday afternoon in seminary. A classmate and I were talking outside his apartment. We heard a crash and ran down the street. We found a man under a motorcycle, crashed into a tree. "Are you okay?" we asked as we came to him. I'll always remember his answer, "I don't know. I can't feel my legs." He had broken his neck. He was hurt so badly, he didn't know how hurt he was.

Imagine two men who fall off a ladder. One breaks his leg and cries out in pain for help. He knows he is hurt, wounded, and needs help. The other man falls and breaks his legs and his back. He feels no pain at all. He thinks he's okay. This is our corruption. This is how deeply we have fallen. The awareness of our own sin is corrupted. Even our conscience is broken.

One of the marks of the fall is that we think we are good. The Pharisees thought they were good, healthy, and didn't need any help. The sinful flesh of humanity thinks it is good and doesn't need a Savior. We are so sick that we think we are healthy, so corrupted that we think we are whole.

The thing that should be the most obvious to us—our sin—is not obvious at all. The most basic truth of the Scriptures—we deserve God's eternal wrath—is the most difficult to grasp. We are so sick that we are delusional. We think we are healthy, "good people."

Martin Luther said, "This hereditary sin is such a deep corruption of nature that no reason can understand it. Rather, it must be believed from the revelation of Scripture" (SA III I 3). We have to be taught our corruption. We have to be shown our sin.

Luther's insight is not only about our sin but is also an insight into the Law.

We need to be shown our sin. The Law

of God does this. The Law shows us our sin. It reveals God's wrath. It proves the deadness of our flesh.

There is a bad theological argument that has been hanging around the Church for centuries. It shows up in slightly different forms in different places and at different times, but it basically goes like this: God would not command what we cannot do. The command to do something implies the ability to accomplish it. The argument says that because there is Law, then there must be the freedom and power to keep the Law.

Erasmus used this argument against Luther. They were fighting about the freedom or bondage of man's will. "If we were not free to keep the Law," Erasmus argued, "then God would be a cruel tyrant to demand of us things that we cannot do, and punish us for not doing them. We must, then, be free to keep the Law."[3] The Law of God, Erasmus argued, proves our goodness, or at least our ability to do good.

Luther's response was (I'm simplifying), "You should read what the Bible says about the Law." Paul writes to the Romans, "Through the Law comes knowledge of sin" (Romans 3:20). The Law shows our sin. The Law reveals God's wrath. The Law is a diagnostic that teaches us the truth that we would otherwise never know: we are sick, fallen, dead in trespasses and sins. We are children of wrath deserving of hell.

Keeping the Law was possible before the fall of Adam and Eve. But it is no longer. While the Law did not change in the fall, its purpose did. After the fall, the chief purpose of the Law is not obedience, but repentance. The Law drags us to the end of ourselves, it demolishes any illusion of our own goodness, it crushes the lie of our freedom, it murders the rumor of our life, and, at last, it shows us the truth of our desperate wickedness.

The Law gives us the diagnosis: we are worse than sick. We are dead, "dead in the trespasses and sins" (Ephesians 2:1). It is the knowledge of this death that makes us ready for the Gospel, ready for Jesus, ready for the resurrection of faith and the new life that the promise of the Gospel brings to us. Until we know we are dead in trespasses and sin, we think we might have something to do with our sal-

---

3   See LW 33:120–21.

vation; but when the Law brings to us the "knowledge of sin," then we know most of all that we need a Savior.

Your Will in Chains

> "The natural person does not accept the things of the Spirit of God, for they are folly to him, and he is not able to understand them because they are spiritually discerned."
>
> (1 Corinthians 2:14)

The question of free will is ancient and ongoing. Are we free or not? To what degree? What are the effects of the fall on our freedom?

The Lutheran theologians made a helpful distinction regarding free will.

Our will is free regarding the things of this life. Our will is bound regarding the things of God. Concerning working, getting married, caring for our neighbor, being a good citizen, and other parts of our creaturely life in this world, we have some freedom. The Lord gives us wisdom and freedom regarding questions like "Where should I live?" or "What should I study in school?" and "Whom should I marry?" These things belong to our free will. Of course, our freedom is very limited. A man can only marry a woman if she agrees to his proposal. The type of job you have depends on your skills, the job availability, and so forth. There is a freedom, as the old theologians said, regarding the things "below us."

We sinners have no freedom, though, regarding the things "above us," the things of God. "The natural person does not accept the things of the Spirit of God, for they are folly to him, and he is not able to understand them because they are spiritually discerned" (1 Corinthians 2:14). Our will is not free to believe in God, to trust Him, or to believe that He hears our prayers and will help us when we are dying. We are not free to fear, love, and trust in God above all things. The unbeliever does not believe in God, and cannot. That is the very definition of *unbelief*. "For the mind that is set on the flesh is hostile to God, for it does not submit to God's law; indeed, it cannot" (Romans 8:7).

American Christianity flips this understanding upside down. There is much consternation about what God's will is for my daily life. "What should I do? Whom should I marry? What color socks should I wear?" There is prayer and fasting to determine what God's will is concerning the small things of this life. There is a constant seeking for private instructions from God regarding the things that God has put in the realm of our free will. On the flip side, there is the assumption that we are free to choose those things above us. Our will is considered free in regards to spiritual things. American Christianity teaches that we can, that we must, make a decision to follow Christ. It assumes we are free to believe in God, to trust His promises, to follow after Him and keep His commandments. Freedom is turned on its head. The American Christian assumes a free will where there is bondage and a bound will where there is freedom.

The confusion of American Christianity regarding the fallen will of mankind is especially seen in the constant call for the unbeliever to "make a decision for Christ." Is this possible? Can the unbeliever make a decision for Christ?

"Have you invited Jesus into your heart?"

This question gushes out of American Christianity. "Have you received Jesus as your personal Lord and Savior?" "Have you dedicated your life to Christ?" Altar calls, times of decision, emotional appeals for the person to respond: all assume we are free to do this. All of these questions have the same premise: the unbeliever has the ability to choose Jesus. But is this what the Bible teaches?

> Altar calls, times of decision, emotional appeals for the person to respond: all assume the unbeliever has the ability to choose Jesus.

WHAT CAN WE DO?

Paul speaks of our conversion as a move from death to life. "And you He made alive, who were dead in trespasses and sins" (Ephesians 2:1 NKJV; see also v. 5 and Colossians 2:13). We are dead in trespasses and sins. Not sick, not crippled, dead. We are, says Paul, dead in our sins, completely unable to choose or decide anything regarding Jesus. Again, Paul writes, "The natural person does not accept the things of the Spirit of God, for they are folly to him, and he is not able to understand them because they are spiritually discerned" (1 Corinthians 2:14). The things of the Spirit of God (and this certainly includes the truth of Jesus and His cross and death for us) are unknown and unknowable to the natural man and the mind of flesh. The Gospel is "foolishness" (1 Corinthians 1:23, 25) to those who do not believe. How, then, could we invite unbelievers to make a decision for that which they think foolish?

They Cannot.

Again, Paul says, "For the desires of the flesh are against the Spirit, and the desires of the Spirit are against the flesh, for these are opposed to each other, to keep you from doing the things you want to do" (Galatians 5:17). Far from accepting the good news of Jesus, our sinful flesh fights against it. Stephen, the first martyr after Jesus' ascension, preaches to the Jews in Jerusalem, "You stiff-necked people, uncircumcised in heart and ears, you always resist the Holy Spirit. As your fathers did, so do you" (Acts 7:51). Such accusation stands over the entire unbelieving world: "They are darkened in their understanding, alienated from the life of God because of the ignorance that is in them, due to their hardness of heart" (Ephesians 4:18).

Far from having a free will to choose or make a decision for Jesus, the Scriptures speak of the natural condition of man as an enemy of God. "For the mind that is set on the flesh is hostile to God, for it does not submit to God's law; indeed, it cannot" (Romans 8:7). The fleshly mind "does not" and "cannot" submit to God's Law. Such sure testimonies answer the question "Can we make a decision for Christ?" The Scriptures plainly tell us "no." Paul quotes the Psalms: "None is righteous, no, not one; no one understands; no one seeks for God. All have turned aside; together they have become worthless; no one does good, not even one" (Romans 3:10–12; cf. Psalm 14:1–3). Jesus testifies, "The light shines in the darkness, and the darkness has not overcome it" (John 1:5).

Adam and Eve, created in the image of God, had the ability to fear, love, and trust in God. But the image of God was lost in the fall, and with it the ability to love and trust in God. Our sinful flesh neither trusts nor loves God, nor does it rightly fear God. It cannot. Our will is bound up in sin and must be rescued and set free. We must be converted.

The Depth of Your Sin and the Dying of Jesus

In this chapter, we have explored the depth of our sin. We have heard the voice of the Law expose our wretchedness, our humility, and our death. We have heard the thunderclap of the Law, which flattens us. It empties us of all pride and any faith in our goodness and ourselves. There is one last word of Law that we need to hear, and it is, surprisingly, the word of the cross.

The pages of the Old Testament are full of sacrifices. Every day, animals were brought to the temple, their blood drained and their bodies burned as a constant reminder of the people's sin and as a constant reminder of the Lord's mercy. When the Israelites took a lamb to the altar, they saw the Lord accepting the death of another in their place. They knew they were sinners, and they should be punished for their

> "But He was pierced for our transgressions; He was crushed for our iniquities; upon Him was the chastisement that brought us peace, and with His wounds we are healed."
> (Isaiah 53:5)

sin. The sinner should be on the altar with blood spilled and body burning, but the Lord had arranged a substitute. This is the theology of the sacrifice, a preaching of the Law and the Gospel. It showed the punishment that the people deserved but did not receive. This preaching of the altar comes into its fullness in the sacrifice of Jesus on the cross. "Behold," preached John the Baptist from his river pulpit, pointing at Jesus, "the Lamb of God, who takes away the sin of the world" (John 1:29).

The cross is the full and final sacrifice offered for sinners. Jesus, on the cross, received the punishment we deserve. Jesus, on the cross, took our place under God's wrath. Theologically this is called the "substitutionary atonement." Jesus was our substitute, our replacement, our blessed stand-in. "He was pierced for our transgressions; He was crushed for our iniquities" (Isaiah 53:5).

If we wonder what the punishment should be for our sin, we only have to ask, "What did Jesus suffer?" That is what we deserve.

A few years back, there was a tragedy in my neighborhood. A man walked into a movie theater and began shooting. A dozen people were murdered, and seventy were wounded. The scene was horrific, the loss devastating, and Aurora, Colorado, was mourning for months. This was a terrible crime. Now, imagine a conversation with the shooter:

"Did you shoot these people?"

"Yes, I did it, and it was wrong."

"So, you acknowledge you've done wrong. What punishment do you think you deserve?"

"Yes, it was a really bad thing to do, and I think that I should have five or six hours of community service as punishment."

When you hear what he thinks his punishment should be, you realize that this man has no idea how bad he is. He has no concept of how horrible his crime was.

Let's imagine this theologically. If we acknowledge we are sinners, what do we think our punishment from God should be? How bad do we really think we are? It is when we begin to fit the punishment to the crime that we see how bad we think we are. Maybe we think the Lord should send us a little trouble because of our sins. Most of us don't think we deserve God's wrath. Most don't think that hell is a fitting punishment for our sins.

When we see Jesus on the cross, we see what we deserve. It should be me, chained to a pole, whipped by a Roman soldier. It should be me blindfolded, spit upon, slapped, crowned with thorns, and mocked. It should be me stripped, nailed hand and foot to a beam, and lifted up to scorn and mockery. It should be me drowning in pain and sorrow. It should be me hanging in the darkness, forsaken by God, smitten by Him, afflicted, suffering God's anger, the object of His holy wrath. It should be me writhing on the cross, gasping for air. It should be me inflicted with God's anger forever in hell. That punishment should be mine, and it should be yours. That is how bad we are.

If hell does not seem like fair punishment, then we do not yet know the depth of our sin. If the cross seems like excessive punishment, then we do not yet know the depth of our sin.

Jesus prayed in the Garden of Gethsemane, minutes before His arrest and hours before His crucifixion, "If it be possible, let this cup pass from Me" (Matthew 26:39). Jesus was asking His heavenly Father for an alternative, for a different plan of salvation. But there was no other option. It was necessary for Jesus to suffer the mockery of man and the wrath of God. He had to endure the punishment of the cross. It was Jesus, or it was us. "According to this, the preaching of the suffering and death of Christ, the Son of God, is a serious and terrifying proclamation and declaration of God's wrath" (Ep V 9).

On the cross, we see, at last, the profound depth of God's anger at sin. On the cross, we see the full manifestation of God's wrath. On the cross, we see what we have earned and deserved; we see the wages of sin. And on the cross, we see Jesus.

He is nailed there in your place.

At the precise moment the fullness of God's wrath is revealed, the fullness of His love also shines forth. This is one of the most beautiful and profound mysteries of the cross. It shows God's wrath, but at the same time, it shows His mercy. On the cross, the depth of your sin is matched with the height of His love. On the cross, your wickedness is revealed and forgiven.

American Christianity is weak on sin, which means it is weak on God's deserved wrath, which means, at last, it is weak on the cross.

In the death of Jesus, we see hell on earth, and we see that we are not in it. We see God's wrath, and we are not suffering it. We see the profound depths of God's anger filled up with the mountain of His compassion. In His mercy, God has not revealed the fullness of His wrath without also revealing the abundance of His grace.

CHAPTER FOUR

THE ONE WHO IS ALWAYS AND ONLY "FOR YOU"

"Fear not, I am the first and the last."
(Revelation 1:17)

People who are sick, or who think they are sick, are always checking their pulse, taking their temperature, measuring their own health. A sick theology does the same. Christians who are constantly measuring and testing their spiritual state are Christians with an unhealthy theology. The focus is in the wrong place—on themselves, their works, their thoughts, their obedience, their nearness or distance from God. This, sadly, is the condition of American Christianity.

I once had a parishioner named Linda, whom I visited on her deathbed. She worried, in her last hours, if her faith was too weak. "Pastor, I don't think my faith is strong enough to save me." I think I surprised her with my response: "You're probably right." She looked at me with a confused expression on her face. "Your faith might not be strong enough, but your Jesus is strong enough." She smiled. "And remember what your Jesus said, Linda. 'If you have faith the size of a mustard seed, you can say to the mountain, "Move over there," and it will move.' " "Well, Pastor," these were almost her last words, "you got me there!"

A strong faith is a faith that rests in Jesus. A healthy theology is a theology that is laser-focused on Jesus.

The Scriptures fix our eyes not on ourselves but on Christ.

> Therefore, since we are surrounded by so great a cloud of witnesses, let us also lay aside every weight, and sin which clings so closely, and let us run with endurance the race that is set before us, looking to Jesus, the founder and perfecter of our faith, who for the joy that was set before Him endured the cross, despising the shame, and is seated at the right hand of the throne of God.
>
> (Hebrews 12:1–2)

Like Peter walking on the water, as soon as our focus wanders from the face of Jesus, we begin to sink (Matthew 14:30), and our theology crumbles into pride or despair.

Our theology begins and ends with Jesus. He is the source and the goal, the Alpha and Omega of the Scriptures, the Author and Perfecter of our faith. Jesus is the Cornerstone of the Church. He is the Good Shepherd of the sheep, the Bridegroom to His Bride, the Vine in which the branches abide, and the Head of the Body. Apart from Jesus, we can do nothing (John 15:5).

Much of American Christianity is focused on the Christian and not on Christ.

This is a sad and dangerous situation. Hope and life and peace are found in Christ, not in ourselves. All true theology begins and ends with Jesus. All true worship begins and ends with Jesus. All true preaching and teaching begins and ends with Jesus.

In this chapter, we will explore the doctrine of Christ and try to restore His person and work, His death and resurrection, to the center of our teaching.

"PREPARE TO DIE"

YOUR END IS THE LAW'S END, WHICH, IN THE END, IS JESUS

Jesus insists on being the Savior. "For the Son of Man came to seek and to save the lost" (Luke 19:10). This is a simple but profound truth. If Jesus is the Savior, then you must be lost. If Jesus is the Savior, then you must need saving.

> "For Christ is the end of the law for righteousness to everyone who believes."
> (Romans 10:4)

I kept a journal of my prayers through college. I was convinced that the Law was keepable and doable. Convinced that I could, with God's help, live a life that was pleasing to Him, I put myself at the center, and Jesus was on the sideline, sometimes coaching, sometimes forgiving, sometimes smiling, but mostly shaking His head in disappointment. I knew I was a sinner, but I didn't know how deep that sin was. I thought I could handle life myself. And this made Jesus my Helper, my

Coach, my Trainer standing at a distance with a disapproving look. Especially, He was my Judge. He was not, in my thinking and in my prayers, my Savior.

I could not have admitted this then, but you could see it in my journal, in my prayers. I was asking for power, not forgiveness. I was looking for victory, not blood. "Let me come to You . . . Let me find Your will for my life . . . Let me serve You . . . Let me see You . . . " I was striving and grasping for an elusive obedience to God's hidden will. This always ended in failure. Stretching for perfect works meant falling into despair.

This, though, was a tricky kind of despair, a not-quite-enough-despair despair. I didn't despair of myself. I didn't despair that I *couldn't* keep the Law, only that I *didn't* keep it. I would fail, and then I'd be at it again. Trying. Praying. Striving. Succeeding? Failing! Weeping. Doubting. Fearing. Singing. Reading. Trying. Trying again and again and again.

Pride was hidden behind this despair: the thought that I could do it. I could keep the Law. I could bring a smile to God's face. Without even knowing it, I was working to be so good that I didn't need Jesus. Denying the depth of my own sinfulness, I was trying to be my own savior.

This is where the theology of American Christianity brought me, the ugliness

of PRIDE WEARING THE MASK OF DESPAIR. This, at last, is where God's Law does its most important work. It crushes us, destroys us, and teaches us despair of self.

The Law of God should not be the last word. When "every mouth [is] stopped" (Romans 3:19), when the incessant attempts to justify ourselves wreck or run out of gas, then the Lord speaks another word. When we come to the end of our pride and ourselves, His voice is full of comfort and peace for us. This word of God is the promise of the Gospel: the news of the death of Jesus for you. It is the basic assertion of the Scriptures. Jesus, the Son of God, is Savior.

Any denial of the depth of our sin strips Jesus of this title, *Savior*. Any thinking or imagining that we can take care of our own sin takes from Him the office of Savior. Any attempt we make to justify and save ourselves robs Jesus of His most precious work.

On the other hand, if we know the depth of our sin and acknowledge our sickness unto death, then we know that our only hope is in another. "The sick," says Jesus, "need a doctor" (see Matthew 9:12). We are the sick. Jesus is the Great Physician. We are the sinners. Jesus is the Savior.

THIS IS WHY THE CROSS OF JESUS IS THE FULCRUM OF THE SCRIPTURES. The saving work of Jesus is His death. He is our Savior in His death. He is our Savior on His cross.

Every word in the Bible is either pressing toward or flowing from the cross. All of the Old Testament types and promises are building to this horrible and holy crescendo: Jesus in our flesh and in our place. On the cross, Jesus is forsaken by God (Psalm 22), beaten and stricken by God (Isaiah 53), the darkness of God's wrath pouring over Him as every ounce of comfort and joy is ripped away. All of this to save you. He drains the cup of God's wrath to the dregs for you (Isaiah 51:17).

Every New Testament book is a preaching of the cross. Paul claimed, "I decided to know nothing among you except Jesus Christ and Him crucified" (1 Corinthians 2:2). Matthew, Mark, and Luke spend one-third of their Gospels recounting the last week of Jesus' earthly life. The Gospel of John has even more; over half of his Gospel is about the Passion of Jesus.

But it's not just the Gospels that proclaim Jesus' Passion.

"Jesus died" is the central message of the Bible, its basic and fundamental assertion, and its chief truth. Every word in the Scriptures

> "The first and chief article is this: Jesus Christ, our God and Lord, died for our sins and was raised again for our justification (Romans 4:24–25). He alone is the Lamb of God who takes away the sins of the world (John 1:29), and God has laid upon Him the iniquities of us all (Isaiah 53:6). All have sinned and are justified freely, without their own works or merits, by His grace, through the redemption that is in Christ Jesus, in His blood (Romans 3:23–25)." (SA II I 1–3)

is hovering around this truth. Without the cross, the Bible doesn't hold together. "The cross alone is our theology," said Martin Luther (WA 5:176.32). The Scriptures are not first about our life. They are first about God's death.

Without the death and resurrection of Jesus, the Bible is a heartless book. Without the cross, the teaching of the Church is wind. Without the cross, our faith is empty. The cross teaches us about ourselves and what we deserve for our sin. And more, the cross teaches us about God. He is love. He is merciful and compassionate. He is flesh and blood, dead and buried and raised. Jesus is Savior.

Blood from Start to Finish, a Book about Jesus

> "Paul, a servant of Christ Jesus, called to be an apostle, set apart for the gospel of God, which He promised beforehand through His prophets in the holy Scriptures, concerning His Son, who was descended from David according to the flesh." (Romans 1:1–3)

The Old Testament is about Jesus.

American Christianity, together with almost the entire modern church, reads the Old Testament without the Gospel, without Jesus or the forgiveness of sins. American Christianity reads the Old Testament like a Jewish book, a Law book. Jesus might be in the Old Testament, but He is there in the shadows. This is a cold and dangerous reading of the Prophets. We can do better.

There are three beautiful and compelling New Testament texts that teach us how to read the Old Testament. They teach us, especially, that the Old Testament is about Jesus.

The first is John 5. Jesus is arguing with the Pharisees. He says, "You search the Scriptures because you think that in them you have eternal life; and it is they that bear witness about Me, yet you refuse to come to Me that you may have life" (John 5:39–40). The Scriptures (and here Jesus is talking about the Prophets, the Old Testament) "bear witness about" Jesus. When we hear the Old Testament, we are hearing the prophets bear witness of the coming Messiah. What is their witness concerning Him?

Luke gives us more. After His resurrection, Jesus walks with two of His disciples on the road to Emmaus. They were sad about the death of Jesus. They had hoped that He would rescue and deliver them, but now (they think) He is dead and buried.

> [Jesus] said to them, "O foolish ones, and slow of heart to believe all that the prophets have spoken! Was it not necessary that the Christ should suffer these things and enter into His glory?" And beginning with Moses and all the Prophets, He interpreted to them in all the Scriptures the things concerning Himself. (Luke 24:25–27)

Jesus gives a Bible study on the road to Emmaus. He brings out the words of the prophets and shows these disciples the promises of the Messiah. He must suffer and die before He enters into glory. The Old Testament is not only about Jesus, but it is also about His suffering, death, and resurrection. The Old Testament is about the cross.

There is one last text to consider, and it is even more specific. Peter is preaching in the seaport of Joppa. Summarizing the Old Testament witness to Christ, he says, "To Him all the prophets bear witness that everyone who believes in Him receives forgiveness of sins through His name" (Acts 10:43). Not only did the prophets preach the Messiah, His suffering, death, and resurrection, but they also preached salvation through faith in His name. They promised the forgiveness of sins through faith alone in the name of Jesus. The Old Testament is about justification.

The New Testament says the Old Testament is ABOUT THE GOSPEL, but is this confirmed when we read the Old Testament? Where do we see these promises of forgiveness?

There is a key Old Testament passage that, if understood correctly, unlocks the Gospel in the Old Testament. It is the font from which all the preaching and praises flow. The text is Genesis 3:15, the protoevangelium, that is, the "First Gospel."

Here's the context: God creates Adam and Eve and plants a garden for them, the Garden of Eden. He puts them in Eden to have children and have dominion over creation. In the middle of this garden, God plants a tree with a threat, the tree of the knowledge of good and evil. "In the day that you eat of it you shall surely die"

(Genesis 2:17). This tree is Adam and Eve's church. Adam and Eve are to see the tree and believe God's Word. Every other tree in the garden is given for their eating. This tree is there for their believing.

But Satan attacks God's Word. He attacks their faith. He calls God a liar. "You will not surely die" (Genesis 3:4). Eve is deceived. She eats. She shares with Adam. He eats. His bite breaks the backbone of the cosmos. Everything is wrecked. Adam and Eve break creation.

Adam and Eve sinned, and with sin came death. Death replaces life. Corruption replaces beauty. Sorrow and loss and pain and shame and strife take the place of joy. With sin comes shame. Adam and Eve see their nakedness. They are ashamed.

Adam and Eve attempt to cover their shame and sin with flimsy fig leaves. Imagine them, there with Satan, wrapped in those leaves. They think they've fixed the problem and made everything right. "How do I look?" Eve asked Adam. "These are my fall colors." Oh, how the devil would have encouraged them. "You guys look fantastic. See how well you've used your wisdom and creativity." All seems well, but then they hear something, the sound of God walking in the garden. We've spoken of this text already. It is the first picture of death. Instead of running *to* God, Adam and Eve (with the devil) run *from* Him. With God and His holiness here, the fig leaves are not sufficient.

These fig leaves are a fitting picture of every man-made religion. They are the attempt to cover our shame and sin by our own efforts. Those fig leaves are every attempt at self-justification, every act to impress God, every effort to be holy by our own works. Apart from Christianity, every world religion is nothing more than fig-leaf fashion, tailoring the garments of death to hide our rotting self.

Adam and Eve cannot hide from God. He finds them (with the devil), stands them up before His face, and makes a judgment. Here comes the surprise. Adam and Eve had just broken the universe, wrecked everything God had made, ruined the very goodness of God's creation. They deserved condemnation. But God gives them grace. Here we come to our verse, the fountain of all God's promises. God turns to the devil and says,

"I will put enmity between you and the woman, and between your seed and her Seed. He shall bruise your head, and you shall bruise His heel" (Genesis 3:15 author's translation)

This text is a riddle that needs to be unpacked.

- First, these words are spoken to the devil. The "you" in the text is Satan. The "your seed" is the offspring of the devil: sin and death. (Remember that neither the angels nor the demons have children.)

- Second, when Adam and Eve ate the fruit, there was enmity and violence everywhere. Adam and Eve were at enmity with each other, with God, with the entire creation. In fact, the only place there was peace was between Adam, Eve, and the devil! The Lord does not let this stand. "I'm putting enmity between you, Devil, and Eve." When the Lord promises to put enmity between the devil and the woman, He is promising He will make peace between Himself and Eve, between Himself and Adam. In fact, God is here promising to reconcile Himself with all humanity.

- Third, many translations of the Bible use the word *offspring* in this text. "Seed" is the more literal translation, and it is helpful. In every other place in the Scriptures, this word refers to the offspring of a man, "Abraham's seed," "Jacob's seed," and so on. Here, though, God says, "her Seed," the seed of the woman. This is an indication that the devil-crushing child of Eve would be born without the help of a man. (Isaiah will make this promise even more explicit when he speaks of the virgin birth in Isaiah 7:14.) The New King James Version is especially helpful when it capitalizes "her Seed," indicating this is a promise of the Messiah.

- Fourth, the Seed of the woman will "bruise" (or crush) the head of the devil. He will destroy the devil and his works. This is good news. Instead of destroying Adam and Eve, the Lord is making plans to destroy the devil, and sin and death with him. Notice that this Seed of Eve will have the power and authority to destroy the devil. While Adam and Eve in their perfection could have resisted the devil, they did not have the strength to destroy him. Only God can destroy the devil. Only God can crush Satan. It must be that this man will also be God!

- Fifth, in destroying the devil, the promised Seed will have His heel "bruised" (or crushed). The devil receives a deathblow to the head. The Seed receives a deathblow to the heel. He will die, but He will not stay dead. Here God promises the death and resurrection of the Messiah. God takes the threat, "In the day that you eat of it you shall surely die," and turns it into a stunning promise: You ate of it; *I* will die!

Putting it all together, God promised Adam and Eve the birth of a child without a father who would also be God, who would die to destroy the devil and his kingdom, and who would rise from the dead. Amazing! After hearing the promise of Genesis 3:15, Adam and Eve could confess the Apostles' Creed. These words, spoken in the wake of Adam and Eve's sin, are a full and wonderful preaching of the Gospel. From the promise of the devil-destroying Seed, all the preaching of the Old Testament follows.

God promised both Abraham and Isaac, "In your seed all the nations of the earth shall be blessed" (Genesis 22:18; 26:4 NKJV). "When your days are fulfilled and you rest with your fathers, I will set up your seed after you, who will come from your body, and I will establish his kingdom," God promises David (2 Samuel 7:12 NKJV). And from Abraham's and Isaac's and David's seed came *the* Seed. This promise of the Seed, first given to Adam and Eve in the Garden of Eden as they stood in the ruins of a dying universe, is the blood-red ribbon that runs through the pages of the Old Testament. It is the hope of all of the Lord's people, and it is their salvation.

GOD ESTABLISHED SACRIFICE IN ORDER TO PREACH THIS PROMISE

Back to the garden. Even after God promises the death of Jesus, Adam and Eve are still standing there in their useless fig leaves. But God has a solution. He takes an animal, kills it, skins it, and wraps it around Adam and Eve. This must have been horrifying—the first death, the first blood spilled, all at the hands of God. Imagine Eve's face as the Lord hangs this animal upside down and its bowels spill out on the ground. "This is what it takes to cover our sin?" The blood of bulls and goats can never take away sin. It will take the death of God Himself. Every sacrifice on every altar offered by every priest is a preaching of this first promise. Every burnt offering is a picture of the cross where the blood of God (Acts 20:28) will flow. The tabernacle and then the temple in Jerusalem are all established to preach the promise of Genesis 3:15.

This is the theology of the sacrifice. So much of the Old Testament is about sacrifices.

THERE IS FORGIVENESS IN THE BLOOD OF THE SACRIFICE, BECAUSE THAT BLOOD IS BOUND UP TO THE PROMISE OF JESUS.

Atonement requires death, the death of God Himself.

Your works, like fig leaves, cannot cover your sins. God will provide Himself as the sacrifice to win mercy and God's grace. The entire Old Testament is preaching this glorious promise.

Many old Bibles have the edges of the pages painted red, almost as if the Bible is bleeding. This is a helpful reminder. This is a bloody book, stained with the blood of Jesus, which washes away our sins.

American Christianity misses the heart of the Old Testament. It misses Jesus. But He is there in the promises and the sacrifices, forgiving, saving, and rescuing His people and comforting them with Himself and His kindness.

THE CROSS ALONE IS OUR THEOLOGY

> **"We preach Christ crucified."**
>
> (1 Corinthians 1:23)

In ancient times, a road cut across the plain from Athens to Corinth, about a fifty-five-mile walk. Paul walked that road (Acts 18:1). He was leaving Athens, having preached on Mars Hill to the philosophers, the Epicureans, the Stoics, and the people who worshiped in the temples. He preached about God the Creator of all, about judgment, and about the resurrection. His sermon made an impression, but few people believed him. As far as we can tell, Athens was the only city Paul visited where a Christian congregation was not established. He then left for Corinth.

Somewhere along that fifty-five-mile trek, he determined something, resolved something. "And I, when I came to you, brothers, did not come proclaiming to you the testimony of God with lofty speech or wisdom. For I decided to know nothing among you except Jesus Christ and Him crucified" (1 Corinthians 2:1–2). Paul came to Corinth preaching Jesus, only Jesus crucified for sinners.

Martin Luther was picking up on this teaching of Paul when he quipped the phrase I mentioned earlier, "The cross alone is our theology." Apart from the preaching of the cross, we do not truly know God. On the cross, the very heart of God is shown. We know who He is because of what He does. We know that "God is love" because we know that Jesus has died.

Apart from the preaching of the cross, we do not know the full depth of our sin, nor do we know the astounding height of the Lord's mercy. Apart from the preaching of the cross, we have no forgiveness, no salvation, no eternal life. (This is not to say that the people of the Old Testament had no salvation—they did, but not apart from the preaching of the cross. For them, it was a preaching of the sacrifice to come, as discussed in the previous pages. Their faith was in the promise of a death to come; our faith is in a death that has already occurred. But it is the same faith that justifies us both; only the death of Jesus on the cross wins the forgiveness of sins.)

{ *The cross alone is our theology.* —Martin Luther }

The cross must be our theology. It must be the object of our preaching and teaching. It must be the content of our meditating and our prayers. Paul's resolution to know nothing but Christ crucified ought to be a mark of the Lord's Church.

It is not. It seems to me that there are preachers who have made a sort of anti-Paul resolution: they know everything *but* Christ crucified. American Christianity is often a Christless and crossless place.

Reverend Todd Wilken, host of the radio show *Issues, Etc.*, has a four-question sermon diagnostic tool to help determine if the sermon is a preaching of Jesus. The first question is shockingly simple: "Is Jesus mentioned?" It is amazing that this is even a question. It is more amazing how often the answer is "No." God and His goodness are preached. Our living according to the Law is preached. We hear how to be a better person and how to love our neighbor. But Jesus never shows up. If there is no Jesus, there is no Gospel, no forgiveness, no Good News. If Jesus is not preached, there is no salvation.[4]

It is amazing that the question "Is Jesus preached?" has to be asked. But this is the situation in American Christianity. The words of Jesus in Revelation, some of the most misquoted and misapplied words in the Bible, actually apply here: "Behold, I stand at the door and knock" (Revelation 3:20). This is not the door of your heart, but the door of the Church in Laodicea (see Revelation 3:14–22). Jesus is saying to His Church, "I'm outside!" If there is anywhere we should find Jesus, it ought to be in and with His Church. But He's not here. Jesus is knocking on the door. He's trying to get in.

> Jesus is saying to His Church, "I'm outside!" . . . Jesus is knocking on the door. He's trying to get in.

This is an apt picture of much of American Christianity. The crosses have been removed from the sanctuaries, but worse, the cross has been removed from the teaching and preaching. Revivalism, pietism, mysticism, and enthusiasm marginalize the cross, pushing it to the side. The man with a good and free will has little need for a dying Savior.

---

4   Wilken's other questions: (1) If Jesus is mentioned, is He the subject or object of the verbs? Is Jesus the one acting, or the one being acted upon? (2) If Jesus is the one doing the acting, what is He doing? What are the verbs? (3) Finally, what is the preacher telling me my problem is, and what is the solution?

The cross is God's answer to our sin, but we think we are not *that* bad. The cross is God's answer to His wrath, but we think God is a nice guy. The cross is God's answer to hell, but we quit believing in judgment years ago. The cross is

God's answer,

but American Christianity is not asking the right questions.

The teaching of the Scriptures centers on the cross, pushes to and grows from the cross, begins and ends at the cross. On the cross, God's anger meets His love. His righteous wrath collides with boundless compassion, and the result is your salvation.

> ## "My God, My God, why have You forsaken Me?"
> (Psalm 22:1;
> Matthew 27:46;
> Mark 15:34)

Forsaken by God, Really Forsaken

We know that the suffering of Jesus on the cross is important. But how is it that the suffering and death of Jesus wins my salvation? Martin Luther has helpfully identified three distinct types of suffering Jesus endured on the cross: physical pain, shame, and spiritual agony.

Suffering, Part 1

The physical suffering is well known. The scourging of Jesus was promised to us already in the Old Testament: "With His wounds we are healed" (Isaiah 53:5). We will consider it briefly. (This is gruesome business. Please skip the next few paragraphs if this bothers you.)

The soldiers beat Jesus as He stood before the Jewish Council. He was struck on the face and hit with a rod. In what looked like an attempt to elicit sympathy from the crowd that was clamoring for Jesus' crucifixion, Pilate then had Him whipped. There was a Jewish custom of giving thirty-nine lashes (forty was supposed to kill you), but the Romans had no such custom. They had perfected the art of crucifixion as an excruciating punishment. They would take their leather whips, the "cat of nine tails," and dip them in tar, then shards of glass, bone, or rock, before the whip was thrashed across the criminal's back. This lashing would rip away skin and muscle, often exposing bone and organs. Jesus endured this lashing and was then loaded down with a crossbeam and led outside the city for crucifixion.

Physical suffering

Crucifixion itself consisted of tying or nailing a man to a cross and leaving him to die. Nine-inch nails would be driven through a person's hands or wrists and feet to hold them to the beam. Suspended at awkward angles, the victim's shoulders would pull out of socket, taking away all arm strength. Breathing was also constricted. To breathe, the crucified would push up on their legs. (This is why the soldiers could hasten death by breaking the victim's legs.) With nothing to eat and very little to drink, strength would fail, the victim's lungs would fill with fluid, and the heart would burst.

To die by crucifixion could be a days-long ordeal. It was such a brutal death that Roman law excluded its citizens from this form of capital punishment.

The physical pain of crucifixion was agonizing. Surprisingly, the Gospels say very little about this suffering. In fact, the most careful description of the physical suffering is found in the Old Testament.

> I am poured out like water, and all My bones are out of joint; My heart is like wax; it is melted within My breast; My strength is dried up like a potsherd, and My tongue sticks to My jaws; You lay Me in the dust of death. For dogs encompass Me; a company of evildoers encircles Me; they have pierced My hands and feet—I can count all My bones—they stare and gloat over Me. (Psalm 22:14–17)

The physical suffering alone does not save us. It cannot. The two thieves crucified on either side of Jesus suffered the same physical duress. You and I could suffer the same physical agony that Jesus endured on the cross. This would not win our salvation. There must be more to the suffering of Jesus.

SUFFERING, PART 2

The four Gospels focus on the second type of suffering: the shame of the cross. The Book of Hebrews tells us specifically that Jesus despised this suffering: "[He] endured the cross, despising the shame" (12:2). The shame of the cross is the mockery, the reviling, the nakedness, the false accusations, and the blasphemy. Jesus was crowned with thorns (Matthew 27:29). This would not be comfortable, but worse than the physical pain of it is the mockery of His kingship and His kingdom. Jesus was blindfolded and struck on the face. This is the mockery of His prophetic office. "Prophesy to us, You Christ! Who is it that struck You?" (Matthew 26:68). The purple robe, the mock homage, the reed in His hand, and the jokes of the soldiers—all of this is the shame of the cross.

Shame

"They spit in His face" (Matthew 26:67). We cringe when we read these words, not because it is physically painful, but because it is full of shame. I've asked a number of Bible classes if they would prefer to be punched in the face or spit upon by an enemy. It is a very revealing question. The spit won't give you a black eye or a broken nose. Why is this even a choice? Why would we rather suffer physical pain than the spit? To be spit upon is a different kind of suffering; it is shame. It is an attack on your name. It says, "You are dirt to me." Jesus, remember, despised the shame of the cross (Hebrews 12:2). (The answers I get in Bible class, by the way, are about 50/50, slightly more people preferring to be struck than spit upon.)

> Christians rejoice in all of the mockery of the cross, knowing that Jesus is in fact King. His crown of thorns is a true crown, glistening with drops more precious than jewels: His blood. His throne is the cross where He is lifted up to gather all people to Himself (cf. John 12:32). Pilate's sign, if he knew it or not, is true. Jesus is the King of kings.

Another question to help decipher the difference between physical suffering and shame is this: would you rather your enemy punch you in the face or pull off all of your clothes? In the Bible, shame is often bound to nakedness. (Consider Revelation 3:18 or Noah in Genesis 9:20–27.) This is true of the cross. The victim of crucifixion hung naked for all the world to see. The soldiers, remember, gambled for Jesus' garments (Matthew 27:35). Almost all religious art shows Jesus with a cloth wrapped around His waist. This is a matter of piety, not history. This public nakedness is the stuff of nightmares. Jesus is exposed before the entire world.

Crucifixion always took place in a public place, normally by the gate to the city. Everyone coming and going would see the crucified. This added to the shame. It reminded the people of the punishment for a crime. This is why the charges were posted above the heads of the crucified. Jesus' "crime" adds to His shame, the mockery written in Hebrew, Latin, and Greek: "This is the King of the Jews" (Luke 23:38; see also Matthew 27:37; Mark 15:26; John 19:19).

The shame of the cross is profound. In many ways, it is worse than the physical suffering of the cross. And Jesus is holy and perfect. He deserved none of these things. This, though, is not all. There is an even more profound suffering.

SUFFERING, PART 3

The third and most severe suffering of Jesus is spiritual. On the cross, Jesus suffers the wrath of God. More than the whip and nails, more than the spit and taunts, more than the devil's assaults: Jesus suffers at the hand of God's holiness and justice. The physical suffering and the shame come from mankind, but the spiritual suffering comes from God.

Two biblical texts capture this the best, and we will consider them both: Psalm 22 and Isaiah 52–53.

Spiritual suffering

We know from comparing all four Gospels that Jesus spoke at least seven things from the cross, but Matthew and Mark have only one statement, one prayer, the "Cry of Dereliction": "My God, My God, why have You forsaken Me?" (Matthew 27:46; Mark 15:34). This prayer is the first verse of Psalm 22, and we understand that He is, in fact, praying the entire psalm. Reading the psalm in this context shows us the agony of Jesus' spiritual suffering.

> My God, My God, why have You forsaken Me? Why are You so far from saving Me, from the words of My groaning? O My God, I cry by day, but You do not answer, and by night, but I find no rest.
>
> Yet You are holy, enthroned on the praises of Israel. In You our fathers trusted; they trusted, and You delivered them. To You they

cried and were rescued; in You they trusted and were not put to shame.

But I am a worm and not a man, scorned by mankind and despised by the people. All who see Me mock Me; they make mouths at Me; they wag their heads; "He trusts in the LORD; let Him deliver Him; let Him rescue Him, for He delights in Him!" (Psalm 22:1–8)

Jesus is forsaken by God. Abandoned. Heaven has turned its face.

Jesus knows that God is merciful. God had always heard the cries of His people and delivered them. But here is Jesus, always faithful, having lived the perfect life, and the Lord is forsaking Him. Jesus prays, cries out for help, but there is no comfort for Him, nothing but darkness and silence.

"Why?" Jesus asks. The cross doesn't make sense. He doesn't know why God is not helping Him, but we know. We know why He suffers, the righteous for the unrighteous: to bring us to God (1 Peter 3:18). The sin of the world has been heaped on Jesus, and now Jesus is experiencing the punishment for that sin. As Jesus bears the sins of the world, He bears God's anger toward that sin.

Martin Luther has beautiful insight into this passage:

> There is no doubt that in the spirit David is here looking at Christ as He struggles with death in the garden and cries out on the cross, "My God, My God, why hast Thou forsaken Me?" (Matt. 27:46.) For that is His real, sublime, spiritual suffering, which no man can imagine or understand. In the garden He Himself says, "My soul is very sorrowful, even to death" (Matt. 26:38). This is what He wants to say: "I have such sorrow and anguish that I could die of sorrow and anguish." He withdraws from His disciples about a stone's throw (Luke 22:41), kneels down, and prays. In the prayer He begins to struggle with death, and He prays more fervently. His sweat becomes like drops of blood that fall on the ground. David is talking here about this sublime, spiritual suffering, when Christ fought with death and felt nothing in His heart but that He was forsaken of God. And in fact He was forsaken by God. This does not mean that the deity was separated from the

humanity—for in this person who is Christ, the Son of God and of Mary, deity and humanity are so united that they can never be separated or divided—but that the deity withdrew and hid so that it seemed, and anyone who saw it might say, "This is not God, but a mere man, and a troubled and desperate man at that." The humanity was left alone, the devil had free access to Christ, and the deity withdrew its power and let the humanity fight alone. . . . The Man and Son of Man stands there and bears the sins of the world (John 1:29), and because He does not give the appearance of having divine consolation and power, the devil set his teeth over the innocent Lamb and wanted to devour It. Thus the righteous and innocent Man must shiver and shake like a poor, condemned sinner and feel God's wrath and judgment against sin in His tender, innocent heart, taste eternal death and damnation for us—in short, He must suffer everything that a condemned sinner has deserved and must suffer eternally. . . . But He does this for our great benefit and for His own great joy. (LW 12:126–27)

Our second text, Isaiah 52:13–53:12, is even more explicit. This is the fourth Servant Song of Isaiah. It describes the suffering of Jesus and the benefit of that suffering with beautiful clarity. From ancient times, the Church has heard these words on Good Friday, the day we especially remember the crucifixion. Jesus is suffering in our place. His sorrow is our joy. His death is our life. His punishment is for our sins and for our forgiveness.

Two verses in this section are particularly important. The first is Isaiah 53:4. "Surely He has borne our griefs and carried our sorrows; yet we esteemed Him stricken, smitten by God, and afflicted."

Jesus, says Isaiah, was "smitten by God." It was not the Roman hammer and nail and whip that struck the worst blow, but the very hand of God. Imagine it! Jesus is not only beaten by men, but also by God. Here the forsakenness of God is active, and acting on Jesus in our place.

A few verses later, we read: "Yet it was the will of the LORD to crush Him; He has put Him to grief" (Isaiah 53:10).

It is the Lord who crushes Jesus. God wanted Jesus crushed, demolished, dead. All of God's wrath over sin, over your sin and mine, is spent on Jesus. All of heaven's fury over humanity's assault on God's holiness is spent on the Son of God. This is stunning, an overwhelming act of mercy.

Modern theology is hesitant to speak of the wrath of God, but without God's wrath for sin, there is no making sense of the cross. God's wrath is poured out, not on me, but on His Son. On the cross, the Son of God Himself suffers God's wrath. In the suffering of Jesus on the cross, God's wrath is propitiated. It is satisfied.

Jesus is smitten by God and afflicted so that we might be forgiven and loved. Jesus prays Psalm 22, "My God, My God, why have You forsaken Me?" so that we might pray Psalm 23, "Even though I walk through the valley of the shadow of death, I will fear no evil, for You are with me" (v. 4). In the profound threefold suffering of Jesus, the holiness of God and the love of God find their full expression, and the result is our life.

The cross, the simple teaching that Jesus died for sinners, is the heart of the Scriptures. It should be the heart of our theology. American Christianity has failed to keep the cross at the center. American Christianity has failed to make Christ the beginning and the end. This failure is profound. If results in confusion, pride, despair, and a vacuum of comfort and peace. It does not have to be this way. Jesus continues to preserve His Church. Jesus will preserve the preaching of the cross until His return. While the suffering and death of Jesus might not be the center of the teaching in American Christianity, the cross remains the central event in history, the central teaching of the Scriptures, and the central focus of the Lutheran Church.

CHAPTER FIVE

YOUR NAME: RIGHTEOUS

"Therefore, since we have been justified by faith, we have peace with God through our Lord Jesus Christ."

(Romans 5:1)

I remember the first time the profound truth of the Gospel struck my mind. It was in the middle of the night. I was on a bus traveling to a youth camp and reading the Book of Romans, in which St. Paul talks about the righteousness of God given to us as a gift. I was so excited, I couldn't contain myself. I ran to the front of the bus and woke up the pastor.

"Pastor, Pastor . . . "

"What's wrong?

"Pastor, I'm perfect," I said.

"What?"

"I'm perfect. All my sins are forgiven. Jesus gives me His perfection. That's what the Bible says, and that means I'm perfect."

He smiled. "You're right," he said, "and I'm sure you'll still be perfect in the morning. Let's talk about it then."

This teaching is what the Bible calls "justification." It is one of the most important teachings in the Scriptures. The Lord graciously gives us His perfection. He calls us righteous. The Lord takes the obedience of Jesus and applies it to our account. We are imputed with Christ's righteousness. Jesus shares His holiness with us. Justification is the article upon which the Church stands or falls.

Justification is what the argument was about in the Reformation. It is what Paul was arguing about with the Judaizers, what Jesus was arguing about with the Pharisees, what the apostle John was arguing about with the Gnostics, and what the prophets were arguing about with the Baalists. The devil is always attacking the truth and comfort of this biblical doctrine, because in this doctrine, we see the great glory of Christ, the work of the Holy Spirit, and the comfort that the Lord wants us to have in life and in death.

> The doctrine of justification is the most important teaching of divine revelation. The apprehension of this doctrine by Luther made him the divinely equipped reformer of the Church.

We often think of the forgiveness of sins in negative terms. The Lord takes away our sins and leaves us with a blank slate. There is more to forgiveness. Not only does the Lord take away our sin, but He also gives us something: the righteousness of Jesus. Imagine a chalkboard covered with all of your sins. Forgiveness is more than wiping the board clean. When the Lord forgives your sins, He takes up the chalk and writes the perfection of Jesus, His perfect keeping of the Law, on the board. Jesus' perfection is imputed to your account. "For our sake He [God the Father] made Him to be sin who knew no sin, so that in Him we might become the righteousness of God" (2 Corinthians 5:21).

Martin Luther called this "the Great Exchange."

If you give me a dirty sock and I, in return, give you a new car, that is a good exchange—at least for you! If you give me a trash can full of dirty diapers, and I in return give you a new home, that is a good exchange. Here is how it is with Jesus: we give Him our sin, our punishment, our death, our grave, the wrath of God that we deserve; and He gives us His mercy and grace, His forgiveness, His eternal life, His name, His Spirit, His blessedness, His righteousness, and His perfection. That is a great exchange indeed. Our sin is imputed to Christ. Christ's righteousness is imputed to us. The Holy Spirit brings this righteousness in the Word. We hear the promise of the Gospel, and faith believes it and has it. The power of God's Word, the depth of our sin, and the death and resurrection of Jesus all come together in the doctrine of justification. If American Christianity has failed in these three previous teachings, that failure continues here.

In this chapter, we will consider justification, the preaching of the Gospel, and the profound benefits the Lord has for us in this preaching.

THE WORD OF PROMISE, CHRIST FOR YOU

A lot of American Christianity's older preaching of the Gospel was a call to return to the cross. "At the foot of the cross, I lay my burdens down." "The old rugged cross." There are two problems with this. First, we can't get to the cross. There is a church built over the traditional place of the crucifixion, and if you crawl under the altar, you can reach through a pane of glass and touch the hole where the cross was planted. But there is no more wood, no cross. There is nothing there. We cannot go back in time to that dark Friday afternoon. Second, even if we could go back in time to the cross, it would do us no good.

> "But the Scripture imprisoned every-thing under sin, so that the promise by faith in Jesus Christ might be given to those who believe."
> (Galatians 3:22)

In the previous chapter, we emphasized the centrality of the cross. On the cross, Jesus takes our place under God's wrath. He wins for us the forgiveness of sins and life everlasting. He sheds His blood as the sacrifice for sinners. Without the cross, there is no salvation. But the salvation won for sinners on the cross is not delivered to sinners through the cross.

Consider this: Plenty of people were there on Good Friday, walking by, mocking Jesus, marveling at the spectacle. This did not forgive their sins. Imagine the Roman soldiers who had crucifixion duty that day. They would be covered with the blood of Jesus. Did this blood benefit them? Were they saved because they touched the blood of Jesus? No.

Jesus on the cross atones for our sins, propitiating the wrath of God. On the cross, Jesus *wins* the forgiveness of our sins. But Jesus does not *deliver* forgiveness to us from the cross. Jesus has another way to get His forgiveness to us. It is delivered in the Word.

Martin Luther, in a glorious little essay titled "Against the Heavenly Prophets," makes this distinction:

> We treat of the forgiveness of sins in two ways. First, how it is achieved and won. Second, how it is distributed and given to us. Christ has achieved it on the cross, it is true. But he has not distributed or given it on the cross. He has not won it in the supper

or sacrament. There he has distributed and given it through the Word, as also in the gospel, where it is preached. He has won it once for all on the cross. But the distribution takes place continuously, before and after, from the beginning to the end of the world. (LW 40:213–14)

THE DEATH OF CHRIST MUST BE PREACHED. FORGIVENESS MUST BE PREACHED. THE GOSPEL IS NOT THE FACT OF THE CROSS OR THE EVENT OF THE CROSS. It is the word of the cross, the promise of the cross.

Neither you nor I could ever know anything about Christ, or believe on Him, and have Him for our Lord, unless it were offered to us and granted to our hearts by the Holy Spirit through the preaching of the Gospel [1 Corinthians 12:3; Galatians 4:6]. The work of redemption is done and accomplished [John 19:30]. Christ has acquired and gained the treasure for us by His suffering, death, resurrection, and so on [Colossians 2:3]. But if the work remained concealed so that no one knew about it, then it would be useless and lost. So that this treasure might not stay buried, but be received and enjoyed, God has caused the Word to go forth and be proclaimed. In the Word He has the Holy Spirit bring this treasure home and make it our own. Therefore, sanctifying is just bringing us to Christ so we receive this good, which we could not get ourselves [1 Peter 3:18]. (LC II III 38–39)

Here is Luther driving the point home:

Christ on the cross and all his suffering and his death do not avail, even if, as you teach, they are "acknowledged and meditated upon" with the utmost "passion, ardor, heartfeltness." Something else must always be there. What is it? The Word, the Word, the Word. . . . Even if Christ were given for us and crucified a thousand times, it would all be in vain if the Word of God were absent and were not distributed and given to me with the bidding, this is for you, take what is yours. (LW 40:212–13)

I remember a time when a member of the congregation came into my study to show me a book. He handed it to me, and I thought he was giving it to me as a gift. "Thank you," I said, like a fool. "I've been thinking about getting this book." "Pastor," he said, a bit sheepishly, "you can borrow it when I'm done. But, it's not for you." Oops. The book wasn't "for you."

Those words make all the difference. Think of these two sentences: "There is a million dollars in the bank." Ho-hum. "There is a million dollars in the bank for you." Pow!

"For you" is the sound of the preaching of the Gospel. "This Jesus, this suffering, this cross, this death, this resurrection, this atonement, this smile from heaven, this eternal life, this righteousness, this is *for you.*" Dear reader, it is for you! The Gospel is a promise, the delivery of the Lord's death for sinners. The victory of the cross is delivered in the preached Gospel. This is the Good News.

It is a promise.

God's Word, remember, can be divided into commands and promises. A command is kept by doing it. A promise is kept by believing it. If I give you a command, "Stand up and do ten jumping jacks," it would make no sense for you to say, "Bryan, I believe you." I didn't give you a promise to believe, but a commandment to do. If I give you a promise, "Jesus is coming back," it makes no sense for you to stand up and do ten jumping jacks. I didn't give you a command to do but a promise to believe.

The Gospel is a promise. There is nothing to do. No command. No work. No requirements. In fact, all commands and works are excluded. Everything is already accomplished.

{ The victory of the cross is delivered in the preached Gospel. This is the Good News. It is a promise . . . *for you.* }

This is why justification is "by faith" and not by works: forgiveness is a promise. "For if the inheritance comes by the law, it no longer comes by promise; but God gave it to Abraham by a promise" (Galatians 3:18). If God had offered salvation through a command, then we would be saved by keeping the command. We would be saved through works. But salvation is given to us through a promise. "By grace you have been saved through faith" (Ephesians 2:8).

The Gospel is a promise. Salvation, therefore, is by faith.

> But now the righteousness of God has been manifested apart from the law, although the Law and the Prophets bear witness to it—the righteousness of God through faith in Jesus Christ for all who believe. For there is no distinction: for all have sinned and fall short of the glory of God, and are justified by His grace as a gift, through the redemption that is in Christ Jesus, whom God put forward as a propitiation by His blood, to be received by faith. This was to show God's righteousness, because in His divine forbearance He had passed over former sins. It was to show His righteousness at the present time, so that He might be just and the justifier of the one who has faith in Jesus. Then what becomes of our boasting? It is excluded. By what kind of law? By a law of works? No, but by the law of faith. For we hold that one is justified by faith apart from works of the law. (Romans 3:21–28)

Preaching Jesus without preaching the promise is not preaching the Gospel. Preaching the cross without preaching forgiveness is not preaching the Gospel. If the promise of forgiveness is not preached, then there is nothing to believe. But when the Gospel is preached, faith is born.

> For I am not ashamed of the gospel, for it is the power of God for salvation to everyone who believes, to the Jew first and also to the Greek. For in it the righteousness of God is revealed from faith for faith, as it is written, "The righteous shall live by faith." (Romans 1:16–17)

American Christianity talks about faith, but faith in what? If there is no promise, there is nothing to believe. American Christianity dangerously misses the promise through which Jesus delivers forgiveness and comfort to His people.

REPENTANCE IS NOT WHAT YOU THINK; IT IS BETTER

"Repent" is the basic preaching of the Church. John the Baptist came preaching repentance and the forgiveness of sins (Mark 1:4). Jesus followed in his footsteps. "Jesus came into Galilee, proclaiming the gospel of God, and saying, 'The time is fulfilled, and the kingdom of God is at hand; repent and believe in the gospel'" (Mark 1:14–15).

REPENTANCE IS THE REQUIREMENT AND THE RESULT OF GOD'S Word coming to mankind.

But what is repentance? In American Christianity, repentance is the requirement that I change. Defined as "doing a U-turn with your life," to repent means I stop doing sinful things and start doing godly things. Repentance is my free will accomplishing some degree of good works. Repentance is often understood as a onetime event, or at least as a monumental event in our spiritual lives. If I am caught up in some sort of sin and come to myself, I repent, that is, I resolve to stop sinning and do better. As with so many other things in American Christianity, this understanding of repentance brings us back to the shaky foundation of our own resolve. Repentance is my work, and the sincerity of my repentance is brought into question by my failure to keep God's Law.

> "I tell you, there will be more joy in heaven over one sinner who repents than over ninety-nine righteous persons who need no repentance."
> (Luke 15:7)

The Bible gives us a different picture of repentance.

Luke 15 is the record of three related and beautiful parables of Jesus. The first is the parable of the lost sheep. It is really the parable of the seeking and finding shepherd. The parable is about Jesus.

> So He told them this parable: "What man of you, having a hundred sheep, if he has lost one of them, does not leave the ninety-nine in the open country, and go after the one that is lost, until he finds it?" (Luke 15:3–4)

There is always a surprise in the parables of Jesus. We see it right away in this text. No normal shepherd would risk the lives of the ninety-nine sheep in the open country to look for one lost sheep. A single wolf or bear could destroy the entire flock. This is no normal shepherd! This is Jesus. His business is to rescue the lost. He does what no shepherd would do. He leaves the ninety-nine and goes after you, the lost one. But the surprise grows:

> And when he has found it, he lays it on his shoulders, rejoicing. And when he comes home, he calls together his friends and his neighbors, saying to them, "Rejoice with me, for I have found my sheep that was lost." (Luke 15:5–6)

The shepherd doesn't return to the flock. He goes home and calls together his friends and neighbors for a party. This is incredibly odd behavior.

I imagine losing my dog. She gets out of the backyard and runs all over town. I chase after her, in the dark and the rain, looking everywhere. I'm not sure "rejoicing" would describe my attitude when I find her. I think it would be some very potent mixture of relief and anger. I certainly don't think I would go around the neighborhood and gather all the people to come over for drinks because I found my dog. This seems absurd. That is the point. This seeking and finding shepherd is absurdly merciful to the one lost sheep and absurdly happy about finding it.

This, dear friends, is repentance! Jesus teaches, "Just so, I tell you, there will be more joy in heaven over one sinner who repents than over ninety-nine righteous persons who need no repentance" (Luke 15:7).

The lost sheep is the "sinner who repents." Amazing. What did the sheep do except wander away from the flock and the shepherd, get lost in the woods to his own great peril, and then be found by the shepherd? It was the shepherd who did all the work. The shepherd searched, found, rescued, picked up, carried home, and gave a party for the sheep. Repentance is being found by Jesus.

The same theme is found in the next parable, the parable of the lost coin. We can rename this too. It is really the parable of the sweeping and finding widow (Luke 15:8–10). Jesus says:

> Or what woman, having ten silver coins, if she loses one coin, does not light a lamp and sweep the house and seek diligently until she finds it? And when she has found it, she calls together her

friends and neighbors, saying, "Rejoice with me, for I have found the coin that I had lost." (vv. 8–9)

The lost coin did nothing to be found by the widow. It sat on the floor under the dust. The widow did it all. The same relentless seeking, the same joyful finding, the same over-the-top rejoicing, and the same point: "Just so, I tell you, there is joy before the angels of God over one sinner who repents" (v. 10).

We considered the parable of the running, forgiving, sweeping-up-in-arms-of-mercy-and-killing-the-fatted-calf father already in chapter 2, but consider it again in the context of our discussion of repentance. We might say, "Here is a more comfortable picture of repentance. This boy realizes what he's done wrong, and he comes back to the father. He does something. Repentance is his work." But this parable is really a rebuke of this understanding of repentance.

The prodigal son has his repentance speech all worked out, "Father, I have sinned against heaven and before you. I am no longer worthy to be called your son. Treat me as one of your hired servants" (Luke 15:18–19). This is the perfect example of the American Christian understanding of repentance. It is our effort and our resolve. The merciful father won't even let him finish! "Here is the ring, the robe, the feast, the joy of heaven, none of it deserved, all of it a gift!" This is the point: repentance is a gift. Repentance is something that the Lord gives to us.

The rest of the Scriptures confirm this. Peter is called before the Jewish Council to account for the miracles he performed in Jerusalem. He ended his testimony with this description of Jesus: "God exalted Him at His right hand as Leader and Savior, to give repentance to Israel and forgiveness of sins" (Acts 5:31). Far from our own work, it is the work of Jesus to give repentance. This comes up again in Acts as the disciples in Jerusalem consider the conversion of the Samaritans. "When they heard these things they fell silent. And they glorified God, saying, 'Then to the Gentiles also God has granted repentance that leads to life' " (Acts 11:18).

Of all the biblical texts about the Lord's work of repentance, Psalm 80 is perhaps the most poignant. The theme of the psalm is repeated in verses 3, 7, and 19. Most English translations use the words *turn* or *restore*, but it would be best translated, "Grant us repentance us, O God; let Your face shine, that we may be saved" (Psalm 80:3 author's translation). The Lord grants repentance, gives repentance. He turns us. In repentance, God is the actor and we are His subject.

THE TWO PARTS OF REPENTANCE

The Bible teaches that repentance has two parts: contrition and faith.

Contrition is knowing that we are sinners deserving of God's wrath.

Contrition is the awareness both of our sins and our sinfulness, both the things we've done wrong and the wrongness that corrupts our nature. Contrition includes the sorrow and fear that follow this awareness. Contrition is a terrified conscience feeling the full force of the preaching of the Law.

It is helpful to distinguish between a troubled conscience and a terrified conscience. A troubled conscience has an awareness of sin. A terrified conscience has an awareness of God's wrath over sin. Anyone, Christian or not, can have a troubled conscience. We know when we've made mistakes, hurt people, said and done the wrong things. A terrified conscience has its sin put in the context of God's holiness, and it knows God is angry about sin.

A troubled conscience says, "I have sinned." A terrified conscience says, "I have sinned and deserve God's temporal and eternal punishment." A troubled conscience asks, "What should I do about my sin?" A terrified conscience asks, "What is God going to do about my sin?" A troubled conscience is natural. A terrified conscience is supernatural, the work of the Holy Spirit to "convict the world concerning sin" (John 16:8). The terrified conscience, then, is the result of the preaching of the Law. It is contrition. This is the first part of repentance.

The second part of repentance is faith. Contrition comes from hearing the Law. Faith comes from hearing the Gospel. Faith knows that all of the sins God hates were died for by Jesus, covered by His blood, forgiven at His word. Faith lifts us out of contrition and fear and gives us hope and confidence. The Gospel comforts terrified consciences with the Good News of the death and resurrection of Jesus.

{ The Bible understands the entire life of a Christian as a life of repentance. }

Without faith, repentance is incomplete. King Saul and King David were both contrite and sorrowful because of their sin. King Saul's sorrow was not mixed with faith, and he died despairing by his own hand (1 Samuel 31). King David's contrition was mixed with faith, and in this the Lord restored him to the joy of His salvation (Psalm 51:12). Judas and Peter were both sorrowful at their betrayal of Jesus. Judas's sorrow had no hope, and he, too, died despairing (Matthew 27:5). But Peter's sorrow was mixed with faith, and Jesus restored him (John 21:15–19). Contrition and faith, these two together make repentance.

Repentance cannot be scheduled. "8:00 a.m., drive to work; 9:30 a.m., meet with Fred; 10:15 a.m., repent of my sins." This is because repentance is not our work. It is God's. Repentance is what happens to us when the Law and the Gospel do their work on us. The Holy Spirit brings the full weight of God's condemning Law, and we are undone, sorrowful, contrite. The Holy Spirit then brings the consolation of the promise of the Gospel and the forgiveness of sins, and we are born again, renewed, and comforted. We are granted repentance.

American Christianity understands repentance as a unique and monumental event, something that happens once (or a handful of times) in a Christian's life. The Bible, on the other hand, understands our entire life as a life of repentance. The Christian life is a life of repentance. We are called to constantly acknowledge, confess, our sinful condition. "If we say we have no sin, we deceive ourselves, and the truth is not in us. If we confess our sins, He is faithful and just to forgive us our sins and to cleanse us from all unrighteousness" (1 John 1:8–9). We daily ask the Lord to "forgive our trespasses." The first of Martin Luther's Ninety-Five Theses says, "When our Lord and Master Jesus Christ said, 'Repent,' [Matt. 4:17], he willed the entire life of believers to be one of repentance" (LW 31:25). Far from a unique moment or monumental experience, repentance is the normal Christian life. We hear the Law and believe what is says. We hear the Gospel and believe what is promises. We know our sin and failures, and we know our Lord and His mercy.

Life without the Gospel is marked by pride and despair. The preaching of the Law turns pride to contrition. The preaching of the Gospel turns despair to faith. The life of contrition and faith, the life of repentance, is the exact opposite of life without the

Gospel. It is a life of truth and joy, a life of terror comforted, despair undone, sin forgiven, a full life as a gift from the Lord.

Conversion: God's Work

There was an early dispute in the Lutheran Church around the question of conversion. "How is a sinner converted to God?" Martin Luther taught that conversion occurs through the Word of God and the Holy Spirit, specifically the Holy Spirit working through the Word.

> "Restore us, O God; let Your face shine, that we may be saved!"
>
> (Psalm 80:3)

Philip Melanchthon was Martin Luther's colleague and the second greatest teacher of the Lutheran Reformation. After Luther died, Melanchthon revisited this question of conversion. The result was bad. Melanchthon added a third thing to the list: man's will. Man's will was now understood as the instrument of conversion and not the object of it.

As the theological conversation progressed through John Calvin, then the radical reformers, and into the revivalists of America, the Word of God lost its place in conversion. American Christianity now understands conversion as the result of the Holy Spirit working together with man's will.

Luther	Melanchthon	American Christianity
Word	Word	
Spirit	Spirit	Spirit
	Will	Will

The Bible says that we cannot choose or turn to God. It teaches that the sinner is completely helpless regarding heavenly things. How, then, are we to believe? How does the sinner come to believe the promises of God? Conversion, turning from death to life and from the devil to God, is a work of God Himself; a work of God alone. We call this teaching *monergism*. God alone is the cause of our salvation; He creates faith (see Ephesians 2:8–10) and gives repentance as a gift. God converts sinners to believers. He opens the heart and gives faith. He calls and turns and claims sinners as His own.

The Bible is very careful to give the credit for faith and believing to the Lord.

> One who heard us was a woman named Lydia, from the city of Thyatira, a seller of purple goods, who was a worshiper of God. The Lord opened her heart to pay attention to what was said by Paul. (Acts 16:14)

Jesus says, "All things have been handed over to Me by My Father, and no one knows the Son except the Father, and no one knows the Father except the Son and anyone to whom the Son chooses to reveal Him" (Matthew 11:27). Again, "To you it has been given to know the secrets of the kingdom of heaven, but to them it has not been given" (Matthew 13:11).

> And we know that the Son of God has come and has given us understanding, so that we may know Him who is true; and we are in Him who is true, in His Son Jesus Christ. He is the true God and eternal life. (1 John 5:20)

Just as the Lord spoke and the universe was created out of nothing, so our faith is created out of nothing. "For God, who said, 'Let light shine out of darkness,' has shone in our hearts to give the light of the knowledge of the glory of God in the face of Jesus Christ" (2 Corinthians 4:6). God's Word alone creates faith. "For I am not ashamed of the gospel, for it is the power of God for salvation to everyone who believes, to the Jew first and also to the Greek" (Romans 1:16). "So faith comes from hearing, and hearing through the word of Christ" (Romans 10:17).

It is the Holy Spirit, working through the Word of God, who gives faith and causes us to trust in Jesus and His cross. God "works in you, both to will and to work for His good pleasure" (Philippians 2:13).

The Small Catechism summarizes this biblical teaching beautifully:

> I believe that I cannot by my own reason or strength believe in Jesus Christ, my Lord, or come to Him; but the Holy Spirit has called me by the Gospel, enlightened me with His gifts, sanctified and kept me in the true faith.

> In the same way He calls, gathers, enlightens, and sanctifies the whole Christian church on earth, and keeps it with Jesus Christ in the one true faith. (SC, Third Article)

OUR FAITH IS A WORK OF GOD THE HOLY SPIRIT THROUGH HIS WORD.

It is plain from the Scriptures that unbelievers cannot make a decision for Jesus or invite Him into their heart, but that the Holy Spirit, through the Word, converts the heart and gives us faith. But does this matter?

Jesus teaches us, "I am the vine; you are the branches. Whoever abides in Me and I in him, he it is that bears much fruit, for apart from Me you can do nothing" (John 15:5). This is a verse of marvelous comfort. Jesus promises that, abiding in Him, we will bear much fruit. In the same verse, Jesus warns us not to think too highly of ourselves. "Apart from Me you can do nothing." Jesus means what He says. We can do nothing good or holy apart from Him.

If we think the unbeliever has the will to choose Jesus or "make a decision for Christ," we undo Jesus' words. Jesus did not say, "Apart from Me you can do nothing except invite Me into your heart." Jesus wants us to have the comfort that He Himself, through the Holy Spirit, has given us repentance and faith.

The Lord's people rejoice that He has made a decision for us. He has decided to die for us, to forgive all our sins, to baptize us into His family, and to call us through His Gospel. Our faith is Jesus' work, and this is our great comfort. "You did not choose Me, but I chose you and appointed you that you should go and bear fruit and that your fruit should abide" (John 15:16).

INTRODUCING PASSIVE RIGHTEOUSNESS

On All Hallows' Eve of 1517, Martin Luther nailed the Ninety-Five Theses to the Castle Church doors in Wittenberg, Germany. Most people identify this event with the beginning of the Lutheran Reformation, and indeed, these theses did start quite a commotion. Reading the Ninety-Five Theses, though, it is clear that Luther did not yet have a grasp of the Gospel, the promise of the forgiveness of sins through Christ's death on the cross. In other words, when he began to protest, Luther was not yet a Lutheran.

The breakthrough moment came a few months later. It is sometimes called his "Tower Experience." Luther writes about it in the preface to his Latin works (see LW 34:336–37). He was a professor teaching the Scriptures, especially the Psalms, but his mind was stuck on Romans 1:17, and particularly one word in the text: *righteousness*. He had learned in school that righteousness is what God requires of us, our keeping the Law, our obedience to His commands. Luther took this seriously. He went to confession multiple times a day. He tortured himself for the slightest breaking of God's commandments. And while he was desperately pursuing the righteousness of God externally, his heart was turning away from God, and bitterness was turning to hatred.

> "For I am not ashamed of the gospel, for it is the power of God for salvation to everyone who believes, to the Jew first and also to the Greek. For in it the righteousness of God is revealed from faith for faith, as it is written, 'The righteous shall live by faith.'"
> (Romans 1:16–17)

Luther writes about it himself:

> Meanwhile, I had already during that year returned to interpret the Psalter anew. I had confidence in the fact that I was more skillful, after I had lectured in the university on St. Paul's epistles to the Romans, to the Galatians, and the one to the Hebrews. I had indeed been captivated with an extraordinary ardor for understanding Paul in the Epistle to the Romans. But up till then it was not the cold blood about the heart, but a single word in Chapter 1[:17], "IN IT THE RIGHTEOUSNESS OF GOD IS REVEALED," that had stood in my way. For I hated that word "righteousness of God," which, according to the use and custom of all the teachers, I had been taught to understand philosophically regarding the formal or active righteousness, as they called it, with which God is righteous and punishes the unrighteous sinner. (LW 34:336)

The Law, Luther knew, demanded righteousness. But now Paul comes along and demands even more. This was a common understanding of the "Gospel" in the monasteries. The Gospel was understood as an intensified law called the "Evangelical Councils." The Law said, "You shall not steal," but the "Gospel" said, "If anyone would sue you and take your tunic, let him have your cloak as well" (Matthew 5:40). The Law says, "You shall not commit adultery," but the "Gospel" says, "Everyone who looks at a woman with lustful intent has already committed adultery with her in his heart" (Matthew 5:28). The Law says, "You shall not kill," but the

"Gospel" has a higher standard, "Everyone who is angry with his brother will be liable to judgment" (Matthew 5:22). Luther understood the righteousness of the Gospel to be a higher standard than the Ten Commandments.

The Ten Commandments are like ten concrete blocks that we carry around in a backpack, and now the "Gospel" comes along and piles on even more blocks, demands more righteousness, and requires more obedience, until we are crushed. (This might sound familiar to many people in American Christianity, where the "Gospel" means a life of growth in good works and obedience.) Luther labored under this weight. It was devastating. Not only did Luther hate the word *righteousness*, but he also hated the God who demanded that righteousness. This is a shocking admission, almost difficult to read, but it is true. Luther continues:

> Though I lived as a monk without reproach, I felt that I was a sin-
> ner before God with an extremely disturbed conscience. I could
> not believe that he was placated by my satisfaction. I did not love,
> yes, I hated the righteous God who punishes sinners, and secretly,
> if not blasphemously, certainly murmuring greatly, I was angry
> with God, and said, "As if, indeed, it is not enough, that miserable
> sinners, eternally lost through original sin, are crushed by every
> kind of calamity by the law of the decalogue, without having God
> add pain to pain by the gospel and also by the gospel threatening
> us with his righteousness and wrath!" Thus I raged with a fierce
> and troubled conscience. (LW 34:336–37)

Can you imagine it? Luther, the great reformer of the Church, talking about his hatred for God. This is the real and true condition of a conscience that doesn't know the forgiveness of sins. There is only the pride in the illusion of obedience or despair in the knowledge of our failures. Luther knew despair. The weight of the Law crushed him, and he raged against the wrath of God pressing down on him. Then something happened.

(As an aside, it is important to note that what we normally hear in these kinds of stories is some miraculous or supernatural event. We expect Luther to tell us an angel appeared to him or he had a vision or there was a flash. But there is none of that. Luther will say, simply, that he paid attention to the words. The importance of this cannot be overstated. Almost every church lays claim to some supernatural revelation. Luther says only that he finally saw the words that were right there in front of him all along.)

> Nevertheless, I beat importunately upon Paul at that place, most ardently desiring to know what St. Paul wanted.

> At last, by the mercy of God, meditating day and night, I gave heed to the context of the words, namely, "In it the righteousness of God is revealed, as it is written, 'He who through faith is righteous shall live.'" (LW 34:337)

Luther sees the word *faith* there in the neighborhood of the righteousness revealed by the Gospel. Luther knows that "faith" is how you keep a promise, and not a command. If this righteousness comes by faith, it cannot be a commanded righteousness. It must be a promised righteousness. This righteousness revealed by the Gospel, then, is not a righteousness that is achieved; rather, it is given by God as a gracious gift. You can hear the excitement in Luther's words as he reports this breakthrough.

> There I began to understand that the righteousness of God is that by which the righteous lives by a gift of God, namely by faith. And this is the meaning: the righteousness of God is revealed by the gospel, namely, the passive righteousness with which merciful God justifies us by faith, as it is written, "He who through faith is righteous shall live." Here I felt that I was altogether born again and had entered paradise itself through open gates. There a totally other face of the entire Scripture showed itself to me. Thereupon I ran through the Scriptures from memory. I also found in other terms an analogy, as, the work of God, that is, what God does in us, the power of God, with which he makes us strong, the wisdom of God, with which he makes us wise, the strength of God, the salvation of God, the glory of God.

> And I extolled my sweetest word with a love as great as the hatred with which I had before hated the word "righteousness of God." Thus that place in Paul was for me truly the gate to paradise. (LW 34:337)

The righteousness of the Law is an active righteousness. A righteousness regarding our thoughts, words, and deeds. The righteousness of the Gospel is entirely different. It is a "passive righteousness," that is, it is a righteousness apart from works. The righteousness of the Gospel is the perfection that the Lord imputes to our account apart from anything we do. Luther names this "alien righteousness" because it comes from outside of me. It is a righteousness that belongs to Jesus but is graciously given to us.

{ **The righteousness of the Gospel belongs to Jesus but is graciously given to us.** }

There is a righteousness of the Law, of our own doing, which is never perfect, never complete, and never good enough. And there is the righteousness of the Gospel that comes to us as a promise. "And to the one who does not work but believes in Him who justifies the ungodly, his faith is counted as righteousness" (Romans 4:5). The Lord Jesus, apart from our works and in spite of our sin, gives to us His life-deserving righteousness and perfection. To know this is to be born again; the doors of heaven are thrown open, and our love for God is born in His incomprehensible love for us.

> "So Jesus said to them again, 'Peace to you! As the Father has sent Me, I also send you.' And when He had said this, He breathed on them, and said to them, 'Receive the Holy Spirit. If you forgive the sins of any, they are forgiven them; if you retain the sins of any, they are retained.'"
>
> (John 20:21–23 NKJV)

This is the heart of the Reformation and of the Lutheran teaching. Luther discovered (or uncovered) the clarity of the Gospel. This doctrine was worth fighting and dying for, because this teaching alone gives comfort and peace to sinners. The righteousness required to be saved is the righteousness of Jesus given to us as a free gift.

Get Out of Jail Free

I remember my first visit to a liturgical Lutheran church as an adult. I was a disappointed American Christian, but my theology still followed the contours of American Christianity. I was balking at this guy standing up front in robes. "What is he talking about? Why is he turning his back to us? What is all this kneeling and crossing and chanting? What is all this mumbo-jumbo?" The thing that troubled me most was when the pastor said to the congregation, "By virtue of my office as a called and ordained servant of the Word, and in the stead and by the command of my Lord Jesus Christ, I forgive you all your sins, in the name of the Father and of the Son and of the Holy Spirit."

"Who does this guy think he is, forgiving my sins? That's God's job!" I was angry and offended. I asked him after the service, and he did the most wonderful and helpful thing. He opened his Bible and showed me John 20:

"If you forgive the sins of any, they are forgiven them" (John 20:23).

This is an astounding and important text.

Jesus had risen. The grave was empty. His work had been accomplished and salvation won. He appears to His disciples and there is a word echoing in the air: "Peace!" "Peace be with you!" The peace Jesus is talking about is bound up to the cross. His peace is the forgiveness of sins. The war between heaven and earth is ended. The reign of sin and death is over. The tomb is empty. Christ is risen indeed. Jesus has peace to distribute because He has just won the victory. "Peace!"

This is the peace of the forgiveness of sins. "It [righteousness] will be counted to us who believe in Him who raised from the dead Jesus our Lord, who was delivered up for our trespasses and raised for our justification. Therefore, since we have been justified by faith, we have peace with God through our Lord Jesus Christ" (Romans 4:24–5:1). The resurrection of Jesus is confirmation that His sacrifice on the cross is acceptable to God. His resurrection is the confirmation of His "It is finished" (John 19:30).

Here's the picture, which is a bit trite, but hopefully gets the point across. In a football game, the running back scores a touchdown as soon as he crosses the goal line. His work is finished. He can dance around, spike the ball, and celebrate with the team. But the points are not awarded until the official raises his hands and signals the touchdown.

Jesus, in His death, crosses the goal line. His work is accomplished. The Father, in the resurrection of Jesus, gives the points to the team. He applies the sacrifice of Jesus to the sin of humanity. In the resurrection, we get the signal from God the Father: "It is good." The sacrifice is acceptable. Justice is satisfied. Wrath is propitiated. Salvation is won. This truly is the Lamb of God who takes away the sin of the world (John 1:29). The world is reconciled to God, and God to the world (2 Corinthians 5:18–19). The warfare waged between sinners and God is ended (Isaiah 40:1–2). "Peace be with you."

Jesus would have the word of this peace spread throughout the entire world. Therefore, He sends out the disciples and establishes the Church in every corner of the world. In Matthew 28:18–20, He sends them to make disciples by baptizing and teaching. In Mark 16, He sends them to "proclaim the gospel to the whole creation" (v. 15). In Luke, Jesus says that "repentance and forgiveness of sins should be proclaimed in His name to all nations, beginning from Jerusalem" (24:47). The peace of the cross and the empty tomb spreads throughout the world by preaching and Baptism.

John records Jesus' specific instructions for expanding this peace to the world, "He breathed on them, and said to them, 'Receive the Holy Spirit. If you forgive the sins of any, they are forgiven them; if you retain the sins of any, they are retained' " (John 20:22–23 NKJV). Jesus is giving His Church the authority to forgive and retain sins, and we call this authority "The Office of the Keys."

There are two other texts that explicitly give this teaching, both in Matthew:

> And Jesus answered [Peter], "Blessed are you, Simon Bar-Jonah! For flesh and blood has not revealed this to you, but My Father who is in heaven. And I tell you, you are Peter, and on this rock I will build My church, and the gates of hell shall not prevail against it. I will give you the keys of the kingdom of heaven, and whatever you bind on earth shall be bound in heaven, and whatever you loose on earth shall be loosed in heaven." (16:17–19)

> Truly, I say to you, whatever you bind on earth shall be bound in heaven, and whatever you loose on earth shall be loosed in heaven. (18:18)

The "keys" here given are the opening and closing of heaven. The Keys are the preaching of Law and Gospel. There is a fantastic definition of the Office of the Keys in the Small Catechism: "The Office of the Keys is that special authority which Christ has given to His church on earth to forgive the sins of repentant sinners, but to withhold forgiveness from the unrepentant as long as they do not repent" (SC, Confession).

This authority is most often exercised in the Absolution, that is, the declaration of the promise of the forgiveness of sins. Speaking the absolution is a practice that is foreign and troubling to American Christianity, but it is a comforting and joyful gift given by Jesus to the Church.

The forgiveness given in the Absolution is not man's forgiveness, but God's. What, really, does it matter if I forgive you? It is nice to have one another's forgiveness, but we all need the forgiveness of God. Jesus wants to make sure we know we have it. Jesus breathed on His disciples and gave them the Holy Spirit and the charge to forgive sins.

Here's the picture. Imagine you are in jail. The judge across the street in the courthouse is hearing your case. He declares you innocent. He then gives the bailiff the key to your jail cell with the charge to set you free. The bailiff comes to you, unlocks your cell, and says, "I am setting you free." You, of course, say, "Hey, that's not your job! The judge is the only one who can set me free. I'm staying right here!" The bailiff comes with the word of the judge for you. He is delivering to you the verdict of the court. He has the key and the command from the judge to set you free.

Things, of course, could go wrong. Imagine the judge declares you innocent and free, but the bailiff goes and plays golf. There you sit, a free man in jail. Or imagine the judge declares you guilty, but the bailiff has different ideas and lets you go. You walk around like a free man, but you are not truly free. The bailiff's office of the key only works if he acts rightly upon the judge's decree.

This is how it is with the Office of the Keys. This is how it is with the Absolution. The Absolution, the declaration of sins forgiven, is sure and valid because Christ has died and been raised, because His blood availed before the Father's throne, and because He has commanded His Church to forgive sins. The "I forgive you all your sins" spoken to the repentant sinner in Jesus' name is just as true as the "It is finished" spoken from the cross.

THE ABSOLUTION, THEN, IS TRULY A HEAVENLY AUTHORITY. THE DECLARATION OF THE FORGIVENESS OF SINS IN NOT ONLY. DESCRIPTIVE, IT IS ACTIVE. The Absolution declares something, promises something, accomplishes something. SINS ARE TRULY FORGIVEN. COMFORT IS TRULY RENDERED. *Delivery of Jesus*

The Absolution is strong medicine for the terrified sinner. It is a strong defense against the assaults of the devil.

The devil is always lurking around our conscience, sowing seeds of doubt. Doubt in God's Word, doubt in God's love, doubt, especially, in God's mercy. The devil uses our sins to assault our confidence in the Lord's mercy. Even when we know the love of God in the cross of Jesus, the devil tempts us to think His love is not for us. "Your sin is too bad. Your shame is too much. You sin all the time, and you think God still loves you?" Against this temptation, the Lord Jesus has given us the gift of Absolution, the Gospel "for you," pressed into your ears and heart such that there is no room for doubt. "If you forgive the sins of any, they are forgiven them" (John 20:23). This forgiveness is as sure and certain on earth as it is in heaven.

In American Christianity, the Absolution is extinct. (It is sadly rare even in Lutheran congregations where the teaching is preserved.) Jesus established the Absolution for His people, for our comfort, and for establishing us in His promised mercy. The recovery of this treasure will give the Church the strength to endure the trouble of these last days.

> "How much more will the blood of Christ, who through the eternal Spirit offered Himself without blemish to God, purify our conscience from dead works to serve the living God." (Hebrews 9:14)

As a Lutheran pastor, I now understand the question I once asked when I first visited a Lutheran church. "Who is this pastor to forgive me my sins?" "No one," is the answer. Whenever anyone asks me that question, I open my Bible to John 20, and rejoice that Jesus has given such a treasure as the Absolution to us.

THE COURTROOM OF THE CONSCIENCE AND THE COMFORT OF TRUTH

We've talked a lot in this book about the conscience; it's time to dig in and sort out what the conscience is, how it works, and how our teaching affects the conscience. Lutheran teaching is unique in that it focuses on the conscience, especially delivering the comfort of the Gospel to terrified consciences.

WHO DUG THAT PIT IN YOUR STOMACH?

The sick feeling we get when we've done something bad is due to our having a conscience. The conscience is our internal referee that makes judgments about the things going on around us. The conscience is a gift from God. Like reason and emotions, the conscience is given to every person in creation. It is part of our humanity. The conscience works like a little courtroom in our heart. Thoughts and actions are tested, and verdicts are pronounced. Our conscience makes judgments on our own thoughts, words, and deeds. Our conscience especially makes judgments on the way other people treat us. Our conscience judges the way people treat others, and it also suggests there is something wrong in the world.

Comparing the conscience to a courtroom lets us consider how it should be ordered, and how it might become disordered.

In a rightly ordered conscience, the Lord sits as judge. The Ten Commandments are the Law. We are the accused. The devil is the accuser. (*Satan* is a Hebrew title meaning "accuser.") This, no doubt, is a terrifying picture. We are guilty of sin and should be condemned. This is why we try so hard to manipulate what is happening in the courtroom of our conscience.

We try to remove ourselves from the accusations of our conscience. We try to put our neighbors on trial instead of ourselves (and make judgments on their lives and actions). We try to take the devil's place and act as the accuser. Or we try to take God's place and act as judge. We invite our peers into our conscience to create our own new law and standards to take the place of the Ten Commandments. We might try to be our own defense attorney. When our sin is brought before the court, we defend ourselves, or we make excuses. We compare our actions to others. "No one was hurt" or "No one knows about it" or "Everyone is doing it."

These are all attempts to silence the accusing sentence of our conscience. It is called "self-justification." The more we practice this, the better we get, but this is not how our conscience is supposed to function. The more we justify ourselves in our conscience, the more twisted and broken our conscience becomes.

The other option available to sinners in the conscience is to accept the guilt of our sin and then become our own judge, pronouncing the sentence. I've hurt others, so I have to hurt myself. We sentence ourselves to self-loathing. "I've sinned, and now I have to pay for it in some other way. If I can be good enough, environmentally conscious enough, politically correct enough, disciplined enough, then I can atone for my sins." We try to pronounce our own sentence. We live in our self-made prisons in an attempt to appease our conscience. This is "self-atonement," and it is a false atonement, a laboring under the delusion that a conscience can be made good or whole through our own sacrifice and suffering.

Self-justification is the distortion of the conscience through pride. Self-atonement is the distortion of the conscience through despair. All of this is based on the fundamental error that "a conscience can be made good by good works." This is utterly false, but it is a profoundly difficult error to resist.

There is a legion of different ways things can go wrong in the conscience. The courtroom of the conscience is out of order. But even when a conscience is working properly, it doesn't mean that it is a good conscience. Apart from Christ, the best our conscience can do is hear the Law and know the depth of our sin, know we deserve God's wrath and punishment. This, in fact, is the first function of our conscience.

Jesus also has a proper place in the courtroom of our conscience. He is our defense.

This teaching is captured in the Greek word *paraklētos*, or in English, *paraclete*. A paraclete is an official friend who goes with you to court. A paraclete is a legal counsel, a defense attorney. The paraclete advocates for the defendant before the court and comforts the defendant with his kindness. In 1 John 2:1, we read, "But if anyone does sin, we have an advocate [paraclete] with the Father, Jesus Christ the righteous." Jesus is our Paraclete who stands before the Father in the heavenly court, pleading our case.

Jesus ascended into heaven forty-three days after His crucifixion. He brought with Him the victory of His cross. Jesus stood before the judgment throne of God with His blood (see Hebrews 9:11–12). His blood is the evidence of His sacrifice and our righteousness. God the Father receives that evidence. We are declared innocent and righteous. Jesus continues to sit at the Father's right hand as our Advocate with the Father. He continues to plead His death for our sake (see Hebrews 7:25; Romans 8:34).

Jesus is not the only Paraclete. From His seat at the Father's right hand, Jesus sends the Holy Spirit to be our Paraclete on earth. In John 14:16, 26 and 16:7, the Holy Spirit is called the Paraclete. "And I will ask the Father, and He will give you another Helper [Paraclete], to be with you forever, even the Spirit of truth, whom the world cannot receive, because it neither sees Him nor knows Him. You know Him, for He dwells with you and will be in you" (John 14:16–17).

While Jesus is our Paraclete in the heavenly courtroom, the Holy Spirit is our Paraclete in the courtroom of our conscience. The Holy Spirit speaks the words of Jesus to our conscience. He comes into the courtroom of our conscience and brings with Him the same evidence that Jesus brings into the heavenly court: the death and blood of Jesus. The gracious drama of the heavenly court is echoed in our conscience, and the verdict spoken in heaven is brought to us in the Gospel. It is difficult to imagine anything more wonderful! The result is faith and life and joy and comfort.

Comforting the terrified conscience is the stated goal of the Lutheran teachers. "But in this controversy, the chief topic of Christian doctrine is treated. When it is understood correctly, it illumines and amplifies Christ's honor. . . . It brings necessary and most abundant consolation to devout consciences" (Ap IV [II] 2). The Lutheran theologians are looking for more than truth. They are looking for the truth that comforts, the truth that forgives, the truth that saves.

This has led to a unique focus on the conscience in Lutheran theology and worship. "Where's the comfort?" is the question we ask when we open the Bible, when we go to church, when Christians talk with one another. "Where is the comfort?" We can't find it in our own doing, in our obedience, in our resolve, in our works. We find true comfort in Christ alone.

By the Holy Spirit, Jesus takes a stand in the middle of our conscience and presents the evidence of His sacrifice, and the verdict is spoken: "Forgiven."

This courtroom drama continues through the life of a Christian. The devil brings the evidence of our sin into the court of our conscience. The Holy Spirit speaks up, "Objection, that sin is died for!" "Sustained!" says the Father, and the devil is off in his restless and futile attempt to find some sin that will overthrow the death of Jesus. But there is nothing for the devil to accuse. "There is therefore now no condemnation for those who are in Christ Jesus" (Romans 8:1). Everything is forgiven. "Who shall bring any charge against God's elect? It is God who justifies. Who is to condemn? Christ Jesus is the one who died—more than that, who was raised—who is at the right hand of God, who indeed is interceding for us" (Romans 8:33–34).

We cannot achieve a good conscience. A good and clean conscience is the gift of God in Christ, in His death, His blood, His mercy.

Paul writes to Timothy: "The aim of our charge is love that issues from a pure heart and a good conscience and a sincere faith" (1 Timothy 1:5). Hebrews says, "And since we have a great priest [Jesus Christ] over the house of God, let us draw near with a true heart in full assurance of faith, with our hearts sprinkled clean from an evil conscience and our bodies washed with pure water" (Hebrews 10:21–22).

A good conscience is a conscience that knows the death of Jesus. A good conscience is a conscience where the voice of Jesus is heard. A good conscience is *not* a conscience without sin; it is a conscience where sin is forgiven, covered with His blood. A good conscience is wrapped in the white robes of Christ's righteousness. A good conscience is a forgiven conscience.

> A good conscience is *not* a conscience without sin. . . . A good conscience is a forgiven conscience.

The devil tries to fill our conscience with a false verdict. Misusing the Law, he declares us good enough. "I'm a good person, so surely I will go to heaven." Wrong. There is no good conscience without Jesus. Or the devil (again misusing the Law) says, "You'll never be saved. You've sinned too much. You are too wicked." Wrong. It is God who judges, and He gave your death sentence to His Son so you would have life.

The devil is right when he calls us sinners. He is wrong when he condemns us to hell. Jesus has suffered. Jesus has died and risen again and ascended to God's right hand. Jesus brings before the Father the evidence of His blood, His cross. The testimony of our sin is struck from the record. We are absolved, declared righteous and holy by the heavenly court. If the blood of Jesus stands in this courtroom, then it stands in our consciences as well.

With its focus on the works of the Christian, American Christianity tries to fill the courtroom of the conscience with our own efforts. The resulting verdict is pride or despair. Comfort is elusive. Peace is absent.

Jesus has something better for us. "How much more will the blood of Christ, who through the eternal Spirit offered Himself without blemish to God, purify our conscience from dead works to serve the living God" (Hebrews 9:14). He has life, mercy, kindness, love, hope, peace, and a cleansed conscience. He has His finished work, His victory over sin and death, His promise of eternal life spoken in heaven and into our ears and hearts, "Your sins are forgiven."

CHAPTER SIX

GO PLAY OUTSIDE

"Whenever our heart condemns us, God is greater than our heart, and He knows everything."

(1 John 3:20)

IN AMERICAN CHRISTIANITY, THE SPIRITUAL LIFE IS ON THE INSIDE. Everything having to do with salvation happens in my heart. It is in my heart where the Lord moves me, touches me, talks to me. It is in my heart that I make the decision to follow the Lord. In my heart I resolve to be better. In fact, in my "decision for Christ," I am both "inviting Jesus to live in my heart" and, at the same time, "giving my heart to Jesus." Everything important, everything having to do with salvation, everything connected to the Gospel is happening on the inside, in the theater of my heart. The locus of God's action is inside.

If God's action is located in the heart, you can understand why American Christianity sees anything happening outside my heart as being disconnected from the Gospel. If it is external, then it is, by definition, a work. If it is outside of my heart, it must be Law. Anything outside must have nothing to do with salvation.

The distinction between external works and internal blessings is fundamental in American Christianity, and it has a number of important theological consequences.

First, American Christianity has no sacraments.

There are, to be sure, ordinances: the ordinance of Baptism and the ordinance of the Lord's Supper. These are symbolic acts and indicators of my faith. They are my works and deeds, not the works of God. American Christianity understands Baptism and the Lord's Supper to be Law, not Gospel. They are works completely disconnected from the forgiveness of sins.

American Christianity teaches that Baptism is the first act of obedience. In Baptism, we publicly testify that we have made a decision for Christ. Baptism is a symbol of our death and resurrection with Christ. The Lord's Supper is likewise a symbol, something we do to remember Jesus and His sacrifice for us.

In the Scriptures, Baptism and the Lord's Supper are bound up to all sorts of wonderful promises and gracious benefits. (We will consider these in this chapter.) American Christianity must conclude that there are no blessings or spiritual benefits in Baptism or the Lord's Supper. Both happen outside your heart.

The second and related theological consequence of denying spiritual benefit to anything external is the loss of certainty and confidence. The human heart is notoriously uncertain. The things on the inside are unsure, always shifting and changing. One moment we are happy; the next we are sad. We are confident and then meek, perceptive and then confused. In one moment we might be confident of God's love, and in the next we are fearful of His wrath.

If God is working only on the inside, then any confidence in the Lord is bound up to my subjective experience. If God brings blessings only to my heart, then my confidence in those blessings is bound up to my feelings. The heart is shifty, unstable, tossed to-and-fro like a ship on the sea. By refusing to see blessing and grace outside of ourselves, American Christianity creates a void of certainty and confidence.

This "certainty void" needs to be filled. American Christianity tries to fill this void with my works or my worship experience.

EVERY KIND OF RELIGIOUS EXPERIENCE SEEKS TO DELIVER CERTAINTY TO ITS BELIEVERS. THEY CANNOT. Any theology that isolates spirituality to our insides is doomed to uncertainty.

The Scriptures, in contrast, begin outside of us. Certainty and confidence are on the outside. The Lord delivers His certain love and unmovable kindness in the *external* Word.

In fact, the Lutheran Church understands that most spiritual action is outside of us. Baptism, the Lord's Supper, the Absolution, preaching and teaching and hearing the Word—all of these begin outside of our heart. The Lord, in His mercy, has bound up all of these things with His promises. These things are sure even when we are not. These things are certain even when we have doubts. When we know the Lord works outside of us, we have some certainty and stability. When we know that the Lord's works are objective, we have a solid foundation on which to build our faith.

This is not to say that Baptism, the Lord's Supper, preaching, or any other external work of God brings us any benefit apart from faith. Faith believes the promises God gives in these gifts. By faith we receive the spiritual benefits and blessings that God promises. But our faith is built on the rock-solid foundations of the works and promises of God, not on the shifting sands of our own heart.

American Christianity emphasizes the internal word and work of God. This leads to uncertainty and doubt. The Lutheran Church emphasizes the external Word, the voice of God that comes from outside of us. This delivers certainty and confidence to our hurting and unstable heart.

HIDE-AND-SEEK WITH THE HOLY SPIRIT

I grew up in a liturgical church, but by the time I was in middle school, it was all praise band all the time. On my journey into the Lutheran Church, my first visit back to the liturgy was a disaster. I mentioned before the distress of my first visit back to a liturgical Lutheran church service. With the robes, the chanting, the turning this way and that, looking this way and that, crossing this way and that, I had no idea what was happening. The Absolution was particularly troubling, and the sermon was not particularly moving. Neither were the hymns and the organ. I boldly pronounced this verdict (after we were out of earshot): "I just didn't feel the Holy Spirit there."

> "The wind blows where it wishes, and you hear its sound, but you do not know where it comes from or where it goes. So it is with everyone who is born of the Spirit." (John 3:8)

I had been trained in the revivalist worship services of American Christianity to sense the presence of the Holy Spirit with my feelings. Goosebumps, a pit in my stomach, "losing myself" in the music or the moment were indicators of the Holy Spirit's presence. If I was "moved," the Holy Spirit was there. In my return to the liturgy, I was not moved. The Holy Spirit had obviously left the building.

But does the Bible train us to hunt for the Spirit with our feelings?

John 3 records an important conversation between Jesus and Nicodemus. Nicodemus was a Pharisee, and a member of the Jewish Council. This Council was the council of judges established by Moses to help rule the nation (see Exodus 18:13). Nicodemus, in other words, was an important man. He comes to Jesus by night (to preserve his reputation), but he seems genuinely interested to know who Jesus is. In fact, Nicodemus would eventually become a follower of Jesus and would assist Joseph of Arimathea in preparing the body of Jesus for burial (John 19:39–42). But this first conversation with Jesus did not begin well.

"Rabbi, we know that You are a teacher come from God, for no one can do these signs that You do unless God is with him" (John 3:2).

Jesus wouldn't be buttered up. Instead, He tells Nicodemus that he is ignorant of the kingdom of God. Jesus gets to the point. Nicodemus must learn how to inherit the kingdom of God.

"Jesus answered him, 'Truly, truly, I say to you, unless one is born again he cannot see the kingdom of God'" (John 3:3).

The Pharisees were about the business of being good enough for God's kingdom. They were going to make it into the kingdom of God by their religious works and observances. Jesus, though, doesn't speak a word about work or our activities. Entrance into the kingdom of heaven, according to Jesus, is God's work. Salvation is a gift. It is a "new birth." This astonishes Nicodemus.

"How can a man be born when he is old? Can he enter a second time into his mother's womb and be born?" (John 3:4).

Nicodemus is thinking about wombs and mothers, our earthly birth. Jesus is teaching about Baptism, water and the Spirit, our heavenly birth.

> Jesus answered, "Truly, truly, I say to you, unless one is born of water and the Spirit, he cannot enter the kingdom of God. That which is born of the flesh is flesh, and that which is born of the Spirit is spirit. Do not marvel that I said to you, 'You must be born again.'" (John 3:5–7)

This birth of water and Spirit, Jesus teaches, is required to enter the kingdom of God. We see here Jesus contrasting the Pharisees' idea of salvation through works with His own divine doctrine of grace.

FAR FROM WORKS,

FAR FROM OUR OWN RIGHTEOUSNESS,

FAR FROM ACHIEVING SOME SORT OF PERFECTION THAT EARNS GOD'S APPROVAL, SALVATION IS BY GOD'S OWN GIFT OF WATER AND SPIRIT.

The kingdom of God comes by promise and faith. And Jesus connects this promise to water.

JESUS BINDS UP SALVATION TO HIS GIFT OF BAPTISM.

Some might protest. "Jesus is not talking about Baptism here." This is using preconceived notions to run from the plain meaning of the text. This conversation with Nicodemus is surrounded with talk of Baptism (see John 1:24–34 and 4:1–2). We'll be talking more about Baptism soon, and we'll pick up the rest of the conversation with Nicodemus in the next section, but Jesus has more to say to Nicodemus about being born again.

"The wind blows where it wishes, and you hear its sound, but you do not know where it comes from or where it goes. So it is with everyone who is born of the Spirit" (John 3:8).

Jesus uses the picture of wind to teach about the Holy Spirit. (In Greek, there is one word that is translated either "word" or "spirit".) You cannot see the wind. You see what the wind does to the leaves or the dust and your newly washed car. You can also feel the wind. But Jesus doesn't mention feeling or seeing. Instead, He says, "You hear its sound." You know the wind is blowing because you hear it. Jesus, remember, is teaching about the Holy Spirit. How do you know where the

Holy Spirit is? How do we know if the Holy Spirit is at work? You hear His sound. The Holy Spirit is heard, not felt. The Holy Spirit doesn't tickle us; He talks to us.

The presence of the Holy Spirit and the evidence of His work is not detected by feeling, but by hearing. The sword of the Spirit is the *Word* of God (see Ephesians 6:17). The Bible never commands us to feel the Holy Spirit. We are commanded to listen to the Word. The Scriptures are inspired by the Spirit, not our feelings (see 2 Timothy 3:16; 2 Peter 1:19–21).

The Holy Spirit teaches. Jesus gives a beautiful promise to His disciples. After His death, resurrection, and ascension, Jesus will send the Holy Spirit. "But the Helper, the Holy Spirit, whom the Father will send in My name, He will teach you all things and bring to your remembrance all that I have said to you" (John 14:26). The Spirit bears witness. "But when the Helper comes, whom I will send to you from the Father, the Spirit of truth, who proceeds from the Father, He will bear witness about Me" (John 15:26). The Spirit will speak. "When the Spirit of truth comes, He will guide you into all the truth, for He will not speak on His own authority, but whatever He hears He will speak, and He will declare to you the things that are to come" (John 16:13). The Holy Spirit works through words. The Holy Spirit talks. And this talking is not inside of us. The Holy Spirit does not communicate through secrets. He teaches by the Word of God. We hear the words of the Holy Spirit when we hear the Scriptures read and preached.

How do you know where the Holy Spirit is? How do you find Him? You listen. Listen for the Word of God. Listen for the Holy Scriptures. Listen for the comforting Gospel message that Jesus has died for you, forgiven you, opened heaven for you. Listen for the preaching of Law and Gospel. You will find the Holy Spirit bound to the very Word of God. This is our great comfort.

If the Holy Spirit were working through feelings and impulses, we could never know exactly what He is communicating. But we *do* know. In the Scriptures we know. We know God's Law. We trust God's Gospel. The Holy Spirit convicts the world of sin and righteousness. Far from playing hide-and-seek with the Spirit, the Holy Spirit is revealed to us by the Word.

I was wrong after I visited that Lutheran service. I might not have been moved. I might not have felt the Holy Spirit. But He was there. He was there in the Word doing His gracious work, even on me. American Christianity teaches us to hunt for the Spirit in the forest of our feelings and experiences, but the Holy Spirit reveals Himself and the mercy of God to us in the external Word. This is our confidence.

Jesus said, "The words that I have spoken to you are spirit and life" (John 6:63).

JUST BECAUSE IT'S PHYSICAL DOESN'T MEAN IT'S LAW

> "And as Moses lifted up the serpent in the wilderness, so must the Son of Man be lifted up, that whoever believes in Him may have eternal life."
>
> (John 3:14–15)

"Stuff can't save you." This is a philosophical argument, not a biblical one, but it creeps around in the shadows of American Christianity. If God works blessings only on the inside, then any kind of physical object will always be disconnected from salvation. "If it is stuff, it is Law." But in the Bible, stuff is always saving us.

When the Israelites were grumbling, God sent snakes to bite and attack them. When they repented, He told Moses, "Make a fiery serpent and set it on a pole, and everyone who is bitten, when he sees it, shall live" (Numbers 21:8). Imagine being one of these people, sitting outside the tent where Moses was crafting this bronze serpent. The smiths are hammering away while you are getting sicker and dying.

"Moses, what's going on in there?"

"We're making a bronze serpent to put on a stick."

"Why?"

"It's what the Lord told us to do. If you look at the bronze serpent on the stick, then you will be saved."

"That's absurd. You should make some antivenom or find some doctors. If the Lord wanted to save us by a miracle, why didn't He just do it? Why all this rigmarole?"

It does seem absurd, but it would be even more absurd if—when the work was completed and the serpent was lifted up on a pole—the people refused to look at it. Looking at a bronze serpent is ridiculous. "Stuff doesn't save us," the people would say. And die.

It pleased the Lord to save the people through the serpent on the pole. It was a very physical thing that brought very real help.

The same thing is established in the tabernacle. There was a real altar with real animals and real blood and real fire. There was the tabernacle and all its furniture, real things in a real place. There were the priests, the Most Holy Place, the incense table, the ark of the covenant, and all the other holy things. Through these physical things, the Lord delivered His mercy and forgiveness to His Old Testament people.

That the Lord uses "stuff" to rescue us comes to its fullness in the flesh and blood of Jesus.

> Since therefore the children share in flesh and blood, He Himself likewise partook of the same things, that through death He might destroy the one who has the power of death, that is, the devil, and deliver all those who through fear of death were subject to lifelong slavery. (Hebrews 2:14–15)

> And by that will we have been sanctified through the offering of the body of Jesus Christ once for all. (Hebrews 10:10)

The blood of Jesus is real blood. His body is a real human body. These real physical things accomplish our salvation. It is the "stuff" that wins us eternal life. When we are tempted to think physical things are Law and not Gospel, we need only remember that the dead body of Jesus is a true physical thing.

God continues to use physical things to save us.

Imagine we are dropped on a desert island. We have a copy of the Bible. Imagine also that the Holy Spirit has given us faith in Christ, but we have no knowledge of the history of the Church. We have never studied theology. We've never heard of the different denominations or the creeds of the Church. We open the pages of the Scriptures and start to read.

We see, first, that we are sinners. God has a standard, and we don't keep it. That much is clear. We also see that Jesus died. A simple reading of the Bible tells you the death of Jesus is important, and it tells you why. Jesus died for sinners. We know, then, that we are sinners, and that Christ has died for sinners. Now we are searching the pages of the Bible for the forgiveness of sins. How does the Lord forgive us? Where is the forgiveness of sins promised? These passages are going to be the most important passages to us.

What do we find?

- First, we see the promise of forgiveness bound up to water. "Repent and be baptized every one of you in the name of Jesus Christ *for the forgiveness of your sins*, and you will receive the gift of the Holy Spirit" (Acts 2:38, emphasis added).

- Next, we see the promise of forgiveness in the cup of Jesus' blood. "Drink of it, all of you, for this is My blood of the covenant, which is poured out for many *for the forgiveness of sins*" (Matthew 26:27–28, emphasis added).

- Third, we see the promise of forgiveness put in the mouth of Jesus' disciples. "If you forgive the sins of any, they are forgiven them; if you retain the sins of any, they are retained" (John 20:23 NKJV).

Our desert-island Christians would look for the forgiveness of sins, and they would find them in the Lord's gifts of Baptism, the Lord's Supper, and the Absolution!

The promise of forgiveness is bound up to stuff, specific stuff: water, bread, wine, the body and blood of Jesus, the preaching of the Word. Baptism, the Lord's Supper, the Absolution—these are so important because Jesus has bound up the promise of forgiveness and mercy to these things. The Lutheran Church calls them the Means of Grace. This is the stuff to which Jesus attaches promises.

If we are reading the Scriptures in simplicity, looking for forgiveness, we find the Sacraments. If we were dropped on an island with faith in Jesus and a trust in the Scriptures, we'd end up Lutheran.

American Christianity does not have the Sacraments. There is the ordinance of Baptism, our "first act of obedience." There is the ordinance of Communion, the symbolic meal of remembrance. These are both purposely and dangerously cut off from the promise of the forgiveness of sins.

Jesus, on the other hand, has bound up His forgiveness to stuff. For our great comfort, He gives us the gifts of Baptism and His own Supper. The next two sections will consider these very specific physical things that Jesus uses to get His grace and mercy to us.

What's the Big Deal about Baptism?

> **"Baptism . . . saves you."**
>
> **(1 Peter 3:21)**

The first time I heard a Lutheran talking about Baptism, I balked. "Forgiveness of sins? Salvation? The covering of Christ?" Impossible. Baptism is an ordinance of the church where I made a public testimony of my faith. It is a symbol of my death to sin and resurrection to new life. It is the first act of obedience in my Christian life. This is what I was taught in American Christianity, and I believed it.

I was baptized as a baby, but by the time my theology had matured in American Christianity, I was certain this baby-Baptism didn't matter at all. Most people who come to this conclusion are "rebaptized," but I never was, and this was because I really despised Baptism. Whenever someone asked me why I had not been baptized as an adult, I responded, "I can demonstrate my faith in better ways than Baptism." (I continue to be embarrassed at how scornfully I thought of and treated the Sacraments, but this scorn is part of the theology of American Christianity.) In one way, though, I was right. Baptism is not a particularly compelling public demonstration of our faith, just as bread and wine are not a compelling symbol of Jesus' suffering and death. Could it be that these gifts of the Lord are, in fact, more than symbolic outward works?

That is what the Lutherans (with whom I was arguing) were saying. They thought that Baptism forgave sins, and I couldn't convince them otherwise. I pulled out my Bible concordance one night to put forth all the Bible passages about Baptism. In the New Testament, there are almost one hundred verses with a form of the word *Baptism*. Many more teach about Baptism without using the word. I looked at them all. Many of these verses are historical (especially regarding John the Baptist), but dozens of passages teach what Baptism is, what benefits it gives. Every single one of these verses binds up Baptism to the Gospel. I was shocked.

The first text I really noticed was Acts 2:38–39. The first part of Acts 2 recounts the day of Pentecost and Peter's inaugural sermon of the New Testament Church. The people gathered in Jerusalem listening to him are "cut to the heart," and they ask Peter, "What shall we do?" (Acts 2:37).

"Peter said to them, 'Repent and be baptized every one of you in the name of Jesus Christ for the forgiveness of your sins, and you will receive the gift of the Holy Spirit' " (Acts 2:38).

In other words, there is nothing *you can do* to be saved. No work can undo your wickedness. You only need repentance and Baptism, and the Lord will forgive all your sins. "Be baptized . . . for the forgiveness of your sins."

It seemed like Peter thought Baptism had something to do with forgiveness. Ananias thought the same thing. When Saul comes to him for shelter after the Lord knocked him down on the road to Damascus, Ananias says to him, "And now why do you wait? Rise and be baptized and wash away your sins, calling on His name" (Acts 22:16). "Wash away your sins" seems a far cry from "make a public testimony of your faith."

As I studied the biblical passages about Baptism, this much became clear: Baptism has something to do with salvation. Text after text confirms this.

Jesus, before His ascension, sends out His disciples to the world, saying,

> Go therefore and make disciples of all nations, baptizing them in the name of the Father and of the Son and of the Holy Spirit, teaching them to observe all that I have commanded you. And behold, I am with you always, to the end of the age. (Matthew 28:19–20)

In Baptism, the Lord's name is put on us, we are adopted into His family, and we put on Christ. "But now that faith has come, we are no longer under a guardian, for in Christ Jesus you are all sons of God, through faith. For as many of you as were baptized into Christ have put on Christ" (Galatians 3:25–27; see also 4:5).

Again, immediately before His ascension, Jesus says, "Whoever believes and is baptized will be saved" (Mark 16:16). Baptism and salvation, again, are neighbors in the same sentence. Salvation, of course, is not without faith. But neither is it without Baptism.

"Truly, truly, I say to you, unless one is born of water and the Spirit, he cannot enter the kingdom of God" (John 3:5). Baptism, teaches Jesus, has to do with entering the kingdom of God. In our Baptism, we are buried with Christ and raised to newness of life:

> Do you not know that all of us who have been baptized into Christ Jesus were baptized into His death? We were buried therefore with Him by baptism into death, in order that, just as Christ

was raised from the dead by the glory of the Father, we too might walk in newness of life. (Romans 6:3–4)

Paul does not say we were "symbolically" buried with Christ. No, he says that in Baptism we "were buried with Christ." Baptism is more than a symbol. It is a real thing. Paul takes up this same theme again in Colossians, comparing Baptism to the circumcision of the heart.

> In Him also you were circumcised with a circumcision made without hands, by putting off the body of the flesh, by the circumcision of Christ, having been buried with Him in baptism, in which you were also raised with Him through faith in the powerful working of God, who raised Him from the dead. And you, who were dead in your trespasses and the uncircumcision of your flesh, God made alive together with Him, having forgiven us all our trespasses, by canceling the record of debt that stood against us with its legal demands. This He set aside, nailing it to the cross. (Colossians 2:11–14)

Again and again the biblical testimony about Baptism seems a far cry from a "first act of obedience" or "the believer's testimony of faith." Again and again, Baptism is bound up to salvation, and faith is bound up to Baptism.

> But when the goodness and loving kindness of God our Savior appeared, He saved us, not because of works done by us in righteousness, but according to His own mercy, by the washing of regeneration and renewal of the Holy Spirit, whom He poured out on us richly through Jesus Christ our Savior, so that being justified by His grace we might become heirs according to the hope of eternal life. (Titus 3:4–7)

We should no longer be surprised! Baptism saves us. Peter says that very thing. Noah and his family were rescued through the ark. Peter compares this ark to God's gift of Baptism: "Baptism, which corresponds to this, now saves you, not as a removal of dirt from the body but as an appeal to God for a good conscience, through the resurrection of Jesus Christ" (1 Peter 3:21).

THE OVERWHELMING TESTIMONY OF THE SCRIPTURES IS THAT

Baptism is Gospel: the gift of God for the salvation of sinners.

This is the doctrine of "baptismal regeneration," and it goes against everything American Christianity teaches. Most of the friends my wife and I lost when we became Lutheran we lost over the doctrine of Baptism.

American Christianity argues against baptismal regeneration. You will notice, though, that most of the arguments do not use the biblical texts about Baptism. Our doctrine of Baptism should come from the biblical texts about Baptism. American Christianity argues like this: "Salvation is by grace through faith apart from works, therefore Baptism cannot save." This is an argument from philosophy, not from the Bible. It really goes back to the discussion at the beginning of this chapter: "If it is physical, then it must be Law." "Stuff can't save."

Jesus can and does use stuff, physical things, to save. He used His body on the cross and His blood poured out to save the world. If He wants to take up water and combine it with His Word to wash away sins, He can do it.

Which is why one of the most important questions to ask about Baptism is "Who does it?" Whose work is it? This is the "Law or Gospel?" question. If Baptism is man's work, then it must be Law and therefore have nothing to do with our salvation. If, on the other hand, Baptism is God's work, then it might be part of His gracious and redeeming work toward us. We could answer this question by observing a Baptism. "Look, I see the preacher standing there with water, pouring it on that baby's head. The preacher is the one who baptizes." The Bible gives us a different insight.

In Ephesians 5, Paul talks about husbands and wives and especially compares them to Christ and His Church:

> Husbands, love your wives, as Christ loved the church and gave Himself up for her, that He might sanctify her, having cleansed her by the washing of water with the word, so that He might present the church to Himself in splendor, without spot or wrinkle or any such thing, that she might be holy and without blemish. (vv. 25–27)

This passage is incredible. Jesus sanctifies the Church, cleansing her of her sins so she would be presented to Him in splendor and holiness. How does He accomplish this cleansing? "By the washing of the water with the word," in other words, with Baptism! Baptism is the work of Jesus.

It might be the pastor's hand pouring the water and his mouth speaking the Lord's name, but the real work is accomplished by God. Baptism is His doing, His name, His adoption, His burying and raising, His forgiving, His clothing, His washing and renewing. Far from being a human work, Baptism is pure and wonderful Gospel.

Luther compares the wonderful gift of Baptism to a doctor who could raise the dead:

> Imagine there was a doctor somewhere who understood the art of saving people from death or, even though they died, could restore them quickly to life so that they would afterward live forever. Oh, how the world would pour in money like snow and rain. No one could find access to him because of the throng of the rich! But here in Baptism there is freely brought to everyone's door such a treasure and medicine that it utterly destroys death and preserves all people alive. (LC IV 43)

WHAT ABOUT THE BABIES?

One of the pressing questions about Baptism is "Who is it for?" Especially, is Baptism for babies? Most of American Christianity withholds Baptism from babies and young children. Should we?

The Bible talks about baptizing children:

> Repent and be baptized every one of you in the name of Jesus Christ for the forgiveness of your sins, and you will receive the gift of the Holy Spirit. For the promise is for you and *for your children* and for all who are far off, everyone whom the Lord our God calls to Himself. (Acts 2:38–39, emphasis added)

Baptism and its promises are "for your children." The promise of forgiveness and the Holy Spirit given in Baptism is "for your children." Further, children are certainly included in the "all nations" in Jesus' institution of Baptism (Matthew 28:19). The Book of Acts has two examples of the Baptism of households, which would include father, mother, servants, and children (see Acts 16:15, 33).

The objection to infant Baptism, then, becomes a purely philosophical (and not biblical) objection. "But babies don't have faith."

I remember talking to a friend who pastored a nondenominational congregation. He was telling me the good news of the birth of his child. "Are you going to baptize your baby?" I asked, obnoxiously.

He answered, "No, Bryan. You know we practice believer's Baptism." It struck me in his answer that American Christianity does not consider babies to be believers. American Christianity excludes infants and babies from faith. Babies can't be baptized because they do not have faith. This, again, is not the teaching of the Scriptures.

Jesus, over and over, makes it clear that babies can and do believe. The applicable texts are Psalm 71:5–6; Luke 1:15, 41; 18:15–17; Matthew 18:1–6; 11:25–27; 21:15–16; and 2 Timothy 3:14–15. Consider Jesus' warning to those who would turn the children away from Him. He warns, "Whoever causes one of these little ones *who believe in Me* to sin, it would be better for him to have a great millstone fastened around his neck and to be drowned in the depth of the sea" (Matthew 18:6, emphasis added).

If our definition of faith excludes infants and children, then our definition of faith is different than Jesus'.

"Believer's Baptism" and "Infant Baptism" are not exclusive categories. The Lutheran Church does not baptize infants because they have faith. Infants are baptized, first, because of the command of Jesus to baptize the nations and, second, because of His promise that this gift is for our children. But we do trust that the Holy Spirit creates and sustains faith in the Word, and that Jesus has bound up His Word of promise to the gift of Baptism.

Years ago, I was presenting to a group comprised mostly of Southern Baptist seniors. We were talking about Philippians and the distinction between Law and

Gospel, but the people in the class were very interested in the Lutheran teaching about Baptism.

"Don't you Lutherans baptize babies?"

"Yes, indeed," I answered.

"How can you do that if they haven't made a decision for Christ?"

"We think of Baptism differently," I responded. "The Baptist faith and message teaches that Baptism is our first act of obedience, that it is our work, our action. We Lutherans understand that Baptism is God's work, His gift of forgiveness to us. Just about the only thing babies are good at is receiving gifts."

To impress the point, I asked, "How many of you are grandparents?" The entire room raised their hands. "Okay, what would you say if I told you not to give gifts to your grandchildren? Their first Christmas: no gifts. Their first birthday: no gifts. In fact, I don't want you to give them any gifts until they reach the age where they can ask for gifts and truly appreciate them."

A dear old grandmother sitting in the back said, with a shaky voice, "Point made!"

Baptism is God's gift to us. In Baptism, God delivers His promised forgiveness, the very same forgiveness won by Jesus in His death. By the death and resurrection of Jesus, and by His institution, Baptism saves.

> Therefore, every Christian has enough in Baptism to learn and to do all his life. For he has always enough to do by believing firmly what Baptism promises and brings: victory over death and the devil [Romans 6:3–6], forgiveness of sin [Acts 2:38], God's grace [Titus 3:5–6], the entire Christ, and the Holy Spirit with His gifts [1 Corinthians 6:11]. In short, Baptism is so far beyond us that if timid nature could realize this, it might well doubt whether it could be true. (LC IV, 41–42)

Feeding on Forgiveness

The Bible's teaching on the Lord's Supper spun me out of the orbit of American Christianity and, at last, brought me into the orbit of the Lutheran Church.

> ## "This is My body, which is for you."
>
> ### (1 Corinthians 11:24)

I learned in American Christianity to take the Bible seriously and read the words literally. This was good. We should believe what the Bible says. But when American Christianity comes to the words of Jesus, "This is My body," teachers trip over themselves backpedaling from the text. "Jesus doesn't mean that the bread is His body, but that the bread symbolizes His body, that it is a picture of His body. See, it says, 'Do this in remembrance.'" That was the argument. That, apparently, was supposed to settle it. By the time the words of Jesus are explained away, it is as if He said, "This is not My body." I didn't buy it. "The words don't mean what they sound like they mean. Jesus didn't mean what He said."

But why? Why can't *is* mean *is*? If Jesus wants to give us His body in, with, and under the bread for the forgiveness of our sins, surely He can.

THAT, IN FACT, IS EXACTLY WHAT IT LOOKS LIKE HE IS DOING.

If we take the Bible seriously and read the words literally, why not give these particularly important words a serious reading?

It is Thursday of Holy Week. Jesus knows His death is hours away. He and the disciples had finished the Passover meal. Jesus had washed their feet. Now He takes bread, breaks it, gives thanks, and says these astonishing words, "Take and eat, this is My body, given for you. Do this in remembrance of Me." He takes the cup full of wine, and when He had given thanks, He gives it to them saying, "Drink of it, all of you. This cup is the new testament in My blood, which is poured out for you for the forgiveness of sins." (See Matthew 26:26–28; Luke 22:19–20; Mark 14:22–24; and 1 Corinthians 11:23–26.)

We will consider these words.

A TESTAMENT

The first word to catch our attention is *testament*. Most English versions translate this word as *covenant*. Certainly the Greek word can be translated either way. The purpose of a covenant is to bind two parties into a firm relationship (see Exodus 6:4–7; Jeremiah 7:32; Ezekiel 37:26–27) based on certain promises. A covenant lasts until the death of one of the parties in the agreement (like marriage, "until death us do part"). A last will and testament becomes effective only after the death of a person and testifies to that person's wishes. So, while some English translations and many Christians—pastors among them—use the terms interchangeably, calling the Lord's Supper a testament better recognizes the unique nature of what Jesus instituted at that first Lord's Supper.

A last will and testament takes the wealth and property of a person and disperses it according to his instructions after his death. This is exactly what Jesus is doing. He is establishing a testament for the disbursement of His treasures that He will accomplish in His death. His treasure is not gold and silver, but His forgiveness, His mercy, His kindness, His Spirit. These are given out in His last will.

The old Lutheran theologians loved to talk about this word TESTAMENT. They knew Jesus was using legal language. While both *covenant* and *testament* refer to a legally binding agreement, Jesus was establishing that which would have enduring effect and benefit. He was establishing a Sacrament that would testify about Him after His death, according to His instructions.

THE NEW KIND OF TESTAMENT

The next word to catch our attention is the word NEW. There is an *old* testimony about what God has done (contained in the Old Testament). This only adds to the confusion about using these terms interchangeably with regard to the Lord's Supper. God established the old covenant with Moses on Mount Sinai. It involved the Passover, the temple, the priesthood, and the sacrifices. The old covenant had circumcision, the blood of bulls and goats, and a lot of forbidden food. The old covenant was always pointing forward to the coming Messiah. The prophets of the old covenant were preparatory, preaching the kingdom of God that was to come.

This old covenant was constantly pointing to Jesus, preaching Him, delivering His promised forgiveness to the people. When Jesus arrived, the promise of the old covenant was rapidly coming to an end. Its purpose was fulfilled. God established something new with the coming of His Christ. The new covenant (contained in the New Testament) between Christ and His Church begins where the old covenant ends: the death of Jesus. The old covenant had the marks of circumcision and the sacrifices at the tabernacle and temple in Jerusalem. The new covenant has the marks of Baptism and especially the Lord's Supper. The Lord's Supper was a formal act that established and instituted the Lord's new testament people: the Church. This new covenant is foretold by God in Jeremiah 31:31–34.

> Behold, the days are coming, declares the LORD, when I will make a new covenant with the house of Israel and the house of Judah, not like the covenant that I made with their fathers on the day when I took them by the hand to bring them out of the land of Egypt, My covenant that they broke, though I was their husband, declares the LORD. For this is the covenant that I will make with the house of Israel after those days, declares the LORD: I will put my law within them, and I will write it on their hearts. And I will be their God, and they shall be My people. And no longer shall each one teach his neighbor and each his brother, saying, "Know the LORD," for they shall all know Me, from the least of them to the greatest, declares the LORD. For I will forgive their iniquity, and I will remember their sin no more.

The prophet Jeremiah preaches to Israel that a new covenant is coming. How wonderful that the forgiveness of sins is the central element of the new covenant! The author of Hebrews loves this sermon from Jeremiah. He understands the promise of Jeremiah to be about the death of Jesus (see Hebrews 8:1–13). There were a lot of sacrifices in the old covenant, but the sacrifice of Jesus on the cross is the sacrifice to end all sacrifices. His death fills up and ends the old covenant. His death is the beginning of the new. "In speaking of a new covenant, He makes the first one obsolete. And what is becoming obsolete and growing old is ready to vanish away" (Hebrews 8:13).

Jesus intends for the new covenant to replace the old. Gone are the sacrifices, the temple, the Passover meal, the priests, and all the ceremonial laws of Moses. In their place is the taking and eating of the body and drinking the blood of Jesus for the forgiveness of sins. This new covenant between God and His people is supposed to endure. How do we know this is true? Jesus established it in the Lord's Supper when He called it "a new testament." It is an expression of His eternal will, and this last testament establishes it forever.

Do This

"Do this," says Jesus, telling His disciples and His Church that this meal is not

a onetime event. The Lord's Supper is an institution. With the words "DO THIS," Jesus puts the Lord's Supper at the center of the Church's life. In the Supper, we receive our inheritance as the Lord's children. We partake of the gifts of His death. This is astonishing. The gifts Jesus gives after His death are the gifts He wins for us in His death, the gifts won in the crucifixion of His body and the shedding of His blood.

Body and Blood

The next words we notice are "My body" and "My blood." "This is My body, given for you." This body of Jesus was handed over to the torture of the cross, to the agony of God's wrath, all for us and our forgiveness. Now Jesus takes that same body and gives it to us. "Take and eat."

Jesus, with broken bread in hand, says to His disciples,

"This is My body." He seems serious about it. He says "is," not "is a symbol." We hear and believe these words in their simplicity. They mean what they say. The bread is the body of Jesus, given for us to eat.

The same is true for the Lord's blood.

"Take and drink, this is the new testament in My blood, poured out for you." This is the blood that won redemption (1 Peter 1:18–19). His blood cleanses us from all sins (Revelation 7:14) and overcomes the devil (Revelation 12:11). In the Lord's Supper, Jesus pours out His blood for us. That is what Jesus says. It is what we believe.

The teaching of the true body and blood was disputed at the time of the Reformation. Martin Luther wrote more about the Lord's Supper than any other teaching. He was constantly defending the teaching that Jesus put His body and blood in the Supper.

> With this Word you can strengthen your conscience and say, "If a hundred thousand devils, together with all fanatics, should rush forward, crying, 'How can bread and wine be Christ's body and blood?' and such, I know that all spirits and scholars together are not as wise as is the Divine Majesty in His little finger" [see 1 Corinthians 1:25]. Now here stands Christ's Word, "Take, eat; this is My body. . . . Drink of it, all of you; this is My blood of the new testament," and so on. Here we stop to watch those who will call themselves His masters and make the matter different from what He has spoken. It is true, indeed, that if you take away the Word or regard the Sacrament without the words, you have nothing but mere bread and wine. But if the words remain with them, as they shall and must, then, by virtue of the words, it is truly Christ's body and blood. What Christ's lips say and speak, so it is. He can never lie or deceive [Titus 1:2]. (LC V 12–14)

"What is the Lord's Supper?" This question is answered in the simplicity of Jesus' own words. It is the true body and blood of Jesus given for Christians to eat and drink.

THE FORGIVENESS OF SINS

When we know what the Lord's Supper is, then we ask another question: "What benefit does the Lord's Supper give?" The answer is in these words: "This is My blood of the covenant, which is poured out for many for the forgiveness of sins" (Matthew 26:28). The forgiveness of sins Jesus wins on the cross is poured out for us in the Supper, given to us there.

THE PURPOSE OF THE NEW TESTAMENT IS THE forgiveness of sins (Jeremiah 31:31–34). American Christianity has tremendous difficulty seeing how the forgiveness of sins could possibly be given to us in the Lord's Supper. After all, the Supper is external, outside us, eating and drinking real stuff. According to the American Christian rule that spiritual things happen only inside us, the Lord's Supper must be Law. But the plain and simple words of Jesus stand against this. He gives us His blood with the promise "poured out for many for the forgiveness of sins."

Forgiveness is what sinners are looking for, longing for, listening for. Here we have it. Jesus is so intent on us knowing our sins are forgiven that He puts His body and blood with bread and wine for us to eat and drink. His true body and blood are there as a pledge to the seriousness of the promise, a down payment for the confidence He wants us to enjoy. "Here is My body. Here is My blood. You can know, then, that this forgiveness stands true."

For You

We talked already about the importance of the words "for you." I remember Christmastime when I was growing up. As soon as a present was wrapped and placed under the tree, my brothers and I would check the tag. "Whose is it? Is it for me?" The only presents that mattered were the ones "for me."

We ask this question of all the Lord's gifts, "Is it for me?" This body and blood, this forgiveness, is it for me? We have a beautiful answer: "This is My body which is for you" (1 Corinthians 11:24).

"For you!"

The kindness of Jesus, His life-giving love, His death and resurrection, His boundless mercy and unfathomable grace all bound up in this meal is for you! All that Jesus accomplishes on the cross is brought to us in the Supper for us to eat and believe and rejoice.

I remember the first time I assisted with the distribution of the Lord's Supper. Trembling, with chalice in hand, I poured the Lord's blood over the parched lips of His forgiven people. The thought kept running through my mind, "One tiny drop of this, the Lord's blood, is enough for the salvation of all mankind." This is a tremendous thought. This is truly a tremendous gift. Here, at His altar, the God of God, Light of Light, very God of very God, the Word made flesh, puts His flesh in bread and His blood in wine for me, for my teeth and my faith, for the forgiveness of all of my sins.

We would never be so bold or daring to take something so precious into our hands or our mouths, but we have His command: "Take and eat; . . . take and drink." There is tremendous comfort in these words. We know just what to do with the body and blood Jesus is giving: take, eat, drink, and believe the promise that here in this meal is forgiveness and new, eternal life. We eat and believe, and in believing we have the life that Jesus gives.

The Lord's Supper is a priceless gift, far beyond anything we could ask for or imagine.

But American Christianity has completely failed to receive and rejoice in the Lord's Supper. They have taken the gracious gift of the Lord's body and blood for the forgiveness of our sins and turned it into a symbolic work. This completely robs the Christian of the gifts and promises Jesus gives in the Lord's Supper: the forgiveness of sins, life, and salvation. The Supper is the Lord's mercy served up for us on a platter.

We sinners are always surprised by the Lord's mercy, and His mercy for us in the Supper is no exception. In the Lord's Supper, the treasures of heaven are unloaded for us. "Take and eat, this is My body, given for you. Take and drink, this is My blood of the new testament, shed for you for the remission of sins." We could respond to these words with a shocked "Forgiveness? For me?" "Yes," says Jesus, "for you."

The Lord's gifts are objective. They are sure. They are not internal spiritual activities, but external gifts and promises. His love is as sure as the water in Baptism, as sure as the bread and wine on the altar, as sure as this word of promise: "Your sins are forgiven." This certainty is our confidence and the foundation of our faith.

CHAPTER SEVEN

THE HOW OF GOOD WORKS

"For we are His workmanship, created in Christ Jesus for good works, which God prepared beforehand, that we should walk in them."
(Ephesians 2:10)

The shelves of the Christian bookstores are full of books about "Christian living." This points to a bigger trend. American Christianity focuses not on the life of Christ but on the life of the Christian. The faith has shifted from "done" to "do," and Jesus' glorious and comforting cry, "It is finished," has become, "Get after it!"

In American Christianity, the good news of the death of Jesus is for the unconverted. Christians get the Law, instructions for living, steps and programs to be a better person. The focus is different. The emphasis is not on what God has done but on what we are to accomplish. If Christianity is about our actions, Jesus is less the Savior and more a personal trainer—Moses dressed like Tony Horton. Jesus encourages us, cheers us on, and looks disappointed or delighted depending on our effort and our success. This is American Christianity, life on the good-works treadmill, going until we're exhausted, falling off, getting back on, smiling through the pain, doubting God's love, knowing our failure, wondering why we are the only people who seem to be struggling and fighting, damning ourselves, excusing ourselves, feeling overcome with frustration with God, with church, with the expectations and the failures, with it all.

The emphasis on the life of the Christian puts one on the pendulum of pride and despair.

THE BIBLE DOES SPEND SIGNIFICANT TIME TALKING ABOUT THE CHRISTIAN'S LIFE OF LOVE AND GOOD WORKS.

American Christianity, though, is confused on the how, the what, and the why of our good works. Regarding the *how*,

American Christianity is confused about the ongoing battle of the flesh and the spirit. It teaches that we accomplish good works with the strength and freedom of our own will. Regarding the *what*, there is confusion about Christian vocation and the role of the Ten Commandments in the world and the Christian's life. Regarding the *why*, American Christianity requires good works for the certainty of salvation and even to earn greater rewards in heaven.

The Lutheran Church has always been accused of being against good works. This is, perhaps, because Lutherans taught the danger of trusting in our good works for salvation. But the accusation is false. Lutherans have always taught the importance and necessity of good works, as well as how they are possible, what they are, and why they are done.

> Furthermore, we teach that it is necessary to do good works. This does not mean that we merit grace by doing good works, but because it is God's will [Ephesians 2:10]. It is only by faith, and nothing else, that forgiveness of sins is apprehended. The Holy Spirit is received through faith, hearts are renewed and given new affections, and then they are able to bring forth good works. Ambrose says, "Faith is the mother of a good will and doing what is right." Without the Holy Spirit people are full of ungodly desires. They are too weak to do works that are good in God's sight [John 15:5]. (AC XX 27–31)

We will especially consider the how, what, and why of good works in the next two chapters. To rightly understand good works, we must consider what it means to have two wills; the connection between faith, the Holy Spirit, and good works; the flexibility of our conscience; and how Jesus hands us over to suffering.

THE DANGER OF BEING A DOG TRAINER

Imagine your uncle has a raging, out-of-control dog. Every time you visit his home, things are in a desperate state of disrepair. The curtains are ripped off the wall, the couch cushions are shredded, food and filth cover the floor, and blood is everywhere. The blood belongs to your cousins and your aunt. They're all in the hospital because this dog attacked them. Your uncle also has wounds from this out-of-control dog: a missing finger, gashes on his face, stitches in his leg. You know if your uncle lives much longer with this dog, he will die.

> "And those who belong to Christ Jesus have crucified the flesh with its passions and desires."
> (Galatians 5:24)

"This is insanity," you say to your uncle through the window, shouting over the dog's growl, "That dog's going to kill you." "Nonsense," he shouts back, "I've just got to work harder training him." Your uncle holds up the books that just came in the mail: *Forty Days of Dog Training Purpose, Your Best Dog Now, Become a Better Dog.*

Anyone observing this situation from the outside can see the absurdity. You cannot train a dog like this. And yet this is how most Christians treat their old Adam, their sinful flesh. They are busy trying to train and reform the sinful flesh.

Insanity. You can't teach the old Adam new tricks.

THERE IS ONLY ONE THING TO DO WITH OUR SINFUL FLESH:
put it to death.

And those who belong to Christ Jesus have crucified the flesh with its passions and desires. (Galatians 5:24)

For if you live according to the flesh you will die, but if by the Spirit you put to death the deeds of the body, you will live. (Romans 8:13)

Our justification puts us at war with the flesh. Paul writes, "Therefore, since we have been justified by faith, we have peace with God through our Lord Jesus Christ" (Romans 5:1). But this peace with God puts us at enmity with the enemies of God: the devil, the world, and our sinful flesh.

When we call the Lord our friend, we call the devil our enemy (AND HE RETURNS THE FAVOR).

> If the world hates you, know that it has hated Me before it hated you. If you were of the world, the world would love you as its own; but because you are not of the world, but I chose you out of the world, therefore the world hates you. (John 15:18–19)

The enmity of the world and hatred of the devil are marks of the Church and marks of the Christian. The Christian is a soldier engaged in a war against the world, the flesh, and the devil: "Share in suffering as a good soldier of Christ Jesus" (2 Timothy 2:3; see Ephesians 6:10–18).

It is no wonder, then, that the Scriptures picture the Christian life as a battle. The ancient war declared by God in the Garden of Eden rages on (Genesis 3:15). We are on the right side of this war. When Adam and Eve sinned in the garden, the Lord could have declared war against them. He did not. The Lord declared war on the devil. Jesus is fighting for us, not against us.

Jesus, the Scriptures tell us, has already won the war against the devil. "The reason the Son of God appeared was to destroy the works of the devil" (1 John 3:8; see Hebrews 2:14–15; Revelation 12:7–9).

We have the confidence that Jesus has won the war, but we are still engaged in various battles. "Beloved, I urge you as sojourners and exiles to abstain from the passions of the flesh, which wage war against your soul" (1 Peter 2:11). Our life is a battle. Outwardly, we fight the world and the devil. Inwardly, we fight our own sinful flesh.

There is a baptismal connection here. When Paul wants to talk about the life of the new man and the death of the old, he almost always points us to our Baptism. Consider these wonderful words from Romans 6:1–7:

> What shall we say then? Are we to continue in sin that grace may abound? By no means! How can we who died to sin still live in it? Do you not know that all of us who have been baptized into Christ Jesus were baptized into His death? We were buried there-

fore with Him by baptism into death, in order that, just as Christ was raised from the dead by the glory of the Father, we too might walk in newness of life. For if we have been united with Him in a death like His, we shall certainly be united with Him in a resurrection like His. We know that our old self was crucified with Him in order that the body of sin might be brought to nothing, so that we would no longer be enslaved to sin. For one who has died has been set free from sin.

Baptism, then, is this death of the flesh and the resurrection of the new man.

> In Him also you were circumcised with a circumcision made without hands, by putting off the body of the flesh, by the circumcision of Christ, having been buried with Him in baptism, in which you were also raised with Him through faith in the powerful working of God, who raised Him from the dead. And you, who were dead in your trespasses and the uncircumcision of your flesh, God made alive together with Him, having forgiven us all our trespasses, by canceling the record of debt that stood against us with its legal demands. This He set aside, nailing it to the cross.
>
> (Colossians 2:11–14)

In Baptism, our sinful flesh is put to death. In Baptism, the new man is raised to newness of life. This death of the flesh and the raising up of the spirit is repentance. Through contrition over our sins, the flesh is put down. Through faith in the promise, the new man rises. We are baptized into a life of repentance.

Luther makes this very clear for us in the Small Catechism:

> What does such baptizing with water indicate?
>
> It indicates that the Old Adam in us should by daily contrition and repentance be drowned and die with all sins and evil desires, and that a new man should daily emerge and arise to live before God in righteousness and purity forever.
>
> Where is this written?
>
> St. Paul writes in Romans chapter six: "We were therefore buried

with Him through baptism into death in order that, just as Christ was raised from the dead through the glory of the Father, we too may live a new life." (SC, The Sacrament of Holy Baptism)

{ Baptism is the battleground of the Christian life. }

The devil is always tempting us to doubt the gifts the Lord gives us in our Baptism. (Consider the temptation of our Lord when the devil tempted Him to doubt the very words spoken to Him by the Father in His Baptism. Compare, for example, the words of God the Father in Matthew 3:17, "This is My beloved Son," with the words of the devil in Matthew 4:3, 6, "If you are the Son of God . . ."). On the other hand, the Lord is always strengthening us in His promises and gifts, bringing us back to the gifts of our Baptism. ("Do you not know that all of us who have been baptized into Christ Jesus were baptized into His death?" Paul says in Romans 6:3.)

This, then, is our Christian life. We are baptized. Our flesh is daily crucified and killed by the Law. The new man daily hears the Gospel, the forgiveness of sins, and rejoices in the gifts of Christ. Our life is a life of repentance and faith. How different this is to the "Do better! Try harder!" of American Christianity. We are not engaged in the insane futility of training and reforming the sinful flesh. We are the joyful objects of God's work, His craftsmanship, shaped through repentance through Law and Gospel.

Our life is marked by this fight between the flesh and the spirit, but praise be to Jesus that this battle will soon end. When the Lord Jesus returns for us, He will set us free from this sinful flesh and completely purify our bodies from temptation, sin, and death. Now we have the Lord's victory over sin and flesh *by faith*. One day soon we will have this victory *by sight*. The resurrection will mark the end of this battle and the complete victory of Jesus over our sin.

In Romans 7, Paul teaches us about the battle between our flesh and spirit. He ends this section with this doxology of hope:

> So I find it to be a law that when I want to do right, evil lies close at hand. For I delight in the law of God, in my inner being, but I see in my members another law waging war against the law of my mind and making me captive to the law of sin that dwells in my members. Wretched man that I am! Who will deliver me from this body of death? Thanks be to God through Jesus Christ our Lord! (vv. 21–25)

Your Two Wills (or Your Will and Your Won't)

The battle of the Christian life rages inside us as we battle with our sinful flesh. The unbeliever has only a fallen and sinful will, the will of the flesh. But the Christian has two wills, the will of the flesh and the will of the spirit. These wills are opposed to one another. They are locked in battle until the day the Lord frees us from sin through death. The two wills of the Christian are aptly described in Luther's phrase *simul justus et peccator*, "simultaneously justified and sinful."

Some theological background is needed here. The Bible makes a distinction between four states of man's will. (We are led in this direction by our Lutheran Confessions: "The will of mankind is found in four different states . . . " [FC Ep II 1].)

> "So then, I myself serve the law of God with my mind, but with my flesh I serve the law of sin." (Romans 7:25)

The FIRST STATE of man's will is after creation before the fall into sin. In the Garden of Eden, Adam and Eve had wills that were free to not sin, but they were also (as the tragedy of history testifies) able to sin. They had the choice to sin and the strength to do what was right.

After the fall, man's will is in a totally different state. In this SECOND STATE, the will of man is no longer free; it is in bondage to sin. Our will is not able not to sin. This is the testimony of the Scriptures about original sin, something we considered at length in chapter 3. "For the mind that is set on the flesh is hostile to God, for it does not submit to God's law; indeed, it cannot" (Romans 8:7).

The THIRD STATE of man's will, after conversion, is our major concern here. What is it like with Christians? What is the state of our will? The Bible teaches that the Christian has two competing and opposing wills, the will of the flesh (or the old Adam), and the will of the spirit (the new man; see Ezekiel 36:26; 2 Corinthians 5:17). These two wills fight each other, oppose each other. They are locked in an ongoing battle.

Paul outlines this battle in dramatic fashion in Romans 7:

> So now it is no longer I who do it, but sin that dwells within me.
> For I know that nothing good dwells in me, that is, in my flesh.
> For I have the desire to do what is right, but not the ability to
> carry it out. For I do not do the good I want, but the evil I do not
> want is what I keep on doing. Now if I do what I do not want, it is
> no longer I who do it, but sin that dwells within me.

> So I find it to be a law that when I want to do right, evil lies close
> at hand. For I delight in the law of God, in my inner being, but I
> see in my members another law waging war against the law of my
> mind and making me captive to the law of sin that dwells in my
> members. Wretched man that I am! Who will deliver me from
> this body of death? Thanks be to God through Jesus Christ our
> Lord! So then, I myself serve the law of God with my mind, but
> with my flesh I serve the law of sin. (vv. 17–25)

Many theologians insist Romans 7 describes Paul before his conversion. Their understanding of the Christian's renewed will won't allow the text to describe a Christian man. The Christian is supposed to be free from sin. If Paul is fighting against the flesh, he must still be an unbeliever. But how does this account for Paul's "delight in the law of God" or the "good" he wants to do? The unbeliever does not (and cannot) delight in the Lord's Law. Paul must be describing the struggles of a Christian. Galatians teaches the same:

> But I say, walk by the Spirit, and you will not gratify the desires of
> the flesh. For the desires of the flesh are against the Spirit, and the
> desires of the Spirit are against the flesh, for these are opposed to
> each other, to keep you from doing the things you want to do. But
> if you are led by the Spirit, you are not under the law. (5:16–18)

We can summarize the capabilities of these two wills as follows: according to our sinful flesh, we are not able not to sin, but according to the new man, we are not able to sin. Consider that! The flesh can do nothing good, nothing right, nothing holy. The spirit can do nothing wrong, nothing sinful. These two opposite and opposing wills fight against each other in the Christian's heart. No wonder this life is full of so much turmoil.

The FOURTH STATE of the Christian's will is after death, in heaven and in the resurrection. Then we are moved beyond the reach of temptation, sin, and the devil. After death, we are finally in perfect freedom and bliss. Our will is totally free to love God and serve our neighbor, and at last we are not able to sin.

These four states of man's will:

Before the Fall	After the Fall (Original Sin)	After Conversion (The Christian Life)	After the Resurrection
Able to sin or not to sin.	Not able not to sin.	Not able not to sin (the old man; the flesh). Not able to sin (new man).	Not able to sin.

This teaching that after conversion the Christian has two wills is uniquely Lutheran. Other confessions differ regarding the states of man's will. The free-will (and semi-free-will) theologies of American Evangelicalism and Roman Catholicism teach that there is no difference in the state of man's will before or after the fall or after conversion. The Calvinist and Reformed traditions agree with the Lutheran Church regarding original sin and man's depravity after the fall. However, in regard to the Christian's will, they teach a renewal of the will to its state before the fall.

The different confessions can be summarized this way:

	Before the Fall	After the Fall (Original Sin)	After Conversion (The Christian Life)	After the Resurrection
Roman Catholic / American Evangelical	Able to sin or not to sin.	Able to sin or not to sin.	Able to sin or not to sin.	Not able to sin.
Reformed	Able to sin or not to sin.	Not able not to sin.	Able to sin or not to sin.	Not able to sin.
Lutheran	Able to sin or not to sin.	Not able not to sin.	Not able not to sin (the old man; the flesh). Not able to sin (new man).	Not able to sin.

There are some agreements. All agree on the state of man's will before the fall. Adam and Eve had the freedom to sin or not sin. Only the Lord knows what things would be like if they had resisted the devil. All agree on the state of man's will after the resurrection. Sin and death are not even a possibility. In the resurrection, we will not be able to sin.

The differences are in the second and third columns. The debate is about man's will in this life before and after conversion.

Consider the second column. Roman Catholics and American Evangelicals do not see a change in the state of man's will, at least not a change in kind. While man's will might move from strong (before the fall) to weak (after the fall), it is still free. Man's will after the fall is sick, but it is not totally depraved. It is alive, not dead. Man is capable of some good. Roman Catholicism and American Evangelicals teach that our wills have a *tendency* to sin, but this tendency is not sin until it is acted upon. This accounts for the important role that man's will plays in conversion (be it with the "altar call" or "decision for Christ" of the Evangelicals, or the cooperation with the grace of God of the Roman Catholics). We considered this in chapter 3 in our discussion on original sin.

The Reformed and Lutherans both teach the fullness of the fall and the completeness of our depravity. The unbeliever is only able to sin.

In the third column, the Lutheran distinction emerges. Our understanding of the Christian's will undergirds our teaching on Christian living. This difference concerning the state of man's will after conversion accounts for the different theologies of sanctification.

If the Christian has a will that is free to sin or not sin, then sanctification is simply going to be a matter of strengthening, supporting, teaching, or training this free will.

If this is your theology of the Christian's will, then your teaching of sanctification often boils down to "Do better!" "Try harder!" Maybe the Lord has some helpful principles or some power-boosting spirit infusion, but the idea is the same. Doing good or doing bad is up to you. Sanctification is about training, coaching, instructing, strengthening, growing, etc., etc., etc., until we obtain some victory.

Not only is this understanding of the Christian's will and sanctification wrong, but it is also dangerous. It invites growth when the Scriptures call for death. It looks for strength where the Scriptures call for repentance. The idea that our wills are renewed leaves the door open for the devil's temptation to pride ("I'm doing it") and despair ("I'll never get it right").

Our sinful flesh cannot be whipped into shape. It cannot be reformed. It can't grow or do good, and trying to do so results only in failure. Remember the uncle's dog? Like with that dog, trying to train and reform the sinful flesh is insanity. Rather, our sinful flesh has to be fought; it has to be killed.

> For if you live according to the flesh you will die, but if by the Spirit you *put to death* the deeds of the body, you will live. (Romans 8:13, emphasis added)
>
> *Put off your old self*, which belongs to your former manner of life and is corrupt through deceitful desires. (Ephesians 4:22, emphasis added)
>
> We know that *our old self was crucified* with Him in order that the body of sin might be brought to nothing, so that we would no longer be enslaved to sin. (Romans 6:6, emphasis added)
>
> But put on the Lord Jesus Christ, and *make no provision for the flesh*, to gratify its desires. (Romans 13:14, emphasis added)

There is no reform here. These passages are not about fixing the flesh or bringing the old man in line. They are about putting to death, putting off, providing no provision, and crucifixion. This death of the old man and resurrection of the new man is our Christian life. It is our lifelong exercise of repentance. We daily die to sin and live to Christ.

> For the death He died He died to sin, once for all, but the life He lives He lives to God. So you also must consider yourselves dead to sin and alive to God in Christ Jesus. (Romans 6:10–11)

The Law puts the old man to death. The Gospel gives the new man life.

The Law shows us our failure, our faults, our impurity, our imperfections. It shows our sin. It exposes the sinful flesh and its shame. Knowing, seeing, and feeling the guilt of our sin produces, in the heart of the Christian, sorrow and contrition. This is the first part of repentance, worked in us by the Holy Spirit through the Law of God (see John 16:8–9; see also Acts 2:37 and the penitential Psalms 6, 32, 38, 51, 102, 130, 143). This is the death of the sinful flesh, its crucifixion.

The Gospel has the opposite effect. While the Law shows us our sin and God's wrath, the Gospel forgives our sins and gives us the love of God in Christ. The Law produces contrition, and the Gospel produces faith (Romans 1:16–17; 10:17). The Lord comes to us with the victory of Jesus on the cross, with His atoning sacrifice, and with the promise of the forgiveness of all of our sins. The Gospel brings forgiveness and life, resurrection.

Repentance is death and resurrection.

Repentance is worked in us by the Holy Spirit through the Lord's Law and Gospel. Repentance is the Lord fighting this battle against our flesh and giving the victory to the new man.

American Christianity teaches that our Christian life is a matter of training, getting better and better through our own strained efforts. The Bible teaches that our Christian life is a life of repentance. The death of the old man and the life of the new through God's Word of Law and Gospel is our sanctification.

BORROWED HOLINESS AND THE WORK OF THE HOLY SPIRIT

> "But I say, walk by the Spirit, and you will not gratify the desires of the flesh."
> (Galatians 5:16)

Our faith grabs on to the righteousness of Christ. By this we are justified, declared righteous and holy by God. This same justifying faith grasps on to the Holy Spirit, the living, active, and working Spirit of God.

Paul, then, warns us about the dangers of beginning our Christian lives by faith but then continuing this life by our works. This is the temptation of American Christianity. American Christianity would preach the Gospel to unbelievers, but the Law to Christians. This makes the Christian life all about doing, obedience, effort, and striving. Paul's warning is as prescient now as it was two thousand years ago:

> Let me ask you only this: Did you receive the Spirit by works of the law or by hearing with faith? Are you so foolish? Having begun by the Spirit, are you now being perfected by the flesh? (Galatians 3:2–3)

Our Christian lives are begun, continued, and ended in the Spirit, in the Lord's work and promises, in the preaching of the Gospel. The Gospel is the power behind our good works. The Law gives shape to our good works of love for God and neighbor (like the banks of a river that keep the water headed for the ocean), but the impulse and power behind our works of service and sacrifice is the Holy Spirit Himself, working in us "both to will and to work for His good pleasure" (Philippians 2:13).

Martin Luther wrote famously about faith and good works in his Preface to the Book of Romans, a passage quoted by the Lutheran Confessions.

> Faith, however, is a divine work in us that changes us and makes us to be born anew of God, John 1[:12–13]. It kills the old Adam and makes us altogether different men, in heart and spirit and mind and powers; it brings with it the Holy Spirit. O, it is a living, busy, active, mighty thing, this faith. It is impossible for it not to be doing good works incessantly. It does not ask whether good works are to be done, but before the question is asked, it has already done them, and is constantly doing them. Whoever does not do such works, however, is an unbeliever. He gropes and looks around for faith and good works, but knows neither what faith is nor what good works are. Yet he talks and talks, with many words, about faith and good works.
>
> Faith is a living, daring confidence in God's grace, so sure and certain that the believer would stake his life on it a thousand times. This knowledge of and confidence in God's grace makes men glad and bold and happy in dealing with God and with all creatures. And this is the work that the Holy Spirit performs in faith. Because of it, without compulsion, a person is ready and glad to do good to everyone, to serve everyone, to suffer everything, out of love and praise to God who has shown him this grace. Thus it is impossible to separate works from faith, quite as impossible as to separate heat and light from fire [LW 35:370–71]. (FC SD IV 10–12)

Faith and good works are bound up to each other. They are inseparable. This connection means that our life, even our Christian life of good works, is bound up to the preaching of the Gospel. We never grow out of the Gospel. We certainly never live such a holy life that we don't need the Gospel. Faith lurks behind every good work. And while it is true that our works have nothing to do with our justification or standing before God, our faith has everything to do with good works. "And without faith it is impossible to please Him [God], for whoever would draw near to God must believe that He exists and that He rewards those who seek Him" (Hebrews 11:6).

If you can stomach it, we will dissect a good work, cut it open to look at its parts. There are, we find, four parts to a Christian good work. A good work is

1. done in faith in God;

2. in obedience to the Ten Commandments;

3. for the glory of God; and

4. for the benefit of our neighbor.

THIS MEANS, FIRST, if we do not have faith, we cannot accomplish a single good work in the sight of God.

It is important here to make the distinction between civil works and Christian works. Civil good works are the outward works of love and kindness that all people are able to perform. A pagan can resist the temptation to kill his neighbor. The unbeliever can be faithful to his wife. We all have a free will in these outward things of human society: to not steal and plunder and riot and cause a ruckus everywhere we go. We can even do heroic and loving things. The atheist can give his life in service to his nation; the heathen can love his children. Love, honor, sacrifice, discipline, service, and sacrifice—all of these virtues are available to all people, and they are good.

But apart from faith in Christ, all of these virtuous acts are so stained with sin that they are not acceptable in God's sight. They are tainted by our unbelief, blemished by our failure to keep the first and fundamental commandment, "You shall have no other gods." "Without faith it is impossible to please Him" (Hebrews 11:6).

With faith, though, something stunning happens. Our good works—still stained with selfish interests and soiled with self-interest—are purified and made holy by the forgiveness of sins. With faith, our minuscule attempts at good works are taken up by the Lord and made glorious in His sight. Imagine the child bringing her "art" to her parent, or the same child who tries to "help" with the dishes, and only makes a bigger mess. This faltering and failing effort is a delight to her parents, not because of the beauty of the art or the goodness of her service, but because of the love of the parent for the child. In a similar way, the Lord takes the weak and halfhearted good works of His children and receives them as a great and glorious gift. This is the key to our Christian good works.

Faith also opens us up to an entirely new realm of works that is not available to those who do not believe. The important parts of the Ten Commandments are locked up behind a door that is opened only by faith.

Consider prayer. The Second Commandment says, "You shall not misuse the name of the Lord your God." This means "we should fear and love God so that we do not curse, swear, use satanic arts, lie, or deceive by His name, but call upon it in every trouble, pray, praise, and give thanks" (SC, Second Commandment). We begin to keep the Second Commandment by praying, but prayer is impossible for the unbeliever. How can you trust God's promises or call on His name if you don't believe in God or know His name? "How then will they call on Him in whom they have not believed?" (Romans 10:14). By faith that we are adopted into God's family, are called His children, and are able to pray. "And because you are sons, God has sent the Spirit of His Son into our hearts, crying, 'Abba! Father!' " (Galatians 4:6). Faith, then, opens up the possibility of prayer. Faith gives the Christian access to the Second Commandment and its good works.

Worship is another example. The Third Commandment requires us to "Remember the Sabbath day by keeping it holy." This means "we should fear and love God so that we do not despise preaching and His Word, but hold it sacred and gladly hear and learn it" (SC, Third Commandment). Unbelievers can walk to church and sit in the pew. They can even listen to the preaching and read the words of the Bible. But to delight in the preaching of the Word and honor it as sacred and holy is impossible apart from faith. "God wants to be worshiped through faith so that we receive from Him those things He promises and offers" (Ap IV [II] 49).

The true worship of God, then, is impossible apart from faith. This is true of all of the good works commanded in the first three commandments and of all the commandments as they govern the actions of our heart.

When we think of the Ten Commandments, we normally think of the outward things of the second table: You shall not kill. You shall not steal. You shall not commit adultery. When the Lutheran theologians talk about Christian good works, they start with the first commandments:

> The Ten Commandments require outward civil works, which reason can in some way produce. But they also require other things placed far above reason: truly to fear God, truly to love God, truly to call upon God, truly to be convinced that God hears us, and to expect God's aid in death and in all afflictions. Finally, the Law requires obedience to God, in death and all afflictions, so that we may not run from these commandments or refuse them when God lays them upon us. (Ap IV [II] 8)

What a profound list of good works: loving God, fearing God, trusting God when we are dying, looking to God for all good. All of these good works are completely impossible without faith. These are the good works that fill the life of a Christian. The Christian stands before God, no longer a slave to the fear of death (Hebrews 2:15), but free to suffer and pray and die, trusting in the Lord and His promises.

{ All good works are completely impossible without faith. }

Faith brings freedom. The Christian life is a life of freedom: freedom from the dominion of the devil; freedom from slavery to sin; freedom from the bondage of self-love; freedom from the fear of death, from the fear of judgment, from the fear of God's wrath. "Now the Lord is the Spirit, and where the Spirit of the Lord is, there is freedom" (2 Corinthians 3:17).

We think of freedom as choice. If I have the opportunity to choose between this or that, I am free. The Bible teaches freedom is the opposite of bondage. If I am locked in a room or bound in chains, I am not free; I am a slave or a prisoner. This is how Jesus talks of slavery to sin. "Truly, truly, I say to you, everyone who practices sin is a slave to sin" (John 8:34). We are born slaves of sin, bound to death and the devil. Freedom comes when the Lord Jesus breaks those chains. "If the Son sets you free, you will be free indeed" (John 8:36). We are free, then, not *to* sin. We are free *from* sin.

Paul says, "For you were called to freedom, brothers. Only do not use your freedom as an opportunity for the flesh, but through love serve one another" (Galatians 5:13). Peter echoes this. "Live as people who are free, not using your freedom as a cover-up for evil, but living as servants of God" (1 Peter 2:16). We are free to love. We will talk more about this in the next chapter, but here it is good to know that the forgiveness that sets us free from sin also sets us free to love God and neighbor. Luther famously noted, "A Christian is a perfectly free lord of all, subject to none. A Christian is a perfectly dutiful servant of all, subject to all" (LW 31:344).

The Christian life is life in the light, lived in the brightness of God's presence and the radiance of His smile. "At one time you were darkness, but now you are light in the Lord. Walk as children of light (for the fruit of light is found in all that is good and right and true)" (Ephesians 5:8–9). Jesus, in His great discourse with Nicodemus, compares the life in the darkness with the life lived in the light:

> And this is the judgment: the light has come into the world, and people loved the darkness rather than the light because their works were evil. For everyone who does wicked things hates the light and does not come to the light, lest his works should be exposed. But whoever does what is true comes to the light, so that it may be clearly seen that his works have been carried out in God. (John 3:19–21)

The life of sin is afraid of the light. This fear is cast out by faith. The forgiveness of sins sets us free from the fear of God's judgment. The verdict has already been given: we are righteous. The Holy Spirit, in giving us the gift of faith, not only throws open the doors of heaven, but He also throws open the Commandments. After faith knows God's love for us, our love for God and our neighbors follows. "We love because He first loved us" (1 John 4:19). Our love is born of faith, born of the Spirit, and is completely bound up to the Lord's love for us.

This is the how of good works; the Holy Spirit, who has us by faith, gives us the freedom to love.

Conscience Training

> "Wage the good warfare, holding faith and a good conscience."
>
> (1 Timothy 1:18–19)

The conscience is incredibly important in biblical theology. We've already discussed the importance of the conscience in receiving the comfort of the Gospel. The conscience is also vitally important to our life of love and good works.

Paul writes to Timothy, "The aim of our charge is love that issues from a pure heart and a good conscience and a sincere faith" (1 Timothy 1:5). What does Paul mean by "a good conscience," and how can we live before God in this manner?

Our conscience, remember, is a gift of God, a part of our created nature. It is our innate and natural ability to know the Law. We might think of the conscience as an internal referee, calling us out when we break the rules and sin against our Lord or our neighbors. When it functions properly, our conscience troubles us when we do something wrong. It pushes us to repentance and trust in the Lord's mercy and grace.

Our conscience doesn't always function properly. Like any referee, it sometimes makes the wrong call. The devil is constantly attacking our conscience, tempting it to make the wrong call, to become calloused or overbearing. A bad conscience distorts our understanding of God and His Word, our neighbor, and even ourselves. A bad conscience always stands in the way of repentance and good works. When we know the dangers to our conscience, we can fight back at the devil, "holding faith and a good conscience" (1 Timothy 1:19). We will consider three dangers to our conscience, and how we counter them with the Lord's Word. The Holy Spirit with the Word of God trains our conscience to function properly.

Danger 1: A Calloused Conscience

Through continued sinning, our conscience becomes calloused or hardened. Paul calls this a "seared" conscience (1 Timothy 4:2). Like scar tissue, a *calloused conscience* has lost the sensation of guilt. It has ceased to feel the pain of sin.

The hardening of a conscience is especially dangerous with habitual sins and addictions. The first time we commit a particular sin, our conscience is troubled. The next time, it is slightly bothered. Each sin registers less and less until finally we've forgotten the thing is even a sin. It could be missing church, living together before marriage, speaking behind someone's back, holding a few dollars back when paying taxes, being angry with your children, or whatever. Addictions and repeated and habitual sin deaden the conscience.

The Lord has help for us. His antidote to a calloused conscience is the Ten Commandments. The Lord's Law works like the video review in a football game. If the referee makes the wrong call, it is examined and reversed. If our conscience does not accuse us of a sin, the Law corrects the call. Or, to put it another way, the Law works like a meat tenderizer that softens our conscience and breaks our heart over our sin. "A broken and contrite heart, O God, You will not despise" (Psalm 51:17; see also Jeremiah 23:29).

If we have missed church for months—and our conscience has stopped getting after us—the Third Commandment still stands: "Remember the Sabbath day by keeping it holy." If we have a habit of speaking poorly of our neighbor, the Eighth Commandment corrects our conscience: "You shall not give false testimony against your neighbor." When sexual sin has wrecked our conscience such that we don't know the trouble we are in, the Sixth Commandment reveals to us what our conscience does not: "You shall not commit adultery."

The Ten Commandments continue to speak even after our conscience has gone mute. And when we consider our life through the lens of the Ten Commandments, the Holy Spirit tenderizes our conscience, shows us our sin and our need of the Lord's forgiveness, and revives our conscience to do its proper work.

DANGER 2: AN EVIL CONSCIENCE

A second danger is an *evil conscience*, that is, a conscience that accuses where it should not. The devil knows Law and Gospel, and he perfectly confuses them to give us an evil, or bad, conscience. Here's how it works. When we are tempted, the devil preaches a false Gospel to us, easing the path to sin. The devil tries to grease the skids for sin by preaching the kindness or indifference of God. He minimizes sin. "Don't worry, God doesn't get mad. No one will be hurt. God wants you to be happy."

Then, after we sin, the devil comes with the Law, accusing our conscience before God. "You call yourself a Christian? Look what you did. You knew you were sinning, and still you kept on doing it. You are a disgrace." The result of this deceptive preaching of the devil is an evil conscience, a conscience in which the Law and Gospel are confused. Like a calloused conscience, an evil conscience cannot hear the instruction and prohibitions of the Law properly. Even more, an evil conscience cannot hear the Gospel in its comforting certainty. The evil conscience is weighed down with guilt and shame and is distorted with uncertainty and fear.

Jesus has medicine for an evil conscience: His sin-forgiving death and resurrection. Our Lord Jesus delivers His forgiveness to sinners through our Baptism, through the preaching of the Gospel, and through the Lord's Supper. The forgiveness of sins makes an evil conscience good. The Lord's mercy cleanses the conscience and makes it pure.

> Since we have a great priest [Jesus Christ] over the house of God,
> let us draw near with a true heart in full assurance of faith, with
> our hearts sprinkled clean from an evil conscience and our bodies washed with pure water. (Hebrews 10:21–22)

It is especially the gift of the Absolution that fights an evil conscience. We stand before our pastor and say, "Look, this sin is really, really bad, and it troubles me. Can even this sin be forgiven?" The Absolution answers, "Yes. I forgive you all your sins" (see John 20:23).

The promise of the Gospel undoes an evil conscience and gives us a bold, good, forgiven one.

There are times when we simply don't feel forgiven or loved by God. Our conscience doesn't register the truth of the Gospel. Our conscience is accusing us of forgiving sins. Our conscience is troubling us with guilt for sins already taken care of by Jesus. In these times, we walk by faith and not by sight (2 Corinthians 5:7), trusting that the Lord's promise of forgiveness is true in spite of our feelings.

By this we shall know that we are of the truth and reassure our heart before Him; for whenever our heart condemns us, God is greater than our heart, and He knows everything. Beloved, if our heart does not condemn us, we have confidence before God; and whatever we ask we receive from Him, because we keep His commandments and do what pleases Him. (1 John 3:19–22)

DANGER 3: A COUNTERFEIT CONSCIENCE

Finally, a *counterfeit conscience* is a conscience that thinks that it becomes good apart from the forgiveness of sins. Most often we attempt to give ourselves a good conscience by good works. When our conscience is troubled, we attempt to mollify it by being good. This is part of our fallen nature. Even non-Christians constantly do good works of charity to "feel good about themselves." This is an attempt to quiet the conscience through the Law, through obedience, and through works.

It is true that doing good works and serving our neighbor often brings satisfaction, but it is not what gives us a good conscience. The forgiveness of sins won by the Lord Jesus through His death on the cross is the *only* way the Lord delivers a good conscience to us. Any other means, from works of service to psychotherapy, only give us the illusion of peace.

{ **The forgiveness of sins is the *only* way the Lord restores a right conscience.** }

The solution to a counterfeit conscience is the Lord's Law and Gospel, and the repentance resulting when the Law and Gospel have their way with us. By the Lord's Law, we are shown the depth of our sin, and by the Lord's Gospel, all that sin is forgiven. This is the one and only way to have a good conscience. We stand before the face of God clothed not in the rags of our own works and efforts, but in the robes of Christ's righteousness made white and pure by His shed blood (see Revelation 7:9).

How much more will the blood of Christ, who through the eternal Spirit offered Himself without blemish to God, purify our conscience from dead works to serve the living God. (Hebrews 9:14)

The devil is always assaulting our conscience, burdening, twisting, hardening, and confusing it. American Christianity says very little about this most important theological topic. Jesus, on the other hand, is particularly interested in our conscience. He purifies, cleanses, and heals our broken conscience, and He gives us a conscience where His forgiving voice echoes with comfort and peace.

SUFFERING AND THE CHRISTIAN LIFE

> **"We rejoice in our sufferings."**
> (Romans 5:3)

American Christianity is focused on Christian living. *Discipleship* and *Jesus follower* and buzzwords like these describe the Christian "living out his faith." The focus is on sanctification. But with all the talk about the Christian life, there is very little talk about suffering. In the Bible, these two go together. The Bible describes the Christian life as a life of suffering.

In fact, many TV preachers describe the Christian life as a life without suffering. The "Health and Wealth" teachers of the "Prosperity Gospel" take this to the extreme. These false teachers present the Christian life as your best life now, a life of spiritual and especially physical blessings in abundance. According to the Prosperity Gospel, sickness, poverty, even too many red lights on the way to work are signs of a lack of God's blessings, and these point to a deeper lack of faith. If you are suffering, you show yourself to be a false disciple of Jesus. This is a horrible and disastrous false teaching.

But there is a subtle "sanctification -means-less-suffering" doctrine in all of us, an inner Buddhist that thinks our suffering means we are far from Jesus and our troubles are indications of God's abandonment. Which is why, I suspect, troubles always stir up questions about God's location. "Where is God in the midst of trouble?" We ask the question because we think (without thinking) that God must keep suffering at arm's length. If we are suffering, God must keep us at arm's length.

THIS IS WRONG, TOTALLY WRONG.

First, God is not a stranger to suffering. The cross shows us this. The prophet Isaiah even gives Jesus the name "man of sorrows" (Isaiah 53:3). No one ever suffered like Jesus suffered in the Garden of Gethsemane and on the cross. All the sins of all humanity—and the wrath of God that goes with them—is piled on Jesus.

When we see Jesus crying out on the cross, "My God, My God, why have You forsaken Me?" then we ought, at least, to know that God is not a stranger to suffering.

Second, Jesus teaches us that the Christian is also not a stranger to suffering. When Jesus is calling His disciples, He doesn't bid them "Take up your La-Z-Boy® and follow Me," but "Take up your cross and follow Me," adding "daily" to the command (see Luke 9:23 and then 14:27). The Christian life is a life of suffering. The yoke of Jesus is an easy yoke (Matthew 11:28–30), not because it lacks suffering, but because it doesn't lack Jesus. It doesn't lack forgiveness.

When we follow Jesus, we follow the One who suffered. The only Bible passage that teaches us to follow the example of Jesus gives us the example of Jesus' suffering:

> For what credit is it if, when you sin and are beaten for it, you endure? But if when you do good and suffer for it you endure, this is a gracious thing in the sight of God. For to this you have been called, because Christ also suffered for you, leaving you an example, so that you might follow in His steps. He committed no sin, neither was deceit found in His mouth. When He was reviled, He did not revile in return; when He suffered, He did not threaten, but continued entrusting Himself to Him who judges justly. He Himself bore our sins in His body on the tree, that we might die to sin and live to righteousness. (1 Peter 2:20–24)

This is astonishing. We have the answer to this old question: "What would Jesus do?" He suffers. He suffers patiently and quietly. If we follow the example of Jesus, we suffer. In a very profound sense, our sanctification is simply getting better at suffering.

This difficult realization opens up all the Bible passages about suffering and the Christian life. The uncomfortable realization that almost every time the Bible takes up the topic of my Christian life it talks about my suffering begins to make sense. I'm supposed to suffer. I'm supposed to be troubled and tempted and weak. I'm a Christian.

Our Christian life, then, is not Jesus removing suffering from us, but Jesus being with us in the midst of suffering. Our comfort is not the lack of trouble, but the promise of Jesus that He, the One who suffered in our place, will never leave us nor forsake us (Matthew 28:19–20; Hebrews 13:5).

{ **Our Christian life is Jesus being with us in the midst of suffering.** }

Third, we see now a purpose in our suffering. Martin Luther taught that three things made a theologian: prayer, meditation on the Lord's Word, and *tentatio*, that is, temptation or suffering. Luther directs us to Psalm 119 to learn these three things.

Psalm 119 is called the great "Torah Psalm." It is a massive acrostic; each of the 22 letters of the Hebrew alphabet have an 8-verse stanza, and in almost every one of the 176 verses, the Scriptures are extolled. It is teaching us how to read the Bible, and it says a lot about suffering. "This is my comfort in my affliction, that Your promise gives me life" (v. 50), and "Before I was afflicted I went astray, but now I keep Your word" (v. 67), and "It is good for me that I was afflicted, that I might learn Your statutes" (v. 71). Affliction, *tentatio*, suffering is good, for it teaches us the Lord's Word. It teaches us to trust in the Lord and to live with hope. Suffering teaches us to pray. In fact, in our suffering, we are being shaped by God.

Consider 2 Corinthians, Paul's treatise on suffering for God's Word:

> But we have this treasure in jars of clay, to show that the surpassing power belongs to God and not to us. We are afflicted in every way, but not crushed; perplexed, but not driven to despair; persecuted, but not forsaken; struck down, but not destroyed; always carrying in the body the death of Jesus, so that the life of Jesus may also be manifested in our bodies. For we who live are always being given over to death for Jesus' sake, so that the life of Jesus also may be manifested in our mortal flesh. (4:7–11)

Jesus' life is manifest in our dying. Jesus' kindness is manifest in our suffering. Paul continues:

> So we do not lose heart. Though our outer self is wasting away, our inner self is being renewed day by day. For this light momentary affliction is preparing for us an eternal weight of glory

beyond all comparison, as we look not to the things that are seen but to the things that are unseen. For the things that are seen are transient, but the things that are unseen are eternal. (2 Corinthians 4:16–18)

In Christ, our suffering is a preparation, a renewal, an instruction, a gift. "For it has been granted to you that for the sake of Christ you should not only believe in Him but also suffer for His sake" (Philippians 1:29).

Fourth, knowing Jesus is with us in suffering, and that suffering is a gift from the ascended Jesus to show us His mercy and prepare us for the resurrection, we then can find joy in our suffering. Acts 5:41 shows this wonderful joy in suffering: "Then they left the presence of the council, rejoicing that they were counted worthy to suffer dishonor for the name [of Jesus]." To rejoice at a beating seems strange to the world, but these disciples know Jesus, and they know the Christian life is a life of suffering.

Romans 5:3–5 also talks about finding joy in suffering:

> Not only that, but we rejoice in our sufferings, knowing that suffering produces endurance, and endurance produces character, and character produces hope, and hope does not put us to shame, because God's love has been poured into our hearts through the Holy Spirit who has been given to us.

We rejoice in the Gospel (Romans 5:1–2), so we rejoice in suffering. Paul loves to talk about this:

> For the sake of Christ, then, I am content with weaknesses, insults, hardships, persecutions, and calamities. For when I am weak, then I am strong. (2 Corinthians 12:10)

> Now I rejoice in my sufferings for your sake, and in my flesh I am filling up what is lacking in Christ's afflictions for the sake of His body, that is, the church. (Colossians 1:24)

The other apostles teach the same. They knew the suffering of Jesus, they knew the suffering of the Christian, and they knew the joy of it all. James 1:2–3 says, "Count it all joy, my brothers, when you meet trials of various kinds, for you know that the testing of your faith produces steadfastness."

Peter says our suffering is more valuable than gold, a badge of honor.

> . . . so that the tested genuineness of your faith—more precious
> than gold that perishes though it is tested by fire—may be found
> to result in praise and glory and honor at the revelation of Jesus
> Christ. (1 Peter 1:7)

Our faith clings to Christ and His promises. Our faith is our strength and our joy. There is joy in the strengthening of our faith.

> But rejoice insofar as you share Christ's sufferings, that you may
> also rejoice and be glad when His glory is revealed. If you are in-
> sulted for the name of Christ, you are blessed, because the Spirit
> of glory and of God rests upon you. But let none of you suffer as
> a murderer or a thief or an evildoer or as a meddler. Yet if anyone
> suffers as a Christian, let him not be ashamed, but let him glorify
> God in that name. (1 Peter 4:13–16)

Christians do not look for suffering, but they don't have to wait long for it to come along. The world, the flesh, and the devil hate the Christian with the rage they have for Jesus. Suffering will come. Crosses will come. Temptations and agony and loss will come. But Jesus has already come, already died, already risen, and He is with us in suffering. He suffered for us, and now He suffers with us. He promises it, and He promises joy in the midst of it.

Jesus says,

> Blessed are those who are persecuted for righteousness' sake, for
> theirs is the kingdom of heaven.

> Blessed are you when others revile you and persecute you and ut-
> ter all kinds of evil against you falsely on My account. Rejoice and
> be glad, for your reward is great in heaven, for so they persecuted
> the prophets who were before you. (Matthew 5:10–12)

There are often terribly false expectations offered to the Lord's people—prom-ises of success, personal prosperity, vanishing temptations, and temporal blessings. These false expectations are dangerous, a setup for "failure," because Jesus promises His followers, again, the exact opposite: "I have said these things to you, that in Me you may have peace. In the world you will have tribulation. But take heart; I have overcome the world" (John 16:33).

We expect suffering. We even rejoice in it. We know Jesus suffered for us, and this is all the comfort we need.

CHAPTER EIGHT

THE GIFT OF A NEIGHBOR
AND THE BEGINNING OF LOVE

"Owe no one anything, except to love each other, for the one who loves another has fulfilled the law. For the commandments, 'You shall not commit adultery, You shall not murder, You shall not steal, You shall not covet,' and any other commandment, are summed up in this word: 'You shall love your neighbor as yourself.' Love does no wrong to a neighbor; therefore love is the fulfilling of the law."

(Romans 13:8–10)

Love is a **dangerous** word. We hear "love" and think "Gospel." Love, after all, is so nice. What better thing in the world is there than love? What higher pursuit than love?

But love, Paul teaches us, is the essence of the Law. "Love is the fulfilling of the law" (Romans 13:10).

A lawyer came to Jesus asking Him about the Commandments:

> "Which commandment is the most important of all?" Jesus answered, "The most important is, 'Hear, O Israel: The Lord our God, the Lord is one. And you shall love the Lord your God with all your heart and with all your soul and with all your mind and with all your strength.' The second is this: 'You shall love your neighbor as yourself.' There is no other commandment greater than these." (Mark 12:28–31)

Love God with everything you have. Love your neighbor as yourself. This is a summary of the Law. If you could take the Ten Commandments and shrink them down to two commands, this is what you would have. And if you kept shrinking, you would end up with one word: *love*.

The command to love is the essence of the Law. As long as we are talking about my love for God and neighbor, we are talking about the Law, which, we have learned, always accuses us. If, on the other hand, we are talking about the Lord's love for us, we are talking about the Gospel. "For God so loved the world, that He gave His only Son" (John 3:16) is the most beautiful and comforting Gospel. "Love your neighbor as yourself" (Leviticus 19:18) is the most convicting Law.

I've often heard Christians say, "You have to learn to love yourself before you can love your neighbor." This is absurd. "No one ever hated his own flesh," Paul says (Ephesians 5:29). We are by nature in love with ourselves. I'll prove it. When I am sitting on the couch watching baseball and I get thirsty, I don't even think about it. I stand up, walk to the kitchen, get something to drink, and go sit down. But if I am sitting on the couch watching baseball, and my son gets thirsty and asks, "Dad, could you get me something to drink?" I moan and groan and say, "During the next commercial." I care for myself without even thinking. I care for my own family with all sorts of trouble. When the Scriptures command us to love our neighbor as ourselves, they are commanding us *out* of a love for self and *into* a love for our neighbor. We must love and serve the people around us just as naturally and unthinkingly as we serve and take care of ourselves.

In fact, in order to love God and my neighbor, I must first be set free from the bondage of my self-love. Christians are often encouraged to love and serve for their own benefit. I recently saw a church sign that read, "Forgive your neighbor, not for his sake, but for yours." This fits perfectly with our therapeutic culture where self-help is the only kind of help you find, but it is an appalling reversal of Christian love. Christian love is sacrifice. Christian love is profound selflessness. Christian love is death. "Greater love has no one than this, that someone lay down his life for his friends" (John 15:13).

{ Christian love is sacrifice. . . . Christian love is death. }

Love should define how we think, speak, and act toward God and toward our neighbor; the kind of love that the Scriptures demand is not the sentimental emotions of Hallmark cards, but an acting, doing, sacrificing, and dying love.

> Love is patient and kind; love does not envy or boast; it is not
> arrogant or rude. It does not insist on its own way; it is not irri-

table or resentful; it does not rejoice at wrongdoing, but rejoices
with the truth. Love bears all things, believes all things, hopes
all things, endures all things. Love never ends. (1 Corinthians
13:4–8)

Love demands everything, so love is never finished. It is never complete. We
cannot check love off the to-do list. There is not a single night when I can put my
head on my pillow and say, "Today I loved the Lord with all my heart, soul, mind,
and strength" or, "Today I loved my neighbor as myself." The Lutheran confessors
said it like this: "The Law always accuses," and that is certainly true of this word
love. It accuses me. It shows me my sin. It demonstrates my selfishness.

But the Bible does not only talk of my love for God and neighbor, it also talks
about God's love for us. This is the sweetest Gospel. "For God so loved the world,
that He gave His only Son, that whoever believes in Him should not perish but
have eternal life" (John 3:16). The love of God compelled Jesus into our flesh and
blood, into our sin and shame, into our death and grave. His love saves us. And His
love sets us free to love our neighbor. God's love sets us free to love our neighbor
because it sets us free to suffer, free to risk, free to die.

The old theologians talked of sin curving us in on ourselves, *incurvatus in se*.

The reason is that our nature has been so deeply curved in upon
itself because of the viciousness of original sin that it not only
turns the finest gifts of God in upon itself and enjoys them (as
is evident in the case of legalists and hypocrites), indeed, it even
uses God Himself to achieve these aims, but it also seems to be
ignorant of this very fact, that in acting so iniquitously, so per-
versely, and in such a depraved way, it is even seeking God for
its own sake. Thus the prophet Jeremiah says in Jer. 17:9: "The
heart is perverse above all things, and desperately corrupt; who
can understand it?" that is, it is so curved in on itself that no man,
no matter how holy (if a testing is kept from him) can understand
it. (LW 25:291)

We say, "If I don't take care of myself, who will? If I don't love myself, who
will?" The Gospel sets us free from this obsession with ourselves, free to love and
serve our neighbor. "For you were called to freedom, brothers. Only do not use

your freedom as an opportunity for the flesh, but through love serve one another" (Galatians 5:13; see also 1 Peter 2:16).

We no longer live for ourselves. We have been purchased by the blood of Jesus, and now our life is poured out in love for our neighbor. This chapter will consider our life of Christian love for our neighbor and faith toward God. This is the *what* and *why* of our good works. Our works find their end and goal in our neighbor's need and God's glory.

When Sin Becomes a Good Work

American Christianity locates the work of God internally in our heart. It is then no surprise that they also locate the Christian life chiefly in the heart. Sanctification, they teach, has to do with spiritual things. On the positive side, quiet times, church services, and evangelism are the major ways I serve God. On the negative side, I maintain my holiness by keeping myself separate from the world, avoiding secular pollution.

> "Only let each person lead the life that the Lord has assigned to him, and to which God has called him."
>
> (1 Corinthians 7:17)

In the Middle Ages, monks cloistered in monasteries to keep themselves from the pollution of the world. They removed themselves from daily life, from marriage, family, and any dealings with money and politics. They focused on the inner life of prayer and meditation. There is a kind of neo-monasticism in American Christianity. Christians gather in their Christian ghetto with Christian music, Christian books, Christian movies, Christian friends, Christian coffee shops, Christian plumbers, and the desire for a Christian government and a Christian nation. If things keep going this direction, we might soon have Christian cars and Christian sunglasses and Christian resorts, where Christians can vacation without temptation and eat Christian hamburgers made from Christian cows and Christian cheese.

American Christianity tends to shun and avoid anything secular. This neo-monasticism disconnects good works from family and day-to-day life and connects them to the church. The list of good and holy things to do is very short, and it normally involves reading your Bible, going on mission trips, or doing churchy things.

There is an even newer movement in the Church that encourages the Christian to do good works in the community. This neo-neo-monasticism makes good works look an awful lot like high school community service. It is, to be sure, good for Christian families to serve their neighbors and in their communities. But we need to be careful that our definition of good works matches the Scriptures' definition.

The Scriptures locate our good works first in our homes and then with our neighbors with whom we live and work. This is the doctrine of vocation. Our vocation is our calling in life. Vocation is much more than our job. Our vocations are the places where the Lord has stationed us to love and serve our neighbor. Our vocations, then, bind us to our neighbor in various and different ways, and our vocations define the way our love looks.

The doctrine of vocation.

All of us have many different vocations. We are the children of our parents. This is the vocation of child. Many of us have brothers and sisters: the vocation of sibling. If we are married, we have the vocation of spouse, and children give us the vocation of parent. Citizenship is also a vocation, of a country, state, county, city, and neighborhood. Our work is a vocation with many different neighbors given to us to love. We also have the vocation of friend. Our Baptism gives us the vocation of being a Christian. We also have the vocation of being a member of a Christian congregation.

In each of these various vocations, my love has a different shape. In all of our vocations, we are to love our neighbor, but love for one person looks much different than love for another. My love for my parents has a different shape than my love for my neighbors. My love for my children has a different shape than my love for the members of my congregation. We love our colleagues at work in a different way than we love the people in our family. The doctrine of vocation helps us with these distinctions.

The Ten Commandments are restrictive; they tell us first what not to do. "You shall have no other gods. You shall not murder. You shall not steal." Our vocations open the doors for the active side of love. It is in our various vocations that we honor our parents and other authorities. We care for our neighbor's physical needs. We protect and improve our neighbor's property and possessions.

Our vocations make what would otherwise be a sin into a good work. Consider these examples. A doctor does all sorts of things that would, in most situations, be sinful: examining here and there, uncovering people's bodies, cutting people open, and giving out all sorts of drugs. If anyone but a doctor did these things, he or she would go to jail. A judge sends people to jail, even sentences them to be killed. If anyone else did this, it would be a terrible sin, but for a judge, this is a good work. Soldiers and policemen act violently in their vocation, which is, for them, a good work. For a couple on their wedding day, what is a sin in the morning is a good work that evening. This list could go on: parents disciplining their children, a city council member making a law, the tax man collecting money, the coach yelling at his team, the friend speaking a harsh word—all of these things are normally sins but are made into good works by the unique bonds of vocation.

Vocation gives us the boldness to do what we would otherwise never dare to do. We cut and shoot and seize and embrace and uncover and rebuke according to our vocation, and this love according to vocation brings forth and supports life in any number of ways.

Our vocations define our good works.

If I am a child, I honor my father and mother; I love and cherish, serve and obey them. If I am husband or wife, I love and cherish my spouse and live faithfully in the bonds of marriage. If I am a parent, I provide for my children's earthly and eternal life. If I am a citizen, I live peacefully with my neighbors and pray for those given the privilege of government. If I govern, I use my reason and authority to serve my neighbor. If I am a student, I listen to my teachers. If I am a Christian, I listen to the Lord's voice in the Scriptures, I go to church to receive the Lord's gifts of the Gospel and the Lord's Supper, I pray, I listen to my pastor. If I am a pastor, I preach and teach, I pray and care for the Lord's people with His Word.

When, then, I ask what I ought to do every day, the answer is found in my vocation. What is my station in life according to the Ten Commandments? That is what I should do. Who is my neighbor in my family, at my work, in my congregation? It is my task to love them according to vocation. It really is that simple, and the Lord really is pleased with these simple works of service in our vocations. It is not glorious; it is not noticed by anyone else; there might be no "Thank-you" card. Our neighbor might not even notice. Works according to vocation are often dirty, small, and completely lacking the glory of more "holy" works, but if these are done with faith in God and love for the neighbor, these small works are great, high, and glorious in the Lord's estimation.

The doctrine of vocation is a tremendous blessing. It sets us free to love and serve in the places where the Lord has placed us with a confidence and joy that is normally missing from the Christian life. Cleaning your room, doing your homework, getting to work on time, doing the dishes, changing the baby's diaper, doing the best work you can at your job, helping your parents move, fixing the fence in the backyard—all of the normal things of this life, when they are done with faith in God and out of love for the neighbor, are glorious good works.

Vocation does not mean we do not sin. Just because it is a good work for parents to discipline their children doesn't mean parents cannot sin against their children. They can. Rulers, according to their vocation, have the authority to wage war, but this does not mean that every war is just and right. No matter what our vocation, we are all sinners. And sins committed in vocation are often the most damaging. Soldiers can assault the wrong people, doctors can betray their patient's trust, the tax collector can take money he should not, pastors can teach false doctrine. Our vocations give us a special obligation. The duty to love opens up the opportunity to harm. Love is always a risk.

So the question "What is my station in life according to the Ten Commandments?" not only tells me what I ought to do today, but it also teaches me what sins I need to confess. Our vocations not only direct our actions toward our neighbor's need, but they also teach us our great need for the Lord's love and mercy.

All of us have multiple vocations. Part of the fun and trouble of this life is sorting out what each vocation means at different times. I am always a Christian, always a husband and father and child, always a pastor, always a citizen, but these different vocations mean different things at different times. Sometimes I'm preaching, sometimes I'm mowing the grass, sometimes I'm praying, sometimes I'm reading a book to the kids, and this moving in and out of the obligations of my vocations is the good stuff, the adventure of a Christian life in this world. Next to the Gospel, the doctrine of vocation gives us the confidence, boldness, and freedom to live and love and serve our neighbor.

Martin Luther (who loved the doctrine of vocation) called the various vocations of the Christian the "masks of God." Through our vocations, God cares for the world and the things in it. Through the vocations of family, children are born and raised. Through the vocations of government, people are protected and afforded the peace needed to provide for life. Through the vocations in the Church, the word of forgiveness and eternal life is preached to sinners throughout the world.

The family, the state, and the Church are the most important realms in which we live according to our vocations. The old theologians called these three realms (family, state, and Church) the "three estates." The Scriptures recognize that all three of these estates are established and instituted by God, and all of them are honorable and good.

The estates order the world. The three estates establish authority. In the family, parents have authority over their children. A husband is placed in authority over his wife and family. In the state, the government exercises authority over citizens. In the Church, the pastor has the authority of God's Word in the congregation. The Bible's teaching of authority is incredibly beautiful and comforting, but our culture is uncomfortable with any talk of one person having authority over another, so a word of explanation will be helpful.

God has ordered the world and established authority in order to distribute and protect His gifts. Parents have authority over their children for the purpose of serving and caring for them, protecting them, and giving them all they need for this life and the life to come. Their authority is for giving gifts. The husband and father has authority over his wife and home so that he might protect his wife and children, provide for them, teach them the Scriptures, and guard them with his prayers. Government has authority over citizens so that it can keep peace and maintain the conditions necessary for a prosperous life on the earth. Pastors have the authority of the Word so that they can give out the gifts of the Lord's grace and mercy, distributing the forgiveness of sins and the Lord's kindness, preaching the Gospel and teaching the Scriptures to the Lord's people. Authority, then, is God's orderly establishment for giving gifts.

Indeed, vocation is God's gift to us. American Christianity misses the comfort of the doctrine of vocation. In grasping for ultra-spiritual good works, the plain and simple works that the Lord has given us are neglected.

According to the Scriptures, and according to our vocation, we have the comfort and freedom of loving and serving our neighbor in simplicity. We break out of the Christian ghetto. The Lord's love makes its way into every corner of this world. And we are comforted with the confidence that the simple daily tasks that mark our lives here below are considered good and right by our Father in heaven, and through them He crushes the devil under our feet (see Romans 16:20).

WORSHIP IS BEING SERVED BY JESUS

> "The Son of Man came not to be served but to serve, and to give His life as a ransom for many."
>
> (Matthew 20:28)

What is worship? This is one of those questions wanting a clear answer from the Lord's Church. Unfortunately, answers are muddled.

American Christianity generally answers, "Worship is my praise and thanks to God for who He is and what He's done." "Worship is the yearning of the heart to be close to God." "Worship is our service of singing and praying to God." The common thing in these answers is this: *We* are the ones acting, praying, singing, praising. We are the givers, and God is the getter. This is what I thought about worship, what I was taught by American Christianity. Worship was deepening my relationship with God, having an experience of God's presence, being moved in my inner being.

In American Christianity, worship is a perfect fusion of moralism and mysticism. My actions and attitudes (with a little help from the praise band) were inducing a "worship experience." God was close, I could feel it, at least most of the time. There were "Holy Spirit goosebumps," the sensation of being lost like a drop in the ocean, hands and voice raised in surrender, and offering myself to God. "Here I am to worship. Here I am to bow down." "Sing like never before, Oh my soul. I'll worship Your holy name." The praise song itself is understood as the sacrifice of praise, offered in the Christian heart to God.

> American Christianity's desire for something new, exciting, and entertaining stands behind the adjective *contemporary*, which is stuck like a leech to the word *worship*.

When we consider the Scriptures, a different picture emerges. The Bible has a different theology of worship.

Rather than our service to Jesus, the Bible teaches that Jesus serves us. Worship is not first or primarily our works, our praises, our yearning and sacrifice, but God's work and Word, His speaking and giving. This is such a radically different picture from our normal understanding of worship that we should hear it again: worship is Jesus serving us. Jesus says, "The Son of Man came not to be served but to serve, and to give His life as a ransom for many" (Matthew 20:28). "Not to be served, but to serve." Jesus came to serve, and He still comes to serve us.

Consider Jesus washing His disciples' feet. The night before His crucifixion, the night of His betrayal and arrest, the night of the giving out of His body and blood for the forgiveness of sins, Jesus stood up from the table, took off His outer robe, wrapped a towel around His waist, and went to wash His disciples' feet (John 13:1–20). This is a shocking display. It is difficult to imagine this text without complete astonishment. Washing someone's feet is a miserably humble job. It was slave's work. But here is Jesus, washing the feet of His followers.

The disciples must have been astounded, stunned. We know Peter is offended that the Lord would do such a thing. He protests. His protest takes two distinct forms, both wrong. First, Peter objects that Jesus is serving him. Second, he tries to tell Jesus how best to serve him. We see in Peter's objections the two ways to misunderstand the Scripture's teaching on worship.

First, Peter objects to Jesus' service. He knows he and the other disciples should be the ones doing the dirty work. Peter should be on his knees washing the feet of Jesus, scrubbing His toes, serving Him. Jesus, after all, is the King of kings, God of God, Light of Light. Jesus created the cosmos, and all things hold together in Him. If there is anyone who should be served, it is Jesus. But here He is, wrapped in a towel, doing the slave's work, wiping the dirt off Peter's feet. He revolts: "Lord, do You wash my feet?" (John 13:6). How can it be that the Lord of all would so humble Himself?

Jesus explains it to Peter: "What I am doing you do not understand now, but afterward you will understand" (John 13:7). It is as if Jesus is saying, "Peter, if you think washing feet is humiliating, just wait until tomorrow! If you think it is horrible that I am here wrapped in a towel, wait until tomorrow when I am stripped and hung on the cross for all to see. If you think pouring water is too lowly for Me, wait until tomorrow when I pour out My blood. If you are troubled by the humility of My washing your feet, you will be appalled at My dying for your sins." Jesus has an even greater humiliation coming. The humility of washing feet is only a prelude to the great humiliation of the cross (see Philippians 2:5–8).

Peter said to Him, "You shall never wash my feet." Peter can't handle it. He can't bear to see Jesus so low, stooping to serve. Peter knows (and he is right) that he should be doing this washing, but Peter's humility is dangerous. Jesus must serve Peter. Jesus warns him, "If I do not wash you, you have no share with Me" (John 13:8).

The humiliation of Jesus is necessary. His serving us is necessary. Jesus came to serve and to give His life as a ransom for many, and unless He serves us, washes our sins away with the cleansing flood of His blood, we have no part in Him.

We are like Peter. We know that we should serve God, but Jesus flips this on its head, turns it upside down. Again, "The Son of Man came not to be served but to serve, and to give His life as a ransom for many" (Matthew 20:28). This is an absolutely shocking truth, and like Peter, we are in danger of not believing it. We think worship is our serving God. We think it must be this way.

But when this truth sinks in, a second theological misunderstanding comes along. If Jesus is serving us, we want to tell Him *how* to do it. "Simon Peter said to Him, 'Lord, not my feet only but also my hands and my head!' " (John 13:9). Peter is saying, "If You are going to serve me, this is what I need."

The more the better, right? Peter thinks that if Jesus is going to serve him, then Peter will be the master. Peter will give instructions to Jesus. Peter will tell Jesus what he needs. This is the Christian who would dictate to Jesus the things he needs for this life, the things that would make him happy. This is the error of the church that decides what Jesus should give to it. This is wrong. Jesus is not a servant; He is the *Master* who *serves*. Because He is the Master, He will determine what we need. "Jesus said to him, 'The one who has bathed does not need to wash, except for his feet, but is completely clean' " (John 13:10). Jesus serves us not according to what we want. He gives us what He knows we need.

{ Jesus is the Master who serves. }

If it were up to us, Jesus would come to serve us with health, wealth, and happiness. If we were calling the shots, we would have all sorts of exciting experiences. But it is not up to us. Jesus knows what we need, and He establishes the worship of His Church so that He can deliver to us what we need. Jesus knows we are sinners whose most desperate need is His promise of forgiveness. So He establishes the worship of the Church so that He can deliver His forgiveness to us.

"Jesus is the one who serves" is an astounding and wonderful truth of the Scriptures. Jesus served us in His suffering and death on the cross. He served us by shedding His blood for our forgiveness. He continues to serve us and bring us forgiveness. He serves us in our Baptism, in the Lord's Supper, in the preaching, in the Word.

Forty days after His resurrection and minutes before His ascension, Jesus speaks these astonishing words to His disciples: "All authority in heaven and earth has been given to Me" (Matthew 28:18). The disciples' minds must have been racing. "What will Jesus do with all that authority? Establish His earthly kingdom? Make us kings? End the Roman occupation? Give us an endless life of miracles?" With all the authority of heaven and earth, you would expect something astonishing, but instead Jesus institutes something incredibly humble. "Go therefore and make disciples of all nations, baptizing them in the name of the Father and of the Son and of the Holy Spirit, teaching them to observe all that I have commanded you. And behold, I am with you always, to the end of the age" (Matthew 28:19–20). What a surprise! That is what Jesus is going to do with all authority in the cosmos: He institutes Holy Baptism using a bit of water with His name, and with "just words," His teaching reveals the mind of His Father and His gracious plan of salvation. Jesus uses all His authority in heaven and on earth to baptize and teach.

Jesus doesn't do the things we expect. He certainly doesn't serve us in the way we expect. He doesn't come in great power and glory. He comes in the humility of the water and the Word to save and rescue us from our sins.

After Jesus had given His last will and testament in the Lord's Supper, He asks His disciples a question, "For who is the greater, one who reclines at table or one who serves?" We know the answer: the customer is always right. The servant is there to serve and give you what you need. The one who sits at the table is greater. Jesus says as much, "Is it not the one who reclines at table?" And then the shock and wonder: "But I am among you as the one who serves" (Luke 22:27). Jesus was among His disciples as the One who serves. He is still with His Church as the One who serves. **The Lord's Supper is His service to us. He is the Host and the Meal. We receive from His fullness grace and mercy.**

The Lutheran Confessions shake it out like this:

> So the worship and divine service of the Gospel is to receive gifts from God. On the contrary, the worship of the Law is to offer and present our gifts to God. However, we can offer nothing to God unless we have first been reconciled and born again. This passage, too, brings the greatest comfort, as the chief worship of the Gospel is to desire to receive the forgiveness of sins, grace, and righteousness. (Ap V [III] 189 [310])

Our Lord Jesus delights in giving, giving Himself and His life for us and our salvation. When we gather to hear His Word and eat and drink His body and blood, this is exactly what He is doing: forgiving our sins, giving us gifts, serving us eternal life.

American Christianity gathers for worship so we might serve God. The Lutheran Church gathers for worship so God might serve us, forgive our sins, and keep us in His mercy and kindness. "What is worship?" There is great joy in having the clear answer from Scriptures. Worship is being served by Jesus.

It's Not a Relationship; It's a Religion

"Religion that is pure and undefiled before God, the Father, is this: to visit orphans and widows in their affliction, and to keep oneself unstained from the world." (James 1:27)

"Christianity is not a religion; it's a relationship." This is perhaps the most ubiquitous cliché of American Christianity. Here's what it is supposed to mean:

"Religion" is about rules, dos and don'ts, our works, and all sorts of outward traditions. Structured worship, ordinances like Baptism and the Lord's Supper, saying the same prayer over and over, these are all the things religion does, and they are bad. Mostly, these are works, and they cannot save you. "Relationship," on the other hand, is much more organic. We believe in Jesus and talk to Him, and He talks to us. He lets us know He is close by, and that He's got our back. We spend time together getting to know each other. Jesus and I are in a committed long-term relationship, and this relationship is deepening and growing.

American Christianity has managed to mix mysticism with moralism, and the result is the understanding of Christianity as a "personal relationship with Christ." We call this "Relationship Theology."

Relationship Theology completely shapes the piety of American Christianity. "Quiet time," "prayer life," "walk with God," being "touched" and "moved" in the church services, and all sorts of other buzzwords grow out of the paradigm of Relationship Theology. Relationship Theology is the reason behind the oft-noted critique that many worship songs could also be sung to your boyfriend or girlfriend. "I'm, I'm desperate for you/And I'm, I'm lost without you." "So heaven meets earth like a sloppy wet kiss/And my heart turns violently inside of my chest."

Relationship Theology reorients our life with God so that we are always measuring how close we are to Him and assessing the status of our relationship. "Am I close to God? Am I growing far from Him? It's time to take the relationship to the next level." With Relationship Theology, the purpose of our "quiet time" is to grow closer to God. The purpose of our prayers is to deepen the relationship. "To have a good relationship, a husband and wife have to spend time together. They have to talk to each other. The same thing is true with our relationship with God." I think I've heard this preached a thousand times. Relationship Theology turns prayer into a two-way conversation. We talk to God, and we listen for Him. American Christianity expects God to talk directly to us in prayer, either through explicit words, impressions, or signs.

There are problems with
RELATIONSHIP THEOLOGY.

The word RELATIONSHIP never appears in the Bible. (A few English versions add it here and there to smooth out the translation, but it doesn't appear in the original.) This means we cannot find a biblical definition of the idea. To be in relationship to something means there are two (at least) objects interacting with each other, and it makes those interactions measurable. We generally speak of a relationship between two people, and we measure their relationship in personal and emotional terms. A relationship can be "good" or "bad" or "complicated." People can be "close to" or "distant from" each other, or have no relationship at all. This is the first danger of Relationship Theology. It assumes the possibility of *not* having a relationship with Christ. This is not true.

Everyone has a relationship with Jesus. Even the unbeliever has a relationship status with Jesus. They are died for by Jesus. They are loved by Him. But, apart from faith, they stand condemned, and He will, on the Last Day, be their Judge. This is a relationship, just not a good one.

The second danger with Relationship Theology is that it introduces the ideas of distance and measurement where they should not be. This can be seen in everyday usage. There is danger, for example, in using the word *relationship* to describe the bond of marriage. The Bible teaches us that husband and wife are not in a relationship with one another, but are "one flesh," brought together and united by God (Genesis 2:24; Matthew 19:6). To ask a husband and wife "How's your relationship?" is, in fact, to put separation and distance between them. It is asking for a judgment, an assessment, a critique. A relationship, after all, could always get better. The union of husband and wife, on the other hand, remains the same in good times and in bad. Try asking a husband and wife these questions: "How is your unity?" "How is your being one flesh?" The questions don't make sense, and that is the joy and confidence of marriage. In other words, the language of "relationship" invites unnecessary critique and questions.

The same thing is true with Christ and His Church. The Church is the Bride of Christ, united to Him (Ephesians 5:22–33; Revelation 19:7). This unity is something established, something sure, bound up to the work and Word of Jesus, no matter how I feel about it. I am united to Christ. If I understand my status with Jesus chiefly in terms of relationship instead of unity, then the sure things become unsure and the established things become uncertain. The confidence of our salvation is weakened under the burden of improving the relationship. "How is your relationship with Jesus?" is an entirely different question than "How is your unity with Christ?"

The third danger of Relationship Theology is that it understands our real problem in emotional terms, rather than guilt and sin. Salvation is understood as the establishment of the relationship. Relationship Theology puts the relationship in opposition to "Religion." Religion is understood to be the Law, the rules and commandments and requirements. "Relationship" is the nice stuff, the friendly Jesus, the spending time together and getting to know each other. But instead of rightly distinguishing Law and Gospel and teaching that our real trouble is our sin and

God's wrath over that sin, our troubles are reduced to our emotional disconnect from God and our emotional distance from the Almighty. If this is the real problem, the solution the Bible offers makes no sense. Why would the Son of God need to suffer and die in the agony of God's wrath if the problem is that we have a bad relationship with Him?

Relationship Theology makes salvation the result of my commitment and continuing resolve to deepen the relationship. It weakens the preaching

of the Law and decimates the preaching of the cross. The Bible teaches us that our problem is sin and the solution is the forgiveness won by the death of Jesus on the cross. Relationship Theology teaches us our problem is distance—we are far from God—and the solution is drawing near to God and deepening our relationship with Him. Relationship replaces repentance, and the Christian life is taken up into the thrill and devastation of a high school romance.

Fourth, Relationship Theology expects things of God that He never promised. It expects God to talk back to us in prayer and direct our lives through direct revelation. It expects we will "feel moved," "touched," "led" by God to do certain things. Or, if we don't feel led, we are waiting to feel led. Relationship Theology teaches us to listen in prayer and expect, even demand, that God will talk back to us. This is a subtle and pious-looking denial of the sufficiency of God's Word, as if we were saying, "God, Your Word might be enough for everyone else, but I need something more. I need You to talk directly to me." The Lord has never promised any of these things. He never promised feelings, greater insight, or a personalized revelation. He gives us His Law and promises and tells us that these are, in fact, sufficient for our Christian life.

Relationship Theology puts our Christian certainty under the domain of our emotions. "I don't feel forgiven" and "I don't feel close to God" have behind them the false expectations of Relationship Theology: that God has promised to give us these feelings of closeness and forgiven-ness. Relationship Theology also expects God's direct intervention in our emotions, and therefore treats emotions as a reliable source of information. "If I feel sure about it, I must be right."

The Bible, on the other hand, puts our emotions under the domain of God's Law. "You shall not covet," for example. This, at the very least, is an acknowledgment that our emotions can be wrong. And, further, the Bible understands our emotions and inner life are affected by the certainty of the external Word. Certainty begins outside of us in the words and works of God. The Lord's promise "You will have eternal life" will normally stir up in the Christian's heart joy and profound comfort. But not always. Sometimes our emotions miss the truth and comfort of God's Word. This does not mean the promise is invalid or untrue. His Word is sure even when we don't feel it. John writes these beautifully comforting words: "Whenever our heart condemns us, God is greater than our heart, and He knows everything" (1 John 3:20). Imagine that—one greater than our heart! Our feelings, in fact, can be wrong and often are. God and His promises are greater than these feelings.

The false expectations of Relationship Theology are dangerous. Like every false teaching, it puts us on the pendulum of pride and despair. If we are "hearing" and "feeling" God, we are proud of our relationship with Him. If we are not, we despair of God's love. While Relationship Theology shapes everything in the Christian life toward deepening the relationship and finding the feelings, biblical piety pushes us to the freedom of repentance and the certainty of the Lord's promises. The certainty of God's Word and promise rule in our heart, and we look for and find comfort in them. His Word promises more than a relationship with Jesus. It unites us with Christ and His undeserved love for us.

A Biblical Picture of Piety

Piety is the way our doctrine looks when it is lived out in our lives. Piety means the shape of our Christian life. Piety is the contour of our prayers, our study, our going to church, our loving the neighbors God gives us. American Christianity has a certain piety, a picture of what it looks like to be a Christian. The piety of American Christianity looks, at times, like biblical piety. Both have open Bibles. Both gather their families around the table to pray. Both are in church on Sunday morning. This is good. But the piety of American Christianity is shaped by Relationship Theology. Biblical piety centers around God's Word and Sacraments, lives in repentance and faith, and results in comfort and love.

The piety of American Christianity centers on the "personal relationship with Jesus," "quiet time," and "prayer time." Even corporate worship in American Christianity is an individual experience: me and God. Biblical piety, in contrast, centers on the corporate worship of the local congregation.

In the Old Testament, this worship was centered on the tabernacle and the temple, where the priests brought the sacrifice to the altar. In the New Testament, this worship is centered on the preached Word and the Lord's Supper, where Jesus dishes up the Absolution, hands us over to a life of repentance, and serves us His body and blood with His promise of forgiveness.

THE PIETY OF AMERICAN CHRISTIANITY SPRINGS FROM OUR DECISION FOR CHRIST AND OUR COMMITMENT TO FOLLOW HIM. Biblical piety springs from the Lord's gift of Baptism and the miracle He accomplished there.

It might seem to us like Baptism is not a particularly important part of our daily Christian life, but a closer look at the Scriptures gives us a different picture. In almost all of his letters, Paul connects Baptism to our Christian life. In fact, as Paul moves in his letters from talking about what we believe to how we live, he connects them by teaching about Baptism. Paul sees Baptism as the fountain and source of our Christian life. (See, for example, Galatians 3:27; Ephesians 4:5; Colossians 2:12; and, in some ways, 1 Corinthians 10:2.)

Consider Romans 6:3–4: "Do you not know that all of us who have been baptized into Christ Jesus were baptized into His death? We were buried therefore with Him by baptism into death, in order that, just as Christ was raised from the dead by the glory of the Father, we too might walk in newness of life." Baptism wraps us up in the life and death of Jesus and sets us into a life of repentance. Baptism puts the flesh to death. Baptism raises the new man to life. All we do, we do in the name of Jesus, the name given to us in our Baptism (see Colossians 3:17; Matthew 28:19).

The piety of American Christianity is reading the Bible looking for instructions, for all the things I am supposed to do in obedience to God. It almost completely misses the comfort of the Gospel. Biblical piety, on the other hand, reads the Bible in its fullness, with the blazing light of Law and Gospel illuminating the words. The Law shows our sins, teaches us repentance, orders the world, and shapes our love for our neighbor. The Gospel also shines forth from the pages of the Bible with glorious and stunning joy and peace. Our sins are forgiven; our conscience is consoled and comforted. The pages of the Scriptures are dripping with the blood and kindness of our Savior. This distinction between Law and Gospel unlocks the Scriptures and gives us the very words of God in their truth and purity.

This biblical piety is, in fact, biblical, but it is important to remember that no-where in the Bible are we actually commanded to read the Bible. Instead, the Lord commands us to treasure His Word, meditate on His Word, and delight in His Word (see, for example, Psalms 1 and 119). We delight in the Lord's Word when we find in the Scriptures the Lord's great kindness and mercy, when we hear His Gospel. If we are reading the Bible without hearing the Gospel, we are missing the entire point.

The piety of American Christianity prays in order to deepen a relationship with God. Biblical piety prays as God's children asking our heavenly Father for the things we need. These are prayers born out of need, prayers from the depths, prayers of people suffering, needing, lacking, falling, sinning, and being sinned against. The Psalms, and especially the Lord's Prayer, show us the prayers of people with enemies, the prayers of people with troubles and tears, prayers from a life of suffering mixed with hope and tears mixed with joy.

American Christianity encourages spontaneity in prayer. Prayers come from the heart. It is true that the Lord loves to hear the cries of our heart, but biblical piety finds the source of our prayers in the command and promises of the Scrip-tures. Our prayers are the Psalms and hymns of the Scriptures that grow out of the Lord's promises. The purpose of biblical prayer is not to deepen our relationship with God. We pray because we are in desperate need of His help, and because He is graciously ready to help us.

In the end, the piety shaped by Relationship Theology results in the roller coaster of pride and despair. God never promised that we would *feel* forgiven. He promises that we *are* forgiven. He never promised that we would *feel* saved. He promises that we *are* saved, even if we don't feel like it. He never promised that we would feel close to Him; He promised never to leave us or forsake us. But, in the beautiful irony of our Christian piety, the feelings of comfort, confidence, and the boldness of faith come from the certainty of these promises.

LOVE BEGUN, NEVER DONE

There is a strain of Christian perfectionism that runs through American Christianity. This is the teaching that the Christian can, in this life, perfectly keep God's Law. Historically, this is the classic theological distinction of the Methodists, born of John Wesley's book *A Plain Account of Christian Perfection*. While most modern Methodists have lost this distinctive, it is carried forward by the Wesleyans and Nazarenes.

There is, though, an unofficial perfectionism that broods underneath most of American Christianity. Repentance is understood as a onetime event. The Law is preached as keepable. Conversion brings the power and ability to keep the Commandments. Comfort is sought in our growth in good works. The work of the Spirit is bound up to our keeping the Law. This pursuit of perfection is dangerous. It is another path to pride and despair. If we convince ourselves that we can, must, and are getting better and better, then soon we don't need to repent. If we keep walking down the path of perfectionism, we eventually don't need Jesus.

> "In this is love, not that we have loved God but that He loved us and sent His Son to be the propitiation for our sins."
> (1 John 4:10)

{ There is a strain of perfectionism that runs through American Christianity. }

Understood correctly, our Christian life of love is a life of humble repentance. Love is never done. The command to love always accuses us. It always shows us our sin. This understanding results in three profound theological truths.

1. First, our life of love is a life of repentance.

2. Second, our works are always and only *begun*, never finished. Jesus, and Jesus alone, can cry out, "It is finished."

3. Third, it is impossible for us to find comfort in our works. We never think we've done enough because we never have done enough.

These are the limitations of our life of love that keeps the Law in its proper place and keeps it from encroaching into the work of the Gospel and the forgiveness of our sins.

A LIFE OF REPENTANCE

We never outgrow repentance. As long as we live in this fallen world, we are and remain sinners. As long as we live in our flesh, we are sinners. We are always desperately in need of the Lord's mercy, which means our Christian life is a life of repentance.

The very first (and perhaps the very best) of Martin Luther's famous Ninety-Five Theses says, "When our Lord and Master Jesus Christ said 'Repent' [Matt. 4:17], He willed the entire life of believers to be one of repentance" (LW 31:25). Repentance is the daily picking up the cross and following Jesus (Matthew 16:24; Luke 9:23).

When discussing the significance of Baptism, Luther says, "It indicates that the Old Adam in us should by daily contrition and repentance be drowned and die with all sins and evil desires, and that a new man should daily emerge and arise to live before God in righteousness and purity forever" (SC, The Sacrament of Holy Baptism).

There is a particularly delightful passage in the Large Catechism where Luther gives advice to the person who doesn't feel his need for the Lord's Supper. He says:

> For those who are of such a mind that they do not realize their condition I know no better counsel than that they put their hand into their shirt to check whether they have flesh and blood. And if you find that you do, then go, for your good to St. Paul's Epistle to the Galatians. Hear what sort of fruit your flesh is: "Now the works of the flesh are evident: sexual immorality, impurity, sensuality, idolatry, sorcery, enmity, strife, jealousy, fits of anger, rivalries, dissensions, divisions, envy, drunkenness, orgies and things like these [Galatians 5:19–21]." Therefore, if you cannot discern this, at least believe the Scriptures. They will not lie to you, and they know your flesh better than you yourself. Yes, St. Paul further concludes in Romans 7:18: "I know that nothing good dwells in me, that is, in my flesh." (LC V 75–76)

Our life of love, then, begins with repentance. In fact, our good works are so bound up to repentance that these works are called the fruits of repentance. "Bear fruit in keeping with repentance" (Matthew 3:8). Our repentance, that is, our sorrow over our sin and faith in the Lord's promise of forgiveness, is the tree from which good works flower and on which its fruits are found.

LOVE ONLY BEGUN

It is a distinct mark of Lutheran theology that it speaks of the *beginning* of love, the *start* of love. Our good works and our lives of sacrifice are only begun, but never finished, never complete. Consider this passage from the Apology of the Augsburg Confession:

> Faith brings the Holy Spirit and produces a new life in hearts. It must also produce spiritual movements in hearts. The prophet Jeremiah shows what these movements are when he says, "I will put My law within them, and I will write it on their hearts" (31:33). Therefore, when we have been justified by faith and regenerated, we begin to fear and love God, to pray to Him, to expect aid from Him, to give thanks and praise Him, and to obey Him in times of suffering. We also begin to love our neighbors, because our hearts have spiritual and holy movements.
>
> These things cannot happen until we have been justified through faith and regenerated (we receive the Holy Spirit). First, because the Law cannot be kept without Christ; likewise, the Law cannot be kept without the Holy Spirit. But the Holy Spirit is received through faith, as Paul declares in Galatians 3:14, "that we might receive the promised Spirit through faith." Also remember, how can the human heart love God while it knows that He is terribly angry and is oppressing us with earthly and endless distress? The Law always accuses us. It always shows that God is angry. God is not loved until we receive mercy through faith. Not until then does He become someone we can love. (Ap V [III] 4–8 [125–29])

It is only by faith that we know the love of God, so it is only by faith that our life of love is begun, our love of neighbor is begun, our prayers are begun. With works begun—but never done—we are free to talk about works without the worry of legalism or pride. Talking about the beginning of works frees us from the dangers of perfectionism. Unlike the perfectionist, Christian works do not fight against repentance, but are precisely where our life of repentance is found. Speaking always of the beginning of works helps keep them in their proper place and maintains the centrality of faith.

The Comfort of Comfortless Works

Finally, the incompleteness and always-accusing-us-ness of our works means we can never take comfort in them. There is always more that we could have done, that we should have done. Our works are never a source of pride. "For by grace you have been saved through faith. And this is not your own doing; it is the gift of God, not a result of works, so that no one may boast" (Ephesians 2:8–9).

Boasting in ourselves and our works is excluded by the Gospel. It is silenced by faith. The pride of works is completely severed from the doing of works by the promise of righteousness. There is no comfort in our doing, our efforts, our works, our determination, our sincerity, or our resolve. We can never do enough. But we don't need the comfort of the Law. We have the comfort of the promise and the confidence of the Lord's forgiveness.

Without the comforting promises of the Sacraments, American Christianity is always looking for comfort in all the wrong places. Good works are often one of these wrong places. "If I do enough, serve enough, pray enough, or grow enough spiritually, I can be sure that God loves me." There is never enough, not according to the Law. We all fall short of the glory of God (Romans 3:23). "If we say we have no sin, we deceive ourselves, and the truth is not in us" (1 John 1:8). We have sin, always, and this sin fights against any comfort we would like to find through obedience.

We find comfort not in the "DO" of the Law but in the "DONE" of the Gospel, in the work of Christ on the cross, in the font, on the altar, in the Word. Our comfort is not in ourselves but in Christ, and this sets us free to love and serve our neighbors—not for our comfort, but for theirs. How wonderful! When the burden of comforting is taken from the Law, then the Law can do its real and wonderful work of defining and giving shape to our serving our neighbor and those in need.

American Christianity pushes us toward certainty through works. The Bible gives us Christ and His kindness and His kingdom. We do not have to attain God's pleasure through works. God is delighted in us through Christ. Knowing that we do not have to work to please God, we can at last work to serve our neighbors and begin to love them as the Lord commands.

CHAPTER NINE

WRESTLING WITH GOD: WHY PRAYER IS SUFFERING

"Your name shall no longer be called Jacob, but Israel, for you have striven with God and with men, and have prevailed."

(Genesis 32:28)

The Christian prays.

In American Christianity, prayer serves to deepen the relationship between the Christian and God. Prayer is thought to be a two-way street, an expression of intimacy with God. Prayer is emotive and motivated by the desire to feel close to God. The Bible gives us a much different teaching and practice of prayer, something we will consider in this chapter.

In this life full of sorrow and trouble, we pray for the Lord's help and deliverance. In this life full of joys and blessings, we thank the Lord for all His benefits. In this life full of forgiveness and mercy, we confess our sins and ask for the Lord's forgiveness.

But prayer is not an easy thing. We learn this by experience, but the Bible teaches it as well.

Consider Jacob. He stole his brother's birthright, ran away for fourteen years, and is, in Genesis 32, headed back to the Promised Land, worried the entire way that Esau will kill him at first sight. So God comes to Jacob as he stands alone on the bank of the river Jabbok. And what does God do with Jacob? Does He teach him? comfort him? show him a miracle? give him a vision so that Jacob will know that the Lord is on his side? No! God grabs ahold of Jacob and begins to wrestle him! (This is the kind of stuff that would get my brothers and me in trouble.)

God wrestles Jacob, and Jacob fights back, and this goes on all night. Eight hours of grappling, circling around to get the best position, diving for the leg, trying to get a better hold, throwing each other in the dirt. God tries to get away, but

Jacob won't let Him go without a blessing. God touches Jacob in the hip and knocks it out of its socket. (Jacob would limp for the rest of his life.)

Whatever you might expect God to do with Jacob, this is not it! A wrestling match that lasts through the night. But this is how it is with the Lord and us. This is how it is with prayer. Prayer is not putting a quarter in the heavenly vending machine and pushing the right buttons so a blessing will fall down upon us. Prayer is wrestling with God, grabbing ahold of His promises, and even if He tries to get away, we don't let go until He gives a blessing, until He keeps His promise.

At last, Jacob prevails, and God gives him a blessing. He even changes his name from Jacob to Israel, which means "wrestles with God."

> But Jacob said, "I will not let You go unless You bless me." And He said to him, "What is your name?" And he said, "Jacob." Then He said, "Your name shall no longer be called Jacob, but Israel, for you have striven with God and with men, and have prevailed."
> (Genesis 32:26–28)

You are Israel, a Christian, one who wrestles with God, one who prays.

PRAYER 101, FOUR THINGS WE NEED TO KNOW FIRST

There are four things we need to know first about prayer. First, prayer is commanded. Second, prayer comes with many wonderful promises. Third, we pray because we have many great needs. Fourth, Jesus teaches us the words to pray.

THE COMMAND OF PRAYER

First, prayer is commanded in the Second Commandment. "You shall not take the name of the LORD your God in vain, for the LORD will not hold him guiltless who takes His name in vain" (Exodus 20:7). When the Lord forbids us from misusing His name, He is commanding us to use it rightly, to call upon Him in trouble, to pray to Him and praise Him and to give thanks. "Let your requests be made known to God" (Philippians 4:6). "Pray without ceasing" (1 Thessalonians 5:17). Prayer is not an option.

> "Call upon Me in the day of trouble; I will deliver you, and you shall glorify Me."
> (Psalm 50:15)

The Lord expects and demands that we pray. This command, like every command, shows us our sin. Our weak and faltering prayers are here exposed to us as sin to be confessed. But there is also a gift in this command to pray. The command to pray emboldens us to stand before the Lord and offer our petitions. The command is an invitation. It gives us the comfort that the Lord wants to hear our prayers.

An audience with a king is a rare privilege. This was true in the ancient world and remains true today. You cannot simply walk up to the king's throne and talk to him. A few months ago, a man jumped over the fence of the White House looking for the president. He was not greeted kindly.

The account of Esther illustrates this. Esther was the favorite queen of King Ahasuerus, and though she had great favor with the king, even she could not approach him unless he called her. When Esther's cousin Mordecai learned of a plot to have all the Jews murdered, he asked Esther to intercede for the people. But this was illegal. To go before the king without an invitation was punishable by death. Esther said to Mordecai, "Go, gather all the Jews to be found in Susa, and hold a fast on my behalf, and do not eat or drink for three days, night or day. I and my young women will also fast as you do. Then I will go to the king, though it is against the law, and if I perish, I perish" (Esther 4:16). The king, it turns out, received Esther favorably, listened to her petition, and the Jewish people were preserved. But think of the law that Esther broke. It was illegal to go before the king without an invitation.

In the command to pray, we have the invitation we need to come before the Lord. When the Lord of the universe commands us to pray, He is giving us the beautiful privilege of standing before Him and presenting to Him our petitions and intercessions. His command emboldens us to stand and speak when we should hide in silence. We know that the Holy Trinity wants to hear our prayers. This is the comfort of the command to pray.

THE PROMISE OF PRAYER

Second, there are promises regarding prayer. God promises to hear and answer them. "Call upon Me in the day of trouble; I will deliver you, and you shall glorify Me" (Psalm 50:15).

Jesus gives a wonderful promise regarding prayer in the Sermon on the Mount:

> Ask, and it will be given to you; seek, and you will find; knock, and it will be opened to you. For everyone who asks receives, and the one who seeks finds, and to the one who knocks it will be opened. Or which one of you, if his son asks him for bread, will give him a stone? Or if he asks for a fish, will give him a serpent? If you then, who are evil, know how to give good gifts to your children, how much more will your Father who is in heaven give good things to those who ask Him! (Matthew 7:7–11)

Because God has promised to hear and answer our prayers, we mix our prayers with faith (see James 1:5–8). When we end our prayers with "Amen," we are saying, "Yes, Lord, I truly believe that You have heard my prayers, and that You will answer them."

{ ## Prayer is wrestling with God, grabbing ahold of His promises. }

Jesus gives promise after promise regarding prayer, and this gives us great boldness and confidence in our prayers. He especially promises to hear and answer prayers offered in His name.

> Whatever you ask in My name, this I will do, that the Father may be glorified in the Son. (John 14:13)

> In that day you will ask nothing of Me. Truly, truly, I say to you, whatever you ask of the Father in My name, He will give it to you. (John 16:23)

> In that day you will ask in My name, and I do not say to you that I will ask the Father on your behalf; for the Father Himself loves you, because you have loved Me and have believed that I came from God. (John 16:26–27)

The name of Jesus is not a magic formula. Tacking the words "in Jesus' name" onto the end of our prayers does not give them some sort of extra power to manipulate the will of God. To pray "in the name of Jesus" means to pray according to His will and from His promises. To pray in Jesus' name, then, is to join our prayers to the petitions of the One who "always lives to make intercession for" us (Hebrews

7:25). To pray in the name of Jesus is to pray like Jesus, to pray for the things He prays for, to desire and ask Him for the things He desires to give to us.

This is why we must be taught what to pray for, and this is why Jesus gives us the words to pray. This is why we use the Psalms as a prayer book. Our prayers are being shaped by the words of Scripture and the promises of Jesus. More on this later.

OUR GREAT NEED

We pray for what we need, but because of our fallen condition, we don't always know the things we need. Martin Luther often spoke of our sinful condition as spiritual leprosy. The disease of leprosy destroys the nerves; you can't feel pain. Leprosy makes you so sick, you don't know how sick you are. We are so sick with sin, we don't know the desperate depth of our condition. This affects our prayers. In our sinfulness, we don't know what we need. We don't recognize how desperate our situation is. We don't know what is good for us.

This is the third thing about prayer: Jesus teaches us what we really need in this life.

Even we sinners have some capacity to know what we need. Our stomach is good at letting us know when we need food. It hurts and cramps up. It shouts, "Feed me!" Our stomach, though, cannot tell us what kind of food we need. A Twinkie or a carrot will both do. Our stomach knows it needs food, but it is a vague and inaccurate knowledge. In fact, so imprecise is our stomach that there are many stories of people who died at sea because they could not resist their thirst, and so they drank seawater.

Jesus tells us what we need. He clarifies the unclear preaching of our stomach and teaches us to pray, "Give us this day our daily bread."

Our conscience also tells us when we have sin trouble. The conscience hurts when we sin or when we are sinned against. But like our stomach, the conscience is an imprecise instrument. Left to ourselves, we invent all sorts of things to soothe the pain of our conscience.

Jesus takes the pain of our conscience and turns it into this right and godly petition: "Forgive us our trespasses as we forgive those who trespass against us."

We know that we are tempted and troubled, and that there is evil and danger in the world, but left to ourselves, we would do all sorts of nutty things to stay safe.

Jesus takes our uneasiness and turns it into these right and godly petitions: "Lead us not into temptation, but deliver us from evil."

In other words, Jesus takes our vague pains and haunting uncertainties and shows us what we really need. This is an incredible gift. Jesus teaches us what our real and true needs are in this life. And there are certain things we need of which we are completely ignorant. In fact, these are the things we need most of all, the things we pray for in the first three petitions of the Lord's Prayer. We have no natural capacity to know we need the Lord's name, His kingdom, His Word, and His Spirit.

Imagine the Lord had given us a stomach for His Word, a little stomach behind our ears. If we skipped our morning devotions and prayers, that little ear-stomach would growl at us. If we skipped church, our kids would grab their ear-stomachs and complain, "I'm starving. When are we going to hear a sermon?" If we listened to false doctrine, we would get ear-stomach poisoning, and we'd be up all night vomiting heresy out of our ears. If we had these ear-stomachs, people would be lined up for church. You would have to call ahead to get a reservation for the 9:00 a.m. service. If we had ear-stomachs, the petition "Hallowed be Thy name" would be as natural for us as "Give us this day our daily bread." Alas, we don't have ear-stomachs. We don't hurt when we skip our prayers and devotions. We don't cramp up if we miss church.

The Lord has to teach us what we need most of all: His name, His Word, His kingdom, and His Spirit.

The seven petitions of the Lord's Prayer do this very thing. "Hallowed be Thy name" teaches us that we need the Lord's name and His Word. "Thy kingdom come" teaches us that we need the Lord's Spirit and His Church. "Thy will be done" teaches us that we need the Lord's will, not ours, to be accomplished. Here we learn that we need the Lord's help to overcome the will of the world, the flesh, and the devil.

The devil tries to prevent our prayers with this little trick, "If God knows what is going to happen, then there is no use in praying." Jesus says the exact opposite when He teaches us the Lord's Prayer. "Because God knows everything, including everything you need, therefore pray."

{ "Do not be like them, for your Father knows what you need before you ask Him. Pray then like this: 'Our Father in heaven . . .' "
(Matthew 6:8–9) }

The Lord knows what we need and teaches us to pray for those very things. Before the petitions of the Lord's Prayer (and the Psalms) become our prayers to God, they are first His Word to us, teaching us what we need and, gloriously, what He wants to give us.

We pray because we are needy. We pray because we cannot manage life with our own resources. And the more we learn from the Scriptures of our desperate need for the Lord's help, the more we are driven to the Lord in prayer to find the help we need.

THE WORDS TO SAY

When we pray the Lord's Prayer, the Psalms, and the other prayers of the Bible, we do not amend our prayers with "if it be Your will." When we pray the prayers of the Bible, we know the things we are asking for are, in fact, His will. We know it is the Lord's will to make His name holy with us, to let His kingdom come, to feed us, forgive us, to lead and deliver us. Praying the words the Lord has taught us gives us great confidence in prayer.

One of the marks of American Christian piety is spontaneity in prayer. To be genuine and spiritual, prayer should be from the heart. In other words, for a prayer to be a real prayer, you have to make it up on the spot. There is, of course, nothing wrong with making up a prayer. But the exaltation of spontaneity disparages printed prayers and praying the prayers of Scripture. In fact, there is a subtle disparaging of the Lord's Prayer because it is "rote" and not "heartfelt."

While there is a certain danger that we might become distracted or disengaged while praying from Scripture or reading prayers from a prayer book, this danger does not mean prepared prayers should be thrown out. We have a treasure in the Psalms and the Lord's Prayer. Jesus has given us the very words to pray, and we rightly thank Him for this great gift.

This is the fourth thing we know about prayer: Jesus has taught us the words to say. "Pray then like this, 'Our Father . . .'" (Matthew 6:9). "When you pray, say: 'Father . . .'" (Luke 11:2).

When we are praying the petitions of the Lord's Prayer and the Psalms, we bring our requests before God with great confidence knowing that these are the words He wants to hear from us, the things He wants us to ask for, and the petitions He wants to answer.

You Shall Covet Your Lord's Promises

Prayer is taught.

This is contrary to our thinking. We value impulse, words straight from the heart. We want to be moved, excited, carried along on a wave of semi-ecstasy. The mark of prayer in American Christianity is that no one knows what is about to be prayed, even the person praying. American Christianity with its emphasis on the heart makes prayer an act of extemporaneity.

> "Lord, teach us to pray."
> (Luke 11:1)

On the other hand, if prayer is something taught in the Scriptures, our prayers arise from the richness of the Lord's Word and not the depravity of our own sinful heart. Prayer is not the overflow of our depraved desires but the imprint of the Lord's Word being brought to God. This reorients prayer away from our heart and toward the Scriptures.

When we read the Lord's Word, we hear His voice, the kind voice of our Good Shepherd who tells us of His mercy and love. We hear His commands and promises, and our prayers grow out of this Word. We hear the Law and ask the Lord for His help to repent of our sins and keep His Commandments. We hear the promises of the Gospel, and we ask the Lord to keep His promises with us. We are asking the Lord to give us the things He has promised to give, to do the things He has promised to do, and to act toward us according to His Word.

Paul teaches us to take up the armor of God (Ephesians 6:10–20). He walks through all of our spiritual equipment: the belt of truth, the breastplate of righteousness, the shoes of readiness to speak the Gospel, the shield of faith, and the helmet of salvation. Last on the list is "the sword of the Spirit, which is the word of God." Paul then teaches us how we are to wield this sword, how we are to use the Word of God: "take . . . the sword of the Spirit, which is the word of God, praying at all times in the Spirit, with all prayer and supplication" (vv. 17–18).

WE USE THE LORD'S WORD IN PRAYER!

When we take up the Lord's commands and promises into our prayer and petitions, we beat back the devil.

{ Prayer is taught. }

The Bible also teaches us to be patient in our prayers and persistent. The Lord does not immediately keep His promises.

> And [Jesus] told them a parable to the effect that they ought always to pray and not lose heart. (Luke 18:1)

> I tell you, though he will not get up and give him anything because he is his friend, yet because of his impudence [persistence] he will rise and give him whatever he needs. (Luke 11:8)

We keep asking, keep knocking, keep seeking, not growing weary in our prayers, but taking hold of the Lord according to His Word. Far from some sort of lifeless repetition, when our prayers grow out of the Scripture, we begin to engage with the Lord in a life-giving conversation. Perhaps our best example of persistent clinging to the Lord's promises in prayer is the Canaanite woman who comes to Jesus (Matthew 15:21–28).

This is what we know about her:

- This woman is a Canaanite, that is, she is not a Jew, but a foreigner. This is a big deal here and throughout the New Testament. The foreigners were not part of the Lord's people. They did not participate in the old covenant. They could not enter the temple. They were uncircumcised and unclean. The Israelites did not consider them partakers of the promises God made to Abraham and Moses. They, in fact, despised them. The Canaanites were supposed to be driven from the land as Joshua brought the Lord's people in to possess their inheritance (see, for example, Joshua 3:10). That there were Canaanites still hanging around is testimony to the people of Israel's disobedience of God's command.

- This woman is a mother. She comes to Jesus praying for her daughter. "Have mercy on me, O Lord, Son of David; my daughter is severely oppressed by a demon" (Matthew 15:22). This woman has the great love of a mother for her children.

- This Canaanite woman has some spiritual insight. She knows the thing that troubles her daughter is not a natural illness but a demon.

- This woman had faith, true faith, in Jesus. We don't know how, but the Word of Christ had reached her ears, and she had believed the promises. She trusted that this man was the one sent from God to rescue sinners. She even calls Jesus the "Son of David," showing that she knew something of the promises that the Jewish people were waiting to be fulfilled.

She knew her trouble, she knew her Lord, and she prayed. This is how it is with all prayers. We know our trouble, we know our Lord, and we pray. We know that we are in need of one who can help, and we know who can help us, so we pray. Our troubles teach us to pray. And they teach us to trust the Lord.

Prayer is need and faith put to words. We know the Lord who hears us and loves us will keep His promises. But it's not easy. In fact, I think this text helps us to escape a very mechanical view of prayer and avoid the temptation of considering prayer a lifeless endeavor. When we pray, we are talking to the Father, or to Jesus or the Holy Spirit, to a person, not a cosmic machine.

Look at how it goes with this woman and her prayers. She comes to Jesus with her request, and He flat out ignores her and acts as though He can't hear her.

> And Jesus went away from there and withdrew to the district of Tyre and Sidon. And behold, a Canaanite woman from that region came out and was crying, "Have mercy on me, O Lord, Son

of David; my daughter is severely oppressed by a demon." But He
did not answer her a word. (Matthew 15:21–23)

We might be put off by Jesus' rudeness. She is not. She continues to put her request to Jesus. She knows Him by faith (and not by sight) to be the One who answers prayers. She pesters Jesus so much, the disciples start to pray to Jesus against this woman! "And His disciples came and begged Him, saying, 'Send her away, for she is crying out after us.' He answered, 'I was sent only to the lost sheep of the house of Israel' " (Matthew 15:23–24).

Jesus talks now, but not to the woman. He tells His disciples that His work is for the Jewish people. But this is enough. The Canaanite woman knows Jesus has heard her, and she knows her prayer is halfway answered. "She came and knelt before Him, saying, 'Lord, help me.' And He answered, 'It is not right to take the children's bread and throw it to the dogs' " (Matthew 15:25–26).

It seems like Jesus is being even ruder to the woman. At first He ignored her, and now He is calling her a dog. But in the contest of prayer, the woman has won. Jesus has spoken to her. He's given her a word. She has a word to trust, to believe. He calls her a dog. It looks terrible to us. It looks like an insult, but she receives it as a promise. She clings to it. And she holds Jesus to this word of promise. "She said, 'Yes, Lord, yet even the dogs eat the crumbs that fall from their masters' table' " (Matthew 15:27). "If you will call me a dog, I'll take it. I'll be a dog and ask only for a dog's due, the crumbs from the table."

This is prayer, taking Jesus at His word, holding it, holding Him to it. This woman had Jesus by the word, which is just what He wanted. He turns to her with delight: "Then Jesus answered her, 'O woman, great is your faith! Be it done for you as you desire.' And her daughter was healed instantly" (Matthew 15:28).

What a wonderful and astonishing picture of prayer! This is not the quiet and sentimental deepening of a relationship. This is wrestling with God, clinging to His Word and not letting go until He keeps His promise and gives us a blessing.

The Canaanite woman teaches us how to pray. The Bible comes along and insults us, calling us sinners. Instead of being put off by this, we grab hold of it and ask Jesus to treat us as He treats sinners, to deal with us according to His mercy, to save us, and give us all we need for this life and the next. "Lord, You said that You came to save sinners. If You call me a sinner, I'll be a sinner, a sinner died for by You. Give me what sinners need, and forgive me. Keep Your promises for me."

Praying against the Devil

"Deliver us from evil."

(Matthew 6:13)

We are tempted to think of prayer as a peaceful event. All is calm, all is quiet and serene. We have a sugary and sentimental picture of prayer.

The Bible's teaching is different. Prayer is warfare. We take up the sword of the Spirit, the Word of God, and we pray. When we pray to the Lord, we are praying against the devil. When we pray for the Lord's kingdom, we are praying against the devil's kingdom. When we pray for the Lord's will to be done, we are praying that the will of the world, the flesh, and the devil would come to nothing.

Martin Luther understood that our prayers to the Lord for His kingdom were also against the devil and his kingdom.

> We need to know this: all our shelter and protection rest in prayer alone. For we are far too weak to deal with the devil and all his power and followers who set themselves against us. They might easily crush us under their feet. Therefore, we must consider and take up those weapons with which Christians must be armed in order to stand against the devil [2 Corinthians 10:4; Ephesians 6:11]. For what do you imagine has done such great things up till now? What has stopped or quelled the counsels, purposes, murder, and riot of our enemies, by which the devil thought he would crush us, together with the Gospel? It was the prayer of a few godly people standing in the middle like an iron wall for our side. Otherwise they would have witnessed a far different tragedy. They would have seen how the devil would have destroyed all Germany in its own blood. But now our enemies may confidently ridicule prayer and make a mockery of it. However, we shall still be a match both for them and the devil by prayer alone, if we only persevere diligently and do not become slack. For whenever a godly Christian prays, "Dear Father, let Your will be done" [see Matthew 6:10], God speaks from on high and says, "Yes, dear child, it shall be so, in spite of the devil and all the world." (LC III 30–32)

Prayer is an act of subversion, an act of treason against the world, an act of rebellion against the devil.

When we are baptized in the Lord's name and transferred into His kingdom, we are also set against the devil and his kingdom of darkness. When Jesus calls us His friends, He makes us the devil's enemies. To be marked with the cross of Christ is to be tattooed with a target for the devil's assaults. We are, therefore, at war, and we wage this war with the Word of God and prayer.

> If we would be Christians, therefore, we must surely expect and count on having the devil with all his angels and the world as our enemies [Matthew 25:41; Revelation 12:9]. They will bring every possible misfortune and grief upon us. For where God's Word is preached, accepted, or believed and produces fruit, there the holy cross cannot be missing [Acts 14:22]. And let no one think that he shall have peace [Matthew 10:34]. He must risk whatever he has upon earth—possessions, honor, house and estate, wife and children, body and life. Now, this hurts our flesh and the old Adam [Ephesians 4:22]. The test is to be steadfast and to suffer with patience [James 5:7–8] in whatever way we are assaulted, and to let go whatever is taken from us [1 Peter 2:20–21]. (LC III 65–66)

{ Prayer is warfare. }

Prayer, then, is our fighting back against the troubles of this life. "Pray" is the positive side of the negative command "Do not worry" (which accounts for the close proximity of Jesus' sermons on prayer and worry in the Sermon on the Mount; compare Matthew 6:7–14 and vv. 25–34). Peter and Paul both admonish us to turn our worry into prayer:

> The Lord is at hand; do not be anxious about anything, but in everything by prayer and supplication with thanksgiving let your requests be made known to God. And the peace of God, which surpasses all understanding, will guard your hearts and your minds in Christ Jesus. (Philippians 4:5–7)

[Cast] all your anxieties on Him, because He cares for you.
(1 Peter 5:7)

Prayer undermines panic. Prayer is a confession that the Lord's promises are true, that His goodness is for us. Worry and anxiety are reminders to pray, and prayer is the antidote to worry.

We live our lives in faith toward God and love toward our neighbor. Our prayers follow the same contours. We pray in faith, trusting the Lord's promises, and we pray for our neighbors. Our prayers are our first good works for our neighbor.

In this way, we also understand prayer as the beginning of what we normally call "evangelism." It is the Christian's desire that more and more sinners would be rescued from the grasp of hell and delivered from their sins through faith in Christ. Knowing conversion of the sinner is the Lord's work, the Church begins the task of evangelism by praying and asking that the Lord's will would be done, that His kingdom would come, that the preaching of His Word would bear the fruit He promised it would (see Isaiah 55:10–11).

THERE IS A "MISSION PANIC" OR "EVANGELISM CRISIS"

that grips American Christianity. Scare tactics are used to motivate and move people, to get them busy doing churchy, evangelistic stuff. American Christianity often invites worry and even fear over the lost condition of sinners. Jesus has not authorized us to worry. He has not sanctioned us to be afraid. He has told us to pray, to love, to fight against the devil, and to trust that He rules and reigns all things for the sake of His Church (see Ephesians 1:22–23).

Crisis, panic, and fear all undermine God's ordering of the world. The Evangelism Crisis is no exception. In God's ordering of the world, preachers preach, parents teach their children the words of Scripture, and friends serve one another in love and speak of the Lord's mercy in their conversations. This good order of things is broken up by the Evangelism Crisis. In a crisis, everyone is a minister, everyone is a missionary, everyone is a preacher and evangelist. American Christianity lives in this crisis mode. Every conversation must be about "sharing Jesus," every act of love must be motivated toward conversion, and the normal stuff of daily living is put on the back burner to serve the urgency of the mission.

This is evangelism motivated by worry and mission driven by anxiety. It is not what is taught by Jesus. Worry and anxiety are undone by prayer. "Thy kingdom come" is a confession that the coming of the Kingdom and the growth of the Church is the Lord's work, not ours. Paul reminded the Corinthians,

> I planted, Apollos watered, but God gave the growth. So neither he who plants nor he who waters is anything, but only God who gives the growth. He who plants and he who waters are one, and each will receive his wages according to his labor. For we are God's fellow workers. You are God's field, God's building. (1 Corinthians 3:6–9)

Faith sets us free to live freely in our vocations, free to love our neighbor without worry, free to speak the Lord's Law and Gospel to our neighbor without panic, and free to fight against the devil in the confidence that his kingdom is already destroyed (Hebrews 2:14).

Faith prays. Christians live in the confidence that the Lord delights in us, that He helps us, that He keeps us and never leaves us. We know that in all the storms and troubles of life and death, God's grace cannot fail. He hears us. He loves us. And He delights in being our Savior.

CHAPTER TEN

THE END OF THE WORLD AS WE KNOW IT

"Now when these things begin to take place, straighten up and raise your heads, because your redemption is drawing near."

(Luke 21:28)

AMERICAN CHRISTIANITY IS OBSESSED WITH THE END TIMES.

It is part of the "crisis" mentality discussed in the previous chapter. American Christianity is filled with "prophecy buffs" and teachers who preach with the Bible in one hand and the newspaper in the other. There is always an eye on current events looking for prophetic fulfillment. In fact, American Christianity is largely caught up in a particular view of the last things called "dispensational premillennialism," a theological system that colors its understanding of the Scriptures. American Christianity, at every turn, fails to distinguish between the Law and the Gospel, and its teaching of the end times is no exception.

The Lord's Church has always lived in the hope of Jesus' return. We live in the "last days" (see Hebrews 1:2), which were inaugurated at His ascension. Jesus promised time and again that He will return to the earth in great glory to raise the dead and judge all people. His return marks the end of this age and the beginning of the new heaven and the new earth where righteousness lives (2 Peter 3:13). His return will be sudden—a horror to all who live confident in their own goodness, but joy and comfort for those who long for His appearing (2 Timothy 4:8). The return of Jesus is the great hope and longing of His people. His coming is the culmination of our salvation; it is our redemption drawing near (Luke 21:28).

The preaching of Jesus' return is a preaching of Law and Gospel, both warning and comfort.

First, the warning. This normally comes to us as the command to "be ready." "Therefore you also must be ready, for the Son of Man is coming at an hour you do not expect" (Matthew 24:44). "And what I say to you I say to all: Stay awake" (Mark

13:37). "But stay awake at all times, praying that you may have strength to escape all these things that are going to take place, and to stand before the Son of Man" (Luke 21:36). The Last Day will be a surprise, and the Christian is warned in order that we would not be caught in sin and debauchery, but rather doing the work the Lord has put before us.

> But the day of the Lord will come like a thief, and then the heavens will pass away with a roar, and the heavenly bodies will be burned up and dissolved, and the earth and the works that are done on it will be exposed.
>
> Since all these things are thus to be dissolved, what sort of people ought you to be in lives of holiness and godliness, waiting for and hastening the coming of the day of God, because of which the heavens will be set on fire and dissolved, and the heavenly bodies will melt as they burn! (2 Peter 3:10–12)

Jesus cannot lie. We know He will return. So we encourage one another to faith and love and good deeds. "And let us consider how to stir up one another to love and good works, not neglecting to meet together, as is the habit of some, but encouraging one another, and all the more as you see the Day drawing near" (Hebrews 10:24–25).

We are warned about the second coming because that day will be a day of wrath and judgment for those not covered in the robe of Christ's righteousness.

> Who then is the faithful and wise servant, whom his master has set over his household, to give them their food at the proper time? Blessed is that servant whom his master will find so doing when he comes. Truly, I say to you, he will set him over all his possessions. But if that wicked servant says to himself, "My master is delayed," and begins to beat his fellow servants and eats and drinks with drunkards, the master of that servant will come on a day when he does not expect him and at an hour he does not know and will cut him in pieces and put him with the hypocrites. In that place there will be weeping and gnashing of teeth. (Matthew 24:45–51)

Jesus intends for us to be warned and ready for His second coming because He loves us and desires our salvation. This is the good news of the Last Day. When Jesus returns, it is to rescue and deliver us, not to punish and destroy us. Especially as we labor under the toil and tears and troubles of this life, the temptations, the weakness, the darkness of death, and the pain of our sins, we look to the Last Day with hopeful expectation, "waiting for our blessed hope, the appearing of the glory of our great God and Savior Jesus Christ" (Titus 2:13).

The return of Jesus is our "blessed hope" because our sins are forgiven. Apart from the grace of God, the Last Day is a day of terror and wrath. But not for Christians. The Day of Judgment does not frighten us, because Christ has died. Jesus took our condemnation in His death on the cross. There is no judgment or condemnation for the Lord's Christians (see John 5:24; Romans 8:1). His return, then, is our salvation. "Christ, having been offered once to bear the sins of many, will appear a second time, not to deal with sin but to save those who are eagerly waiting for Him" (Hebrews 9:28). This is why Jesus tells us not to run for the hills or hide in fear, but to "lift up our heads." The One who died for us is the One returning for us. The One who suffered for our sins is the One coming to deliver us. "Straighten up and raise your heads, because your redemption is drawing near" (Luke 21:28).

In His life, death, and resurrection, Jesus made a place for us in His kingdom. He will return to take us to that place, the eternal home of blessedness.

> Let not your hearts be troubled. Believe in God; believe also in Me. In My Father's house are many rooms. If it were not so, would I have told you that I go to prepare a place for you? And if I go and prepare a place for you, I will come again and will take you to Myself, that where I am you may be also. (John 14:1–2)

Our hope is not simply to be in heaven, or even to make it to the resurrection. Our great hope is to be with Jesus, to dwell where He dwells, and this is exactly what He promises us.

The teaching of the last things is called "eschatology" from the Greek *eschaton*, "last things." We will consider in this chapter the end of all things, the return of Jesus in glory, and the different teachings in the Church about this great Last Day.

{ Jesus intends for us to be warned and ready for His second coming. }

In the Nicene Creed, the Church confesses in simplicity and hope, "He will come again with glory to judge both the living and the dead."

The simplicity of this doctrine has been changed, expanded, and exalted in American Christianity. Congregations who are typically wary of creeds and precise theological articulation make their particular eschatological system a matter of church fellowship. American Christianity has its own dictionary of theological buzzwords dealing with its unique eschatology. Rapture, dispensationalism, pre-trib (or post-trib or mid-trib), great tribulation, the thousand-year reign, and such are the code words for the eschatologically orthodox. American Christianity might not be clear in its teaching that Jesus is both God and man, but it is very clear in confessing that the rapture will be before the tribulation. American Christianity has a very peculiar and strange teaching concerning the end times. It's a great irony that the nuttiest teaching of American Christianity's theology is the rally point upon which its pastors become most insistent on theological agreement.

I know something of this. I was taught to expect the secret rapture of the Church and the thousand-year reign of Jesus on the Church. I was taught that the reconstitution of Israel as a nation in 1948 was the fulfillment of biblical prophecy, as was the establishment of the United Nations. When I learned that the Lutherans didn't teach the pre-tribulation rapture (I'll explain the vocabulary in the coming sections), I almost gave up on them. When I learned that the Lutherans had a different understanding of the thousand-year reign of Christ, I was so distressed that I almost never went back.

I hope, in this chapter, to unfold a biblical eschatology and dispel a number of the non-biblical teachings that have made their way into American Christianity. In the end, the scriptural truths deliver comfort and hope in the Lord's promised return.

> But you are not in darkness, brothers, for that day to surprise you like a thief. For you are all children of light, children of the day. We are not of the night or of the darkness. So then let us not sleep, as others do, but let us keep awake and be sober. For those who sleep, sleep at night, and those who get drunk, are drunk at

night. But since we belong to the day, let us be sober, having put on the breastplate of faith and love, and for a helmet the hope of salvation. For God has not destined us for wrath, but to obtain salvation through our Lord Jesus Christ, who died for us so that whether we are awake or asleep we might live with Him. Therefore encourage one another and build one another up, just as you are doing. (1 Thessalonians 5:4–11)

ONE THOUSAND YEARS OF WHAT?

There are about five different eschatological schools of thought. These grow, chiefly, out of different understandings of a singular passage in the Book of Revelation. Revelation 20:1–10 tells of a one-thousand-year time in which the devil will be bound and the saints will reign with Christ. This one thousand years is called the millennium (from the Latin *mille*, thousand, and *annus*, year). How you understand the millennium relative to today and the second coming determines which school of thought you fall into.

> "Blessed and holy is the one who shares in the first resurrection! Over such the second death has no power, but they will be priests of God and of Christ, and they will reign with Him for a thousand years."
> (Revelation 20:6)

- Premillennialism teaches that Jesus will return to establish His kingdom on the earth.

- Postmillennialism teaches that Jesus will return after a one-thousand-year golden age, which is yet to come.

- Amillennialism (or realized millennialism) teaches that the one thousand years is a description of the time between Jesus' ascension and return.

Most of American Christianity is premillennial (and, in fact, a specific type of premillennialism called "dispensational premillennialism"; more on dispensationalism in the next section). It is a good bet that if you hear a preacher on the radio or television talking about the end times, this teacher is a premillennialist and he is putting forward this teaching as if it was the only way of reading the Bible.

Premillennialists teach that the world is entering a particularly difficult time, that various political events are fulfillment of Bible prophecy, and that Jesus will return to establish an earthly kingdom where He will rule and reign from the throne of David in Jerusalem. In the millennium, people will live to an extreme old age, there will be peace among the nations, and almost everyone will be holy—at least until the end of this thousand years when the devil will be loosed to lead a rebellion against the Lord and His people. When Jesus puts down this last rebellion, He will cast the devil and all his followers into the lake of fire; there will be the resurrection and the last judgment; and after these things, the eternal state will begin. This, at least, is the chronology of the premillennialists. It is not what the Scriptures teach.

We consider the text of Revelation 20 and use Scripture to interpret Scripture. Here is the text:

> Then I saw an angel coming down from heaven, holding in his hand the key to the bottomless pit and a great chain. And he seized the dragon, that ancient serpent, who is the devil and Satan, and bound him for a thousand years, and threw him into the pit, and shut it and sealed it over him, so that he might not deceive the nations any longer, until the thousand years were ended. After that he must be released for a little while.
>
> Then I saw thrones, and seated on them were those to whom the authority to judge was committed. Also I saw the souls of those who had been beheaded for the testimony of Jesus and for the word of God, and those who had not worshiped the beast or its image and had not received its mark on their foreheads or their hands. They came to life and reigned with Christ for a thousand years. The rest of the dead did not come to life until the thousand years were ended. This is the first resurrection. Blessed and holy is the one who shares in the first resurrection! Over such the second death has no power, but they will be priests of God and of Christ, and they will reign with Him for a thousand years. (Revelation 20:1–6)

We will ask two questions that will help open up this text from Revelation.

1. What does the rest of the Bible say about one thousand years?

2. What does the rest of the Bible say about the binding of the devil?

First, what about one thousand years? Should we understand this as a literal one thousand years? Our preference is always to read the Bible as literally as possible, but we also want to understand the text in its context. John, in Revelation (as is in the other apocalyptic texts of the Bible), uses numbers to capture an idea. If we interpret the numbers as a symbol, we are, in fact, understanding the number as John intended it to be understood.

It turns out that the Bible often uses the number 1,000 in a symbolic sense. For example, "For every beast of the forest is Mine, the cattle on a thousand hills" (Psalm 50:10).

What about the cattle on the 1,001st hill? It, too, certainly belongs to the Lord. In fact, all the cattle on all the hills belong to the Lord. That is the point. "A thousand" is used to capture the completeness of the Lord's rule and His utter lack of need. "If I were hungry, I would not tell you, for the world and its fullness is Mine" (Psalm 50:12).

"He is the LORD our God; His judgments are in all the earth. He remembers His covenant forever, the word that He commanded, for a thousand generations" (Psalm 105:7–8). Does the Lord forget His promise on the 1,001st generation? Certainly not. In fact, if we take this to mean a literal one thousand generations, we would be in trouble. According to the Scriptures, we are probably less than two hundred generations from Adam. We are nowhere close to one thousand generations, which would mean (if we read this to mean a literal thousand generations) that this world would need another thirty-two thousand years before the Lord could, in fact, keep this promise. The "thousand generations" of Psalm 105 is to be understood as "forever." The Lord will never forget His covenant.

There are three times that the Bible speaks of "a thousand years": Psalm 90:4; 2 Peter 3:8; and Revelation 20:1–10.

Psalm 90 is the oldest Psalm, the only psalm of Moses. It is a prayer about the mortality of man and the mercy of God. We pray Psalm 90 in the funeral liturgy, sometimes as the lid of the casket is closed before the service. Verse 4 reads, "For a thousand years in Your sight are but as yesterday when it is past, or as a watch in the night." No man ever lived to one thousand years. Methuselah, the oldest we know of, lived to the ripe old age of 969 (Genesis 5:27). But even this great age of a man is nothing to the Lord. One thousand years is as a day, like a few hours. All of the great achievements of man are nothing at all, and we all waste away. This is certainly a symbolic use of "a thousand years."

The second use of "a thousand years" is 2 Peter 3:8, where Peter quotes Psalm 90.

> But do not overlook this one fact, beloved, that with the Lord one day is as a thousand years, and a thousand years as one day. The Lord is not slow to fulfill His promise as some count slowness, but is patient toward you, not wishing that any should perish, but that all should reach repentance. But the day of the Lord will come like a thief, and then the heavens will pass away with a roar, and the heavenly bodies will be burned up and dissolved, and the earth and the works that are done on it will be exposed. (2 Peter 3:8–10)

Notice how Peter uses the text from Psalm 90 to describe the Lord's patience. We expect the return of Jesus at any moment, but the Lord is patient. He desires that none should perish. He waits. Peter uses "a thousand years" to describe the time of the Lord's patient mercy before the second coming of Jesus. The Scriptures consistently use a thousand, and specifically "a thousand years," to indicate the fullness and completeness of something. When we come to the one thousand years of Revelation, we have the same thing. The one thousand years indicates the full and complete time of the Lord's ruling and reigning. In fact, it seems like John is using the phrase the same way Peter did (in 2 Peter 3:8–10), as a description of the Lord's patience between the ascension and second coming.

{ We expect the return of Jesus at any moment, but the Lord waits. }

Using Scripture to interpret Scripture, we understand the one thousand years of Revelation not as a chronological demarcation but as a theological indication of the complete patience of the Lord before His return.

Our second question for Revelation 20 is this: What does the rest of the Bible say about the binding of the devil?

The binding of the devil marks the beginning of the millennium.

> Then I saw an angel coming down from heaven, holding in his hand the key to the bottomless pit and a great chain. And he seized the dragon, that ancient serpent, who is the devil and Satan, and bound him for a thousand years, and threw him into the pit, and shut it and sealed it over him, so that he might not deceive the nations any longer, until the thousand years were ended. After that he must be released for a little while. (Revelation 20:1–3)

If we can determine from other biblical texts when the devil is bound, we will be able to determine when the millennium begins. We should not be surprised that this event is spoken of throughout the New Testament.

American Christianity teaches that the binding of the devil is a future event. It is something that will be accomplished when Jesus returns in glory. The Scriptures, on the other hand, constantly put before us the cross of Jesus as the binding of the devil.

Jesus attracted the demons. The demons make occasional appearances in the Old Testament and the Book of Acts, but they are swarming in the Gospels. Jesus is to the demons like the porch light is to moths. And Jesus fights and contends with the demons. He casts them out and sends them off. He, with authority, sets people free from the influence and trouble of the demons.

The Pharisees noticed this and accused Jesus of deriving His authority from the demons. Jesus responds with an argument and a parable.

> If Satan has risen up against himself and is divided, he cannot stand, but is coming to an end. But no one can enter a strong man's house and plunder his goods, unless he first binds the strong man. Then indeed he may plunder his house. (Mark 3:26–27; and see the parallels in Matthew 12:29 and Luke 11:21–22)

The parable is this: the devil is the strong man. His house is the world. His goods are the unbelieving people throughout the world. The thief is Jesus, who binds the devil in order to rescue sinners from the devil's kingdom and transfer them into His own kingdom (see Colossians 1:13). Jesus talks of His earthly ministry as a "binding" of the devil.

This is confirmed by John in his first epistle. "The reason the Son of God appeared was to destroy the works of the devil" (1 John 3:8). Jesus came, John teaches, to "destroy the works of the devil." Notice, if Jesus *did not* manage to destroy the devil, then He did not finish the work He came to do.

Perhaps the clearest and most profound text in this regard is Hebrews 2. Jesus, Hebrews tells us, is greater than the angels, but still He humbled Himself to be our brother. He has taken on our humanity, our flesh and blood, in order to save and deliver us.

> Since therefore the children share in flesh and blood, He Himself likewise partook of the same things, that through death He might destroy the one who has the power of death, that is, the devil, and deliver all those who through fear of death were subject to lifelong slavery. (Hebrews 2:14–15)

This text is loaded with teaching and loaded with comfort. We are the children of flesh and blood. Jesus, in His incarnation, takes flesh and blood upon Himself in order to die. Notice the result of His death: "through death He might destroy the one who has the power of death, that is, the devil." There is no confusion here: the death of Jesus is the destruction of the devil.

American Christianity objects to this teaching. "Look around! Things are going to pot. This world is falling apart. A glance at the newspaper or ten minutes of the evening news will convince us that the devil is alive and well." This is a theological argument that presumes we can determine spiritual truths with our eyes. We call this theology "Look-Aroundism." We look around to see how it is with the devil, how it is with Jesus, how it is with us. The Look-Aroundist concludes that the devil is loose, ruling, and reigning. The Look-Aroundist assumes that the Lord Jesus must not be on the throne and that the devil is not at all bound.

Hebrews 2 wonderfully anticipates this objection. Quoting Psalm 8, the author notes:

> "You made Him for a little while lower than the angels; You have crowned Him with glory and honor, putting everything in sub-

jection under His feet." Now in putting everything in subjection
to Him, He left nothing outside His control. At present, we do not
yet see everything in subjection to Him. (Hebrews 2:7–8)

Everything is subject to Jesus. All things are under His control. The universe is
under His feet. But notice, "At present, we do not yet *see* everything in subjection
to Him." We see destruction. We see death. We see darkness and trouble. What we
see does, indeed, look like we are living in the devil's kingdom, but this is not true.
Jesus, by His death, has destroyed him "who had the power of death, that is, the
devil." The disorder and turmoil of this world are more of the devil's lies to tempt
us to unbelief and despair.

The Scriptures give us the good news that the Lamb of God, our Jesus, sits on
the throne. The One who died for us now rules and reigns for us. The One who did
not spare His life now orders this world for the good of those who love Him and are
called according to His purpose (Romans 8:28). Jesus triumphed over the devil and
the demons in His death, making a public spectacle of them (Colossians 2:13–15).

Now let's revisit the one thousand years of Revelation 20. Understanding from
the Scriptures how to read the one thousand years and the binding of the devil,
we see that the millennium begins with the death and resurrection of Jesus and
extends until His return. We are in the millennium. And we find ourselves in this
text. We are those who have partaken of the first resurrection by our Baptism (Romans 6:3–4). We are those who rule and reign with Christ! Jesus had made us, His
Church, a kingdom (Revelation 1:5–6), and by faith we are "seated . . . with Him in
the heavenly places in Christ Jesus" (Ephesians 2:6).

What a comforting privilege. Indeed, all things are ours. "For all things are
yours, whether Paul or Apollos or Cephas or the world or life or death or the present or the future—all are yours, and you are Christ's, and Christ is God's" (1 Corinthians 3:21–23). We do not yet see all these things, but we know them by faith, and
when the Last Day comes, we will know them by sight.

Rather than a description of a kingdom to come, the thousand years of Revelation is a beautiful and glorious description of right now, the spiritual reality of the
Church's victory over death and the devil, and our privileged position as Christ's
friends in His kingdom of grace.

DISPENSATIONALISM: WHAT AND WHY NOT?

> "But now in Christ Jesus you who once were far off have been brought near by the blood of Christ. For He Himself is our peace, who has made us both one and has broken down in His flesh the dividing wall of hostility."
>
> (Ephesians 2:13–14)

"Dispensational premillennialism" is a mouthful. This is the name of the theological system that has captured the imagination of American Christianity. Even if you have never heard the name, you most likely will have heard of the teachings. If you've seen the bumper sticker "In Case of Rapture This Car Will Be Unmanned," you've seen the theology of dispensational premillennialism. The "secret rapture of the Church," the Left Behind books and movies, Christian Zionism, and the understanding that the modern nation-state of Israel is a fulfillment of biblical prophecy are all part of the theological uniqueness of dispensational premillennialism.

I was a dispensationalist long before I knew that word. In fact, I think most of American Christianity is dispensational by default; they have never heard any other teaching about the last days. American Christians grow up hearing about the rapture, listening to preachers with the Bible in one hand and the newspaper in the other showing us how biblical prophecy was being fulfilled in the geopolitical machinations in the Middle East. The first time I went to Israel, I distinctly remember thinking, I will see Bible prophecy being fulfilled before my eyes.

Dispensationalism takes the premillennial outline of the end times (discussed in the previous section) and overlays a number of theological presuppositions. Dispensationalism is much more than an eschatology; it is an entire system of doctrine that touches on salvation, the Scriptures, and the Gospel. We can identify three assertions that the dispensationalists claim make their theology unique:

FIRST, DISPENSATIONALISTS MAKE A DISTINCTION BETWEEN ISRAEL AND THE CHURCH.

They teach that Israel is the earthly people of God and the Church is the heavenly people. According to dispensationalists, God works differently in the different "dispensations" of history. In the Old Testament, He had a particular plan to save His people through works and sacrifices. When the Jewish people rejected Jesus as their Messiah, the Lord switched to "plan B," the crucifixion and the establishment of the New Testament Church. This is a shocking thing for most nondispensational Christians to hear. How could the death and resurrection of Jesus be "plan B"?

Some dispensationalists, embarrassed by this teaching, have modified their doctrine and tried to bring the works of God in the Old and New Testament into unity. This is "modified" or "moderated dispensationalism." This theological adjustment is good and should be carried to its conclusion, namely, the abandonment of dispensationalism altogether.

Dispensationalism builds a wall between Israel and the Christian Church. Jesus, the Scriptures teach, tears that wall down:

> Therefore remember that at one time you Gentiles in the flesh . . . were at that time separated from Christ, alienated from the commonwealth of Israel and strangers to the covenants of promise, having no hope and without God in the world. But now in Christ Jesus you who once were far off have been brought near by the blood of Christ. For He Himself is our peace, who has made us both one and has broken down in His flesh the dividing wall of hostility by abolishing the law of commandments expressed in ordinances, that He might create in Himself one new man in place of the two, so making peace, and might reconcile us both to God in one body through the cross, thereby killing the hostility. And He came and preached peace to you who were far off and peace to those who were near. For through Him we both have access in one Spirit to the Father. So then you are no longer strangers and aliens, but you are fellow citizens with the saints and members of the household of God, built on the foundation of the apostles and prophets, Christ Jesus Himself being the cornerstone, in whom the whole structure, being joined together, grows into a holy temple in the Lord. In Him you also are being built together into a dwelling place for God by the Spirit. (Ephesians 2:11–22)

The second dangerous distinction of dispensationalism is the claim of using a "consistent, literal hermeneutic."

Dispensationalists claim to read the Bible literally. If the text says "one thousand years," it means "one thousand literal, historical years." If the text says the Antichrist will exalt himself in the temple; it must mean the literal temple in Jerusalem. (In fact, the dispensationalists are looking for the rebuilding of the temple in Jerusalem in order to fulfill the prophecy of 2 Thessalonians 2:4.) The trouble with the supposed "consistent, literal hermeneutic" is that it does not match Scripture's own interpretation of itself. The Bible, Old and New Testament, is chiefly a book about Jesus, not about Israel.

Jesus says to the Pharisees, "You search the Scriptures because you think that in them you have eternal life; and it is they that bear witness about Me, yet you refuse to come to Me that you may have life" (John 5:39–40). The testimony and witness of the Scriptures is about Jesus, through and through, from "Moses and all the Prophets" (Luke 24:27; see also vv. 25–26, 44–47). This witness of the entire Scriptures is not only about the person of Jesus but also about His work, suffering, death, and resurrection (see Luke 1:69–71; John 1:45; 5:46; Acts 13:32–33; 26:22–23; Romans 1:2; 3:21; and 1 Corinthians 15:3). The central theme of the Scriptures is the death of Jesus (Genesis 3:15). Jesus is speaking literally when He says, "See, we are going up to Jerusalem, and everything that is written about the Son of Man by the prophets will be accomplished" (Luke 18:31). It is in Jerusalem, in our Lord's passion, death, and resurrection, that the prophetic word finds its completion. The center of the Scriptures and the climax of all history is not the earthly millennium, but the cross and resurrection of Jesus.

The New Testament constantly quotes the Old Testament to show that it is fulfilled in Christ. All the promises of God find their "Yes" in Christ (2 Corinthians 1:20). The Bible teaches us a consistent hermeneutic, and it is Christ. Reading the Bible without Christ is like reading a veiled book, but the veil is lifted when we see the Scriptures are about Jesus (2 Corinthians 3:14–16).

Third, dispensationalists claim that the purpose of history is the glory of God rather than the salvation of mankind.

It doesn't matter, they say, if God condemns us or saves us. He is glorified either way, and that is the point of it all.

The strange and dangerous thing here is pitting these two things, God's glory and man's salvation, against each other. The Bible holds them together. When the angels sing to the shepherds at the birth of Jesus, they hold these two doctrines together. "Glory to God in the highest, and on earth peace among those with whom He is pleased!" (Luke 2:14). Jesus speaks of His cross as His glory: "Now is the Son of Man glorified, and God is glorified in Him. If God is glorified in Him, God will also glorify Him in Himself, and glorify Him at once" (John 13:31–32). When the twenty-four elders around the throne of God in heaven fall down to worship the Lamb who was slain, they put the glory of God and the salvation of humanity together: "Worthy are You to take the scroll and to open its seals, for You were slain, and by Your blood You ransomed people for God from every tribe and language and people and nation, and You have made them a kingdom and priests to our God, and they shall reign on the earth" (Revelation 5:9–10).

Dispensationalism is a doctrine of despair. It fails to read correctly the Scriptures. Instead of distinguishing between Law and Gospel, it makes a false distinction between Israel and the Church. It reads earthly Israel into the Scriptures where it should see Christ. And it drives a wedge between God's glory and man's salvation.

It is a wonderful surprise that Jesus is glorified in saving us! He is exalted on the cross. He is lifted up for our salvation. The purpose of history is both God's glory and man's salvation, and both of these are found on the cross.

RAPTURE, RESURRECTION OF THE LIVING

I remember waiting for the rapture. When I was in American Christianity, that was the thing to do. One year in particular stands out: 1993. I had read an article by a "Bible teacher" who had done the math, and based on the date of Israel's becoming a nation (1948) and the average length of a generation in the Bible, this fellow had figured out that 1993 would be the year that Jesus would return. I knew the Bible said no one will know the day or the hour (Mark 13:32), but it didn't say anything about not knowing the year.

> "For the Lord Himself will descend from heaven with a cry of command, with the voice of an archangel, and with the sound of the trumpet of God. And the dead in Christ will rise first."
>
> (1 Thessalonians 4:16)

I remember my anxiousness as the year wound down. After Christmas, I knew there were only six days left. Then came New Year's Eve, and I knew Jesus was coming that day. Night came, so I knew I would be raptured out of bed. The morning came. You can imagine my disappointment until I realized, "It could still be 1993 somewhere in the world." I only had to wait a few more minutes until the rapture.

My experience is not unique. While it is not true that all rapture teachers are setting dates and predicting times, it *is* true that the teaching of the rapture drums up a kind of eschatological frenzy. This is how the relatively new and obscure teaching of the secret rapture has become one of the most popular teachings in many churches and is the backbone of any number of books, movies, and bumper stickers. Most evangelicals who write or speak on the subject of prophecy assume that the key end-time event for Christians is the secret rapture. What is the popular teaching of the rapture? Is it biblical? And, how are we to understand the second coming of our Lord Jesus?

I've already mentioned this popular bumper sticker: "Warning: In Case of Rapture This Car Will Be Unmanned." My wife had one of these on her first car. This friendly warning told all those around her to look out. If the rapture happened while she was driving down the interstate, there would be no one to steer or stop, and the car would go careening into the oncoming traffic. Thus the seven-year tribulation would begin with monstrous traffic jams.

According to the dispensationalist view, the coming of Jesus will happen at two separate times. In the first, Jesus will come secretly, returning halfway to earth to snatch away all Christians to heaven. The true believers will suddenly disappear, while the unbelievers will be "left behind" to receive a second chance. During the following seven-year period, it is said, the Antichrist will come into power. God will select and seal the 144,000 Jews who will then take the Gospel to the whole world, converting countless souls to Christ. After those seven years of tribulation and trouble, Jesus will then come in all power and glory—His second coming. Christ will rule directly over the earth from the throne of David in Jerusalem. Those who ultimately reject Christ even after the rapture and tribulation will be judged and destroyed.

The very popular Left Behind books begin with the rapture and people disappearing from planes, cars, and their beds. A baby disappears from the birth canal and (in a generous ecumenical touch) the pope goes missing, secretly and silently raptured.

Many corners of American Christianity are obsessed with the secret rapture.

Yet this is not what the Bible teaches about the Last Day and Jesus' second coming.

There are two texts to consider: 1 Corinthians 15:50–52 and 1 Thessalonians 4:13–18. Both of these texts are used to teach the secret rapture. Both of these texts have nothing to do with a secret rapture at all. Both are about the resurrection.

When the Scriptures speak of the Last Day and Jesus' second coming, they speak of two major events: the resurrection of the dead and the judgment. Almost every warning, promise, and parable of the second coming concerns these two events. It is troublesome that the Church has lost her robust confession of the resurrection of the body and now tends to speak of our eternal soul in heaven as the end of all things. When Jesus returns to the earth, He will call forth the dead bodies of all people, will reunite them with their souls, and then usher the believers in Him into the eternal new heaven and earth. The Lord's Church will dwell in the resurrection in peace and bliss with the Lord forever.

The resurrection of the dead, then, is central in the teaching of the second coming. When Jesus returns, those who have died will be called out of the grave. The question then arises: What about those who are still alive when Jesus returns? How will they be resurrected? Will Jesus put them to death so that He can raise them to life? Or will they miss the resurrection all together? These are the questions that Paul is answering in these two texts.

First, consider 1 Corinthians 15:50–52:

> I tell you this, brothers: flesh and blood cannot inherit the kingdom of God, nor does the perishable inherit the imperishable. Behold! I tell you a mystery. We shall not all sleep, but we shall all be changed, in a moment, in the twinkling of an eye, at the last trumpet. For the trumpet will sound, and the dead will be raised imperishable, and we shall be changed.

After discussing the resurrection of the dead for the entire chapter, Paul now takes up the question of those who are alive when Jesus returns. He starts by restating the theological problem: "flesh and blood cannot inherit the kingdom of God."

In other words, we who are alive cannot simply walk into the new heaven and the new earth. Our corruption is unfit for eternity. We must first be resurrected, given incorruptible and immortal bodies if we want to enter the eternal kingdom of God.

How will we be given resurrected bodies? "Behold! I tell you a mystery. We shall not all sleep" (i.e., die in the faith), "but we shall all be changed." We who are alive will, along with those who sleep in the grave, be changed. This, then, is how we want to understand the scriptural teaching of the "rapture": it is the mystery of the resurrection of the living, the instantaneous changing into immortal resurrected bodies of those who are alive when Jesus returns. Paul explicitly states this in verse 52: "For the trumpet will sound, and the dead will be raised imperishable, and we shall be changed." We see these two things together, the resurrection of the dead and the "rapture," the resurrection of the living.

Notice also that instead of being a precursor event of an unfolding apocalyptic scenario, the rapture is concurrent with the last trumpet and the resurrection of the dead. Also notice that there is nothing secret about this event. The trumpet of God is sounding, announcing the Last Day.

Second, consider 1 Thessalonians 4:13–18. Paul is answering the same question as before: "How will the living be resurrected?"

> But we do not want you to be uninformed, brothers, about those who are asleep, that you may not grieve as others do who have no hope. For since we believe that Jesus died and rose again, even so, through Jesus, God will bring with Him those who have fallen asleep. For this we declare to you by a word from the Lord, that we who are alive, who are left until the coming of the Lord, will not precede those who have fallen asleep. For the Lord Himself will descend from heaven with a cry of command, with the voice of an archangel, and with the sound of the trumpet of God. And the dead in Christ will rise first. Then we who are alive, who are left, will be caught up together with them in the clouds to meet the Lord in the air, and so we will always be with the Lord. Therefore encourage one another with these words.

Paul talks of two groups of people: those who have fallen asleep (died in the faith) and those who are alive. The dead will rise first (the resurrection of the dead), and "then we who are alive, who are left, will be caught up together with them in the clouds to meet the Lord in the air." The living will be brought up into the clouds to meet with the Lord. We see again that the rapture is the mystery of the resurrection of the living, the means by which Jesus makes fit for eternity those who are alive when He returns.

Also note again that the rapture is concurrent with Jesus' return and the resurrection of the dead. And finally note that Paul seems to take pains in this text to indicate that this event is the precise opposite of a secret. Jesus shouts, the archangel shouts, and God Himself blows the trumpet.

The phrase "left behind" comes from Jesus' teaching concerning His second coming in Matthew 24–25. He says,

> But concerning that day and hour no one knows, not even the angels of heaven, nor the Son, but the Father only. For as were the days of Noah, so will be the coming of the Son of Man. For as in those days before the flood they were eating and drinking, marrying and giving in marriage, until the day when Noah entered the ark, and they were unaware until the flood came and swept them all away, so will be the coming of the Son of Man. Then two men will be in the field; one will be taken and one left. Two women will be grinding at the mill; one will be taken and one left. Therefore, stay awake, for you do not know on what day your Lord is coming. (Matthew 24:36–42)

Teachers of the secret rapture point to this text and say, "Look, there it is. People will be going about their business, and one will disappear. That's the secret rapture." But on closer examination, we see that Jesus is teaching the opposite.

The idea that those who are not taken to the Lord will go about wondering what happened to their friends is nowhere in the text, as if those who were swept away by the flood were puzzled over the whereabouts of Noah. In the days of Noah, the flood came and *took away* all the unbelievers. So it will be on the Last Day. Jesus will return, and the unbelievers will be *taken away* in judgment. To be taken away is the bad thing. To be left behind is what we want, to stand before the Lord in His glory.

This text is a picture of the judgment and separation. Like those who were destroyed by the flood, like the unfaithful servant who is cut in two (Matthew 24:51), like the foolish virgins who are locked out of the wedding (Matthew 25:11–12), like the wicked and lazy steward who is cast into outer darkness (Matthew 25:30), and like the sheep who are sent away (Matthew 25:41), so will be the unbelievers who are in the field or at the grindstone; they will be taken away in judgment.

In referring to the days of Noah, Jesus is teaching that His coming in glory and judgment will be totally unexpected by the unbelieving world. Jesus will return with such severe swiftness that unbelievers won't even have time to stop what they are doing before they know the brunt of God's wrath.

The believer, on the other hand, will escape God's wrath through the blood of His Son, our Lord Jesus. Jesus has been judged and has suffered God's wrath in our place. Like Noah and his family who escaped the flood, like the faithful servant who is called "blessed" (Matthew 24:46), like the wise virgins who are welcomed to the feast (Matthew 25:10), like the good and faithful servants who are commended by their master (Matthew 25:21, 23), and like the sheep who "inherit the kingdom prepared for [them] from the foundation of the world" (Matthew 25:34), so will the believers inherit the blessed promise of life everlasting. These remain unto eternal life.

Notice, again, that the taking and leaving of the text, the judgment of all people, is concurrent with Jesus' second coming. "Therefore, stay awake, for you do not know on what day your Lord is coming" (Matthew 24:42). All of these events—Jesus' return, the resurrection of the dead, the resurrection of the living (the rapture), and the great judgment—occur at the same time. With these words of warning and promise, Jesus would have us, His Church, be ever watchful for His return in glory.

HOW TO READ REVELATION

> "The revelation of
> Jesus Christ . . . "
>
> (Revelation 1:1)

Just like every book of the Bible, the last book of the Scriptures is intended by God to comfort us. This book, though, is especially shrouded in mystery and surrounded with fear and confusion. This is not helped by teachers who bring Revelation to the Church as a chronology of the events preceding the second coming. If we try to understand Revelation through the newspaper, we will certainly miss the comfort and peace that Jesus is delivering to us there.

The visions given to John are often difficult to decode and understand, but we must recognize in this book the voice of Jesus, the Lamb of God seated on the throne. We see in these visions that Jesus, who was crucified for us, is now enthroned for us, and He will, on the Last Day, return to rescue us.

We will, then, consider five rules for reading Revelation, with the hopes that this book will deliver to us the joy of our salvation, and that we would all, when our last hour comes, join the crowd around the throne of Jesus singing His praises.

RULE 1: REMEMBER WHO IS BEING REVEALED: JESUS

The first words are the most important: "The revelation of Jesus Christ . . . " (Revelation 1:1). It is Jesus being revealed. When Jesus ascended into heaven, "a cloud took Him out of [the disciples'] sight" (Acts 1:9). We still cannot see Him. The devil takes advantage of this to tempt us. "Jesus has left you. He has abandoned you. He has forgotten you." Especially in times of trouble or persecution, it is easy to think that the Lord has left us as orphans.

This was the case when John wrote Revelation. John was the bishop in Ephesus, the overseer of all the churches in the region. The Roman emperor was persecuting the Christians. Persecution always started with the bishops and pastors. John, then, was in exile, living in a cave on the little island of Patmos. The Christians were suffering, forced to worship the Caesar or be fined, beaten, or even killed. How easy would it be for the Christians to think that Jesus had forgotten them.

So the Holy Spirit pulls back the veil and gives John a glimpse of heaven, of the throne room of God, and there is Jesus. Still alive. Still in charge. Still loving and serving His Church. This is what Revelation is revealing: Jesus our Savior.

RULE 2: REMEMBER WHO REVELATION IS FOR: THE CHURCH OF ALL TIME

If Revelation is an unfolding of the events immediately preceding the Last Day, it becomes a useless book for the last two thousand years of Church history. But John says that this is the revelation "God gave him to show to His servants the things that must soon take place" (Revelation 1:1). The things revealed were not long-distant, future events. The Church was getting a picture of the spiritual reality of their days. John sees the spiritual contours of the troubles on earth, and He sees the blessed reality of heaven. This vision of heaven is to correct and comfort the Church of all time. The audience of Revelation is not simply the people on the cusp of the apocalypse. It is for Christians in every place and time who are tempted to think that God is far off.

Any interpretation of Revelation that excludes any part or era of the Church is wrong. The entire New Testament era is the "last days" (Hebrews 1:2), and the second coming of Jesus is always, for the Church, right around the corner.

RULE 3: SCRIPTURE INTERPRETS SCRIPTURE

This a rule for reading all of the Bible. It is especially important when reading Revelation. Over half of the verses in Revelation allude to some Old Testament text. It is especially important for us to know the other parts of the Bible when studying Revelation. Revelation uses pictures to communicate, and these pictures are mostly drawn from the other parts of the Bible.

The understanding that Scripture interprets Scripture has further application. Some passages of the Bible are clearer than others. In some places, the Bible speaks directly to a certain doctrine. We use the clear passages to interpret the less clear passages, which mostly means we use the rest of the Scriptures to understand Revelation.

RULE 4: PUT TOGETHER WHAT YOU HEAR AND WHAT YOU SEE

When reading Revelation, it is important to pay attention to what John *hears* and what John *sees*. Oftentimes, John will hear the angel preaching, and then he will see what was being preached about. The seeing and the hearing are quite different, but they are describing the same thing. A few examples will be helpful.

In Revelation 4, John is brought into the throne room of God and sees the heavenly worship. In chapter 5, John sees a scroll in the right hand of God. While the text doesn't tell us what is written on the scroll, we know it is important that the scroll be opened. In fact, when no one is found worthy to open the scroll, John begins to weep. "And no one in heaven or on earth or under the earth was able to open the scroll or to look into it, and I began to weep loudly because no one was found worthy to open the scroll or to look into it" (Revelation 5:3–4). This, it turns out, is the Book of Life, and the reading of this book is our salvation.

One of the elders around the throne comforts John with this news: "Weep no more; behold, the Lion of the tribe of Judah, the Root of David, has conquered, so that he can open the scroll and its seven seals" (Revelation 5:5). John hears the report that the Lion of Judah is worthy to open the seals. Then John looks, and this is what he sees: "And between the throne and the four living creatures and among the elders I saw a Lamb standing, as though it had been slain" (Revelation 5:6). John hears the sermon of the Lion, and then he sees the completely contrary vision of the Lamb. But look, this Lion and Lamb are the same. They are both Jesus. He is the Lion of Judah who overcame death and destroyed the devil. He is the Lamb of God who takes away the sin of the world. Comparing what is heard with what is seen gives us a fuller understanding of the visions.

Another example is in chapter 7. This is a favorite passage of comfort, with the saints coming out of the great tribulation, their filthy robes made white in the blood of the Lamb. John hears, first, the preaching, "And I heard the number of the sealed, 144,000, sealed from every tribe of the sons of Israel: 12,000 from the tribe of Judah were sealed, 12,000 from the tribe of Reuben, 12,000 from the tribe of Gad" (vv. 4–5), and so forth, with 12,000 sealed from each of the tribes. This is a very orderly assembly with the precise number of people drawn up in formation.

Then John sees this assembly:

> After this I looked, and behold, a great multitude that no one could number, from every nation, from all tribes and peoples and languages, standing before the throne and before the Lamb, clothed in white robes, with palm branches in their hands, and crying out with a loud voice, "Salvation belongs to our God who sits on the throne, and to the Lamb!" (Revelation 7:9–10)

The 144,000 is the innumerable multitude, the saints of the Lord brought from death to life in Jesus' name. Again, the thing that is heard and the thing that is seen are described as opposites of each other, but they are, in fact, descriptions of the same thing, in this case, the Church.

Putting together what is heard with what is seen will help piece together the seemingly disparate visions of Revelation.

RULE 5: NOTICE THE MOVEMENT FROM EARTH TO HEAVEN

"Revelation" is a translation of the Greek word *apokalypsis*, or *apocalypse* in English. *Apocalypse* means an unveiling, and that is what the visions of Revelation do. Unseen spiritual realities are unveiled. The curtain is pulled back so we might see the spiritual activity on earth and in heaven.

John gets a glimpse of the troubles of this earth, the work of the devil that is driving the persecution of the Church and the troubles of the Christians. John sees the beast, the false prophet, the whore, the dragon, all the spiritual forces of wickedness gathered together to assault the Church. He sees behind the troubles to the demonic forces pulling the strings. What a mess! We see these realities in his visions and are ready to despair.

But then the angel carries John into heaven to see how things are there, to see if Jesus is still on the throne. The angel takes John (and us) to see the unseen heavenly realities. In heaven, we see the Lamb, the Slain One, the Crucified and Raised Friend of Sinners, and He is on the throne. The saints and angels are still gathered around singing His praises. All is well.

Then we go back down to earth to see more of the trouble: the seals are being opened, the trumpets are being blown, bowls of wrath are being poured out, there is darkness and disease, rivers of blood and piles of corpses. And just when we've had enough, the angels come again to take us back to heaven, to get another glimpse of the throne. There sits Jesus, our Jesus, and all is well.

Notice, when you read Revelation, how the visions move back and forth between earth and heaven. There are visions of earthly trouble and heavenly comfort. The purpose of this back and forth is to assure us, in the midst of all of our troubles, that Jesus is still seated at the Father's right hand. This is our hope and confidence in the midst of affliction, Jesus our Savior sits on the throne. In Revelation, the brightness of heaven shines through the gloom of this earthly life. We get a glimpse of heaven, and Jesus is there. We get a glimpse of eternity, and Jesus is there. We get a glimpse of the judgment throne, and Jesus is there. We get a glimpse of the resurrection, of the eternal state, and Jesus is there. We get a glimpse of life beyond trouble, beyond death, beyond the grave, and Jesus is there, and we are with Him. We "will see His face" (Revelation 22:4).

This revelation of Jesus, then, is a comforting foretaste of the revelation of Jesus and the glory

and kindness that await His people. Jesus is coming soon, and this is our great hope and prayer. "Come, Lord Jesus." Amen.

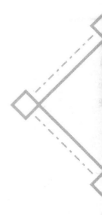

CHAPTER ELEVEN

SURPRISED BY THE GOSPEL

"In Him we have redemption through His blood, the forgiveness of our trespasses, according to the riches of His grace."
(Ephesians 1:7)

The Gospel is never earned, never deserved, never expected. The forgiveness of sins is always a gift, freely given by God in His mercy. This means that the Gospel is always a surprise.

We daily sin much and deserve from the Lord anger and punishment. The more we know about ourselves and the Lord's Law, the more we know what we deserve, and it isn't pretty: death, judgment, condemnation, hell. But instead, we find Jesus—dead, buried, raised for us. He comes to us not in anger, but in kindness; not in wrath, but in weakness and mercy. Jesus is always bearing with us, forgiving us, smiling on us. We always expect judgment, we always deserve judgment, but we always get the cross, an overflowing of mercy, a flood of grace.

> The saying is trustworthy and deserving of full acceptance, that Christ Jesus came into the world to save sinners. (1 Timothy 1:15)

> For while we were still weak, at the right time Christ died for the ungodly. For one will scarcely die for a righteous person—though perhaps for a good person one would dare even to die—but God showed His love for us in that while we were still sinners, Christ died for us. (Romans 5:6–8)

The weak, the ungodly, the sinners: that is you and me, the doomed and despairing, but Jesus came for such as us. He came to die for us, rescue and deliver and save us.

For years, I lived and labored in the theological wasteland of American Christianity, and this was the trouble: there was no hope for me. Everything was centered on me, my works, my life, my experiences and excitement, my resolve and sincerity. There was no kindness and mercy for me. There was no certainty or comfort. There was no Gospel.

But then the Gospel came, the promises, the forgiveness, the surprise of God's love in Christ. And it is still a surprise. It is the most joyous and wonderful constant surprise: Jesus is for me.

Sin . . . Forgiven . . . for You

> "With You there is forgiveness, that You may be feared."
> (Psalm 130:4)

I met a man the other day who told me, "I've done too many terrible things."

"Do you think," I asked him, "that the death of Jesus was only for little sins that don't matter?"

"I don't think I'm savable," he told me.

"Well, if you want to take Jesus off the cross, go ahead and try. But you can't. He will be the Lord crucified for you. He will be the Savior who takes all your sins and punishment, and He is nailed with them to the cross for you. Jesus is a better Savior than you are a sinner." Christ died for sinners.

{ The Gospel is always a surprise. }

We've talked in this book about the pendulum of pride and despair, but we can see, at last, how they are really two sides of the same coin. Despair is a hidden form of pride. If I despair of God's love, then I have an incredibly high view of myself, my power, and my sin—as if my sin is strong enough or great enough to keep me from God. When I despair of God's mercy and kindness, then I am really saying that I know better than God what is true, that He is lying when He tells me His Son died for me and all my sins are forgiven.

Despair, then, is only another face for pride, and pride is idolatry. Pride is fear and love and trust of something other than our gracious God and Savior. "I'm too dirty for Jesus to love. I'm too bad for Jesus to save." Is that right? Is it all about you? Are you that good at being bad?

You are only unsavable if Jesus says you are unsavable. He doesn't. You are only unforgiven if Jesus says you are unforgiven. He doesn't. Jesus over and over in the Scriptures comes to us with kindness and mercy, with promises of life and salvation, with forgiveness of our sins.

"Behold, the Lamb of God, who takes away the sin of the world!" (John 1:29). John the Baptist preached with his finger pointing at Jesus and his words pointed at you. Your sin, all of it, was died for by Jesus and is covered with His blood. Everyone who believes this promise is among the blessed company of those whom "He has delivered . . . from the domain of darkness and transferred . . . to the kingdom of His beloved Son, in whom we have redemption, the forgiveness of sins" (Colossians 1:13–14).

The devil is constantly tempting us to think that our sins don't need forgiving or that our sins can't be forgiven or that the death of Jesus somehow missed us. You know how this is, in your mind and heart and conscience, like we arrived at the airport late and missed the flight to forgiveness. We, though, have the comforting certainty of the Scriptures, the very Word of God. "In Him we have redemption through His blood, the forgiveness of our trespasses, according to the riches of His grace" (Ephesians 1:7).

Martin Luther, reflecting on what the Church is, said, "Everything, therefore, in the Christian Church is ordered toward this goal: we shall daily receive in the Church nothing but the forgiveness of sin through the Word and signs, to comfort and encourage our consciences as long as we live here" (LC II 55).

In your Baptism, the Lord forgave your sins. In the Lord's Supper, the Lord continues to forgive your sins. In the Absolution and the preaching of the Gospel, the forgiveness of your sins is planted in your ears and heart. In the Scriptures, you hear the voice of Jesus, your Good Shepherd, the one who laid down His life for the sheep, calling you to His comfort and peace.

> Come to Me, all who labor and are heavy laden, and I will give you rest. Take My yoke upon you, and learn from Me, for I am gentle and lowly in heart, and you will find rest for your souls. For My yoke is easy, and My burden is light. (Matthew 11:28–30)

We rest in the confidence that God is not mad at us, that God's wrath is spent, that heaven is open, that God smiles at us, that our life is eternal, and that we have the Holy Spirit with His gifts of joy and comfort and peace, all through the death of Jesus, and all delivered to us in the forgiveness of our sins, in the forgiveness of your sins.

Jesus' voice reaches into every corner of our heart and conscience and sweeps out every bit of guilt. The flood of His merciful blood washes away every sin, even the greatest and most horrendous, even the smallest and most innocent, all of it. This is not a onetime event; it is our life, so that even when we reach the eternal joys of heaven, we will be clothed in the white robes of the righteousness of Christ. We will eternally wear the forgiveness of sins. We are forever dressed in the forgiveness of sins. "These are the ones coming out of the great tribulation. They have washed their robes and made them white in the blood of the Lamb" (Revelation 7:14).

Our eternal life is the eternal, glorious, triumphant "therefore" to the forgiveness of our sins.

> *Therefore* they are before the throne of God, and serve Him day and night in His temple; and He who sits on the throne will shelter them with His presence. They shall hunger no more, neither thirst anymore; the sun shall not strike them, nor any scorching heat. For the Lamb in the midst of the throne will be their shepherd, and He will guide them to springs of living water, and God will wipe away every tear from their eyes. (Revelation 7:15–17, emphasis added)

THE DEVIL . . . DESTROYED . . . FOR YOU

> "And the great dragon was thrown down, that ancient serpent, who is called the devil and Satan, the deceiver of the whole world—he was thrown down to the earth, and his angels were thrown down with him." (Revelation 12:9)

When we look at the world and at ourselves, it looks as if everything is falling apart. It looks as if the devil is sitting on the throne and ruling and reigning in this world. If we look around, things look bleak.

If we were "Look-Aroundists," if we got our doctrine from the newspaper and television, we would probably believe that the devil is loose, free, totally unhindered, and in charge. After all, things are bad and getting worse, we are racing toward destruction.

We are not Look-Aroundists. We do not learn what is true and false in the world simply by looking around. We learn what is true from the Scriptures, and there we learn that the devil and his kingdom are destroyed.

Hebrews teaches this in no uncertain terms.

> Since therefore the children share in flesh and blood, He Himself likewise partook of the same things, that through death He might destroy the one who has the power of death, that is, the devil, and deliver all those who through fear of death were subject to lifelong slavery. (Hebrews 2:14–15)

We are flesh and blood, we have bodies, so Jesus partook of the same; He took up our humanity so that He might die. He, the Bible teaches, took up a body so that He could be nailed to the cross. He took up blood so that it could be spilled for us and our salvation. He did these things that "He might destroy the one who has the power of death, that is, the devil."

Jesus, in His death, has destroyed the devil. He has rescued you from the bondage of the fear of death, and He has taken those same chains that held us in fear and used then to bind the devil, to throw him in prison, to demolish his authority.

In the Book of Job, we see a frightful picture. The angels of God present themselves to the Lord, and the devil is there with them (Job 1:6). The devil in heaven? Yes, and he is there doing his devil work. Remember, *Satan* is the Hebrew word for "accuser," and that is exactly what the devil is doing in heaven. He is accusing Job of sin. We see the same frightful scene in Zechariah 3:1. The devil stands before the Lord to accuse the high priest Joshua. The devil has a place in the council of the Lord, and he stands there accusing us of our sin. The worst part of this is that the devil's accusations are true. We are sinners. We are guilty. We do deserve the Lord's temporal and eternal punishment.

{ The devil's accusations are true. We are sinners. We are guilty. }

But the devil is not the only one to stand before the Lord. Revelation 12 gives us a beautiful glimpse into the heavenly court. Jesus was born, died, raised, and ascended into heaven to the right hand of God (12:1–6). This is the result:

> Now war arose in heaven, Michael and his angels fighting against the dragon. And the dragon and his angels fought back, but he was defeated, and there was no longer any place for them in heaven. And the great dragon was thrown down, that ancient serpent, who is called the devil and Satan, the deceiver of the whole world—he was thrown down to the earth, and his angels were thrown down with him. And I heard a loud voice in heaven, saying, "Now the salvation and the power and the kingdom of our God and the authority of His Christ have come, for the accuser of our brothers has been thrown down, who accuses them day and night before our God. And they have conquered him by the blood of the Lamb and by the word of their testimony, for they loved not their lives even unto death. Therefore, rejoice, O heavens and you who dwell in them! But woe to you, O earth and sea, for the devil has come down to you in great wrath, because he knows that his time is short!" (Revelation 12:7–12)

Jesus brings His blood into the heavenly court. He brings His suffering and death as evidence to the Father, and the result is that the devil has nothing to condemn. Everything is forgiven! The blood of Jesus, like a flood, drives the devil from heaven. It silences his accusations. It robs him of his power. The devil's claim on you is broken by the death of Jesus.

{ **The blood of Jesus silences the devil's accusations.** }

Knowing this truth, that the devil's accusations have been silenced, Paul writes some of the most comforting words in the Bible:

> If God is for us, who can be against us? He who did not spare His own Son but gave Him up for us all, how will He not also with Him graciously give us all things? Who shall bring any charge against God's elect? It is God who justifies. Who is to condemn? Christ Jesus is the one who died—more than that, who was raised—who is at the right hand of God, who indeed is interceding for us. Who shall separate us from the love of Christ? Shall tribulation,

or distress, or persecution, or famine, or nakedness, or danger, or sword? As it is written, "For Your sake we are being killed all the day long; We are regarded as sheep to be slaughtered." No, in all these things we are more than conquerors through Him who loved us. For I am sure that neither death nor life, nor angels nor rulers, nor things present nor things to come, nor powers, nor height nor depth, nor anything else in all creation, will be able to separate us from the love of God in Christ Jesus our Lord. (Romans 8:31–39)

By the death of Jesus, the devil is destroyed, for you.

DEATH . . . SWALLOWED UP . . . FOR YOU

"Death is natural." I hear that lie all the time. "Death is part of life." We use these clichés to comfort ourselves in the face of death, but they are not true. Death is not natural. It is not part of life. We are not supposed to die. Adam and Eve were not supposed to die, and neither were you.

> "Death is swallowed up in victory."
> (1 Corinthians 15:54)

"In the day that you eat of it you shall surely die" (Genesis 2:17). Death is the punishment for sin. "The wages of sin is death" (Romans 6:23). We are dying because we are sinners. Death is our enemy. And death is God's enemy.

There is some comfort for us in the fact that Jesus doesn't like death. Jesus wept when He heard Lazarus was dead (John 11:35). He wept because He loved Lazarus, and He wept because He hated death.

The Scriptures call death the "last enemy," and it is an enemy that Jesus fights, that Jesus will destroy. "The last enemy to be destroyed is death" (1 Corinthians 15:26).

Every time Jesus encountered death in His earthly ministry, He undid it. He raised the dead. One of those accounts is in Luke 7:11–17. Jesus and His disciples traveled to a little village called Nain, and a large crowd traveled with Him. As they came to the gate of the town, they met another large crowd coming out of town, a funeral procession.

This was a funeral like any other funeral. There was a dead man and his mourning mother. Luke tells us that this woman was a widow. She had already suffered the loss of her husband, and she was weeping, undone.

These two processions met at the gate. We know what happens when a funeral procession comes down the road. We pull over; we stand to the side. This is what Jesus and His disciples should have done. They should have stood to the side and let the funeral pass, perhaps even join in. Jesus didn't.

Jesus stood there, right in the middle of the road, right in the way, and when the casket reached Him, He reached out His hand and stopped this funeral procession. Imagine being there. Here is some rabbi, a stranger, standing in the middle of the road, stopping a funeral procession, telling you to stop crying, interrupting your son's funeral. This is unheard of.

There is a difference in the way our Lord Jesus thinks of death and the way we think of it. There's a difference between the way the Lord treats death and the way we do.

There's a word used of death in the Bible that will be helpful to bring out here: *reigned*. "Yet death *reigned* from Adam to Moses, even over those whose sinning was not like the transgression of Adam, who was a type of the one who was to come" (Romans 5:14, emphasis added). "Because of one man's trespass, death *reigned* through that one man" (Romans 5:17, emphasis added). Death reigned. Death ruled. Death was in charge, it had its way, it was king.

That is why we stand aside as funeral processions go by. Death is to be reverenced, respected, honored, even feared.

But Jesus isn't concerned with death's honor. In fact, Jesus doesn't care much for death at all, and He's not afraid to bring shame to death. This is important for us to remember: Jesus doesn't like death.

Jesus doesn't come to grips with death. He doesn't accept death. In fact, everything that Jesus does is fighting against death. It is Jesus, after all, who came out of the grave on the third day and put an end to death's rule and reign forever.

But while our Lord looks at death with disdain, He looks quite differently at the victims of death, at us. We have it here in the text, wonderful words that occur often: "And when the Lord saw her [that is, the grieving mother], He had compassion on her and said to her, 'Do not weep' " (Luke 7:13). Jesus saw this woman walking in a veil of tears, mourning the loss of her son (and no doubt her late husband as well), and He felt for her. He was moved, and His guts churned for her.

Jesus hates death, and He loves this dear woman.

How wonderful are these words! We are not only told what Jesus did and what He said, but even what He felt! If we are tempted to think that our Lord and God is distant, aloof, cold, unmoving, and unmoved, this word *compassion* undoes that temptation. Jesus has compassion on this woman, and He has the same compassion for you.

{ The Lord's compassion . . . is behind His hatred of death. }

It is the Lord's compassion for this woman and for you that is behind His hatred of death. Jesus wants to have us in life, even eternal life, and He knows that death stands in the way. But nothing will stop the Lord's compassion. Nothing can stand in the way of His love. There is nothing, not even death and the grave, that will stand between you and your Jesus.

There He was, standing in the middle of the gate of Nain with His hand on the coffin of this dead man, looking with compassion at this woman, when Jesus said, "Young man, I say to you, arise" (Luke 7:14). And the dead man sat up and began to speak, and Jesus gave him to his mother.

Jesus, with a word,

UNDOES DEATH;

UNDOES SADNESS;

UNDOES TEARS;

UNDOES THIS FUNERAL PROCESSION;

UNDOES THE RULING AND REIGNING OF DEATH IN THIS VILLAGE OF NAIN.

Jesus does not step aside and let death pass by; He stands in the way. He stops the great procession of death, the great funeral march that was the history of mankind. Jesus stands there in the way of death and won't let it pass.

There is a problem. Even though we don't like death, we do deserve it. Death is our just wages. "The wages of sin is death" (Romans 6:23). "In the day that you eat of it you shall surely die" (Genesis 2:17). This is a problem, because while both Jesus and you don't want you to die, you must. It is the punishment God has appointed for you and your sins. This man being carried out of Nain to his grave deserved to die; he was a sinner. And you deserve to die. You, too, are a sinner.

> **"For God did not send His Son into the world to condemn the world, but in order that the world might be saved through Him."**
> (John 3:17)

But so great is Jesus' love for you and all mankind that He took care of that too. He died in our place, suffered in our place, hung on the cross in the shame and wrath that belongs to us. Jesus hates death so much that He submitted to death for you. Jesus, on the cross, took the wrath out of death. He took the punishment out of death. He took the judgment out of death. He took the fear out of death.

Because of His resurrection, because Jesus refused to stay dead but rose on the third day, your Jesus won't let you stay dead either. When our last hour comes, we will rest in the grave, our souls carried by the angels into heaven, but this will be only for a little while. Soon, Jesus' voice will ring out over the world and call us all from the grave. That voice will be the fulfillment of all our hopes and prayers. On that great Last Day, the Lord Jesus will have us with Him in life, beyond the reach of sin and trouble and tears, beyond the reach of death and the grave.

ON THE LAST DAY,

our graves will be as empty as the grave of Jesus. He has swallowed up death, destroyed it, for you.

You will be raised, full of life and immortality and light to see the Lord face-to-face and rejoice forever in His kindness and peace.

When the perishable puts on the imperishable, and the mortal puts on immortality, then shall come to pass the saying that is written: "Death is swallowed up in victory." "O death, where is your victory? O death, where is your sting?" The sting of death is sin, and the power of sin is the law. But thanks be to God, who gives us the victory through our Lord Jesus Christ. (1 Corinthians 15:54–57)

Amen

American Christianity starts with me, continues with my works, finds comfort in my closeness to God, and is always looking inside for hope and peace. This is the perfect recipe for pride and despair, for a trust in ourselves or fear of God's judgment. The Scriptures give us something different, something better. In the Scriptures, we find God long-suffering, abounding in steadfast love, with an abundance of mercy for us. And the Lord has preserved this teaching in the world.

It might seem like American Christianity is a vast wasteland, a desert with no comfort and no peace, but there are outposts of the Gospel, streams of living water flowing from pulpits, from fonts and altars where Jesus is pleased to serve His forgiveness. These congregations are normally not very flashy, not very large, and not very exciting. They are humble churches with humble people and pastors whose treasure is the pure Word of God, Law and Gospel, and the Sacraments.

There is an alternative to American Christianity.

I never thought I would end up in the Lutheran Church, but here, in the last place I expected it, was the simplicity of Christ, the clarity of the Scriptures, the sharpness of the Law, and the sweetness of the Gospel. Here, in the Lutheran Church, the Lord's mercy found me, His promises took hold of me, and His Gospel surprised and delighted me. Here my sins are absolved. Here my conscience is comforted. Here I hear the voice of my Good Shepherd, Jesus, surprising me with His mercy and calling me to be His own.

And calling you, also, to come to His rest, the forgiveness of all your sins.

> Come to Me, all who labor and are heavy laden, and I will give you rest. Take My yoke upon you, and learn from Me, for I am gentle and lowly in heart, and you will find rest for your souls. For My yoke is easy, and My burden is light. (Matthew 11:28–30)

Amen.

INTRODUCING THE BOOK OF CONCORD
CONFESSING AND THE LUTHERAN CONFESSIONS

"So everyone who acknowledges Me before men, I also will acknowledge before My Father who is in heaven."
(Matthew 10:32)

One of the slogans of American Christianity is "No creed but the Bible." It is ironic that this little quip is itself a creed!

American Christianity is suspicious of creeds and confessions. Because they are not contained between the covers of the Bible, it is assumed that creeds and confessions are the "doctrines of men," corrupt and full of error. I remember asking once, "Why say the Apostles' Creed when you could say the words of Jesus?"

This suspicion of creeds and confessions also makes a person suspicious of creedal and confessional churches. I remember the first time I saw a Book of Concord, the collection of Lutheran confessional writings. I balked. If you have the Bible, what more do you need? If the Lutherans believed in the Bible alone, why did they add these writings? How is this any different from the Book of Mormon?

"I'm not a Lutheran or a Methodist or a Baptist; I'm a Christian. I follow Christ." Indeed, all of these churches claim to draw their teaching from the Bible alone. But they disagree with one another. They have different doctrines about the Bible, about Jesus and His work, about salvation, Baptism, the Lord's Supper, the second coming, the Christian life, and any number of other things.

There are theological differences between the different denominations—many and important differences. But they are not unlimited; in fact, these differences fall into a handful of categories. The names of the different confessions are simply a shorthand way of speaking of these differences. You could say, "I believe in the Bible as the only source of theology, in man's total depravity, in God's sovereignty in salvation, that God elects some to salvation and others to damnation, that Jesus died only for the elect, that the Lord's Supper is a communion with the divine but not with the human nature of Christ, and that Baptism initiates us into the covenant of grace and unites us with the Church." Or you could say, "I'm a Calvinist." Same thing, just easier to say.

A second result of this anti-confessional attitude is an aversion to studying Church history, or at least an aversion to thinking that Church history actually matters. It is as if, in the mind of most American Christians, there was a time warp between the imprisonment of Paul and the day they were born.

The various names of the different denominations are simply shorthand for a body of teaching, mostly articulated through the history of the Church as various errors tried to creep in. The creeds of the Early Church were especially important in fending off Arianism (the teaching that Jesus was not God, but rather the first and greatest of God's creations) and other errors about Jesus and the teaching of the Trinity.

The confessions of the Reformation took up the teachings of salvation, the Scriptures, the Sacraments, and the Church. The more we know our Church history, the less likely we are to repeat the same errors. The Church of Jesus is always standing up and teaching, confessing, asserting the truth, and resisting untruth.

Jesus tells His disciples, "So everyone who acknowledges Me before men, I also will acknowledge before My Father who is in heaven" (Matthew 10:32). To *acknowledge* something is to *confess* it. Jesus, then, requires the Church to confess. Jesus not only authorizes His Church to have creeds and confessions, but He also demands it. The confessions of a church are its answer to Jesus' question: "Who do you say that I am?" (Matthew 16:15). We rejoice that Jesus puts His truth in our mouths.

{ There is an alternative to American Christianity. }

The Lutheran Church is, then, a confessing church. The official Confession of the Lutheran Church is called the Book of Concord. It is a collection of documents first published in 1580. For a text over four hundred years old, the Book of Concord continues to prove itself incredibly useful today. It has a profound understanding of the Holy Scriptures as well as our human nature, and it brings the Law and the Gospel to bear on the theological disputes of its day.

Lutherans do not consider the Confessions above or equal to the Scriptures. Rather, the Book of Concord sits under the Scriptures, confessing their truth and rejecting the errors they reject. Only the Scriptures are infallible, and we hold to the Book of Concord because it is a correct exposition and application of the Scriptures.

A study of the Book of Concord is a study of the teachings of the Scriptures, and the discovery of this teaching is the discovery of the pure, wonderful, gracious teaching of the Gospel, the death of Jesus for our salvation.

THE THREE ECUMENICAL CREEDS

THE FIRST THREE DOCUMENTS IN THE BOOK OF CONCORD ARE THE THREE ECUMENICAL CREEDS: THE APOSTLES' CREED, THE NICENE CREED, AND THE ATHANASIAN CREED.

The Apostles' Creed is the most ancient summary of the Christian faith. The three articles of the Creed confess God the Father, Son, and Holy Spirit. The First Article confesses God the Father, Creator of the cosmos. The Second Article confesses Jesus, the Son of God, as God and man who was born of the virgin Mary, suffered, died, rose, ascended into heaven, and is coming again in judgment. The Third Article confesses the Holy Spirit, who creates and sustains the Church, forgives our sins, and will raise us on the Last Day and give us eternal life.

Like all the early creeds of the Church, the Apostles' Creed is especially interested in articulating the two natures of Christ—that Jesus is both God and man and our Savior. We don't know the precise origin of the Apostles' Creed, but it was already old in the fourth century.

The Nicene Creed was composed at the Council of Nicaea in the year 325 and expanded in 381 at the Council of Constantinople. Like the Apostles' Creed, the Nicene Creed has three articles about God the Father, Son, and Holy Spirit. This creed was written especially against a number of false doctrines regarding the Trinity and the two natures of Jesus.

The false doctrine of Arius had made inroads into the Church. Arius taught that Jesus was the first and greatest creation of God, but that He was not God, only of "like substance." In the Nicene Creed, the Church confesses Jesus to be "very God of very God, begotten, not made, being of one substance with the Father."

The Athanasian Creed is the longest creed. It is named for Athanasius (c. 296–373), the great defender of the faith. Even though it was probably not written by Athanasius, it is certainly an articulation of his teaching and the orthodox teaching of the Church. The Athanasian Creed is in two parts. The first articulates the teaching of the Trinity, that there is one God and three persons. The second half of this creed confesses Jesus, His person and work.

THE AUGSBURG CONFESSION

The first uniquely Lutheran document is the Augsburg Confession, presented by a number of German rulers to Emperor Charles V on June 25, 1530.

Martin Luther had written and posted the Ninety-Five Theses thirteen years earlier on October 31, 1517, and the debate they sparked resulted in theological divisions throughout Europe. The Turks were invading from the East, and Charles V called a diet (a meeting with the emperor) to settle the theological divisions and reunite the Holy Roman Empire.

The twenty-eight articles of the Augsburg Confession were compiled by Philip Melanchthon, Martin Luther's colleague at Wittenberg University. The first twenty-one articles articulate the Lutherans' theological position and demonstrate that they were not departing from the Scriptures nor from the historic church. The last seven articles discuss abuses that the Lutheran churches had corrected.

The heart of the Augsburg Confession is Article IV on justification. Our churches teach that people cannot be justified before God by their own strength, merits, or works. People are freely justified for Christ's sake, through faith, when they believe that they are received into favor and that their sins are forgiven for Christ's sake. By His death, Christ made satisfaction for our sins. God counts this faith for righteousness in His sight (Romans 3:21–26; 4:5).

THE APOLOGY OF THE AUGSBURG CONFESSION

The Roman Catholic theologians were not impressed with the Augsburg Confession, so they presented a refutation to Charles V. This refutation was read, but the Lutheran theologians were never given a copy. They did have notes, and from these they prepared a defense of their confession called the Apology of the Augsburg Confession. The Lutheran Church Fathers were not saying they were sorry for the Augsburg Confession. Rather, the word *apology* means "defense," as we use it in the word *apologetics*.

The Apology of the Augsburg Confession is the longest document in the Book of Concord. It was also authored by Philip Melanchthon, and it delves into the biblical basis of the Lutherans' teaching, especially justification through faith, the distinction of the Law and the Gospel, and repentance. It was finished in April 1531.

THE SMALCALD ARTICLES

The Lutherans were always asking for a church council. They wanted to argue and defend their teaching from the Scriptures before the entire church. In 1536, Pope Paul III called for a church council to be held in Mantua. There was debate regarding the Lutheran attendance, and it was clear from the beginning that the Roman Catholic Church was interested in exterminating the Lutherans, not in hearing them. Nevertheless, it was determined that Luther should prepare a confession to be heard in a general council. The result was the document called the Smalcald Articles.

The Smalcald Articles have three parts. The first part is a brief confession of the Trinity and the two natures of Christ. These teachings were not in dispute. The second part has four articles, beginning with the "first and chief article . . . Jesus Christ, our God and Lord, died for our sins and was raised again for our justification" (SA II I 1). Luther then contrasts the Roman Catholic teachings with this first and chief article. The third part unfolds the Lutheran teaching in a less polemic and more pastoral way, beginning with the teaching of sin and the Law, and continuing on to the Gospel and the various ways the Lord brings the Gospel to us.

The Smalcald Articles cover a lot of teaching, but the theological center regards how the Lord brings His mercy and grace to us, through the external Word. The Smalcald Articles were written by Martin Luther and adopted by the Lutheran princes gathered in Smalcald in 1537.

THE POWER AND PRIMACY OF THE POPE

The gathering in Smalcald received Luther's Smalcald Articles but wanted to say more about the specific abuses of the pope. Philip Melanchthon then prepared the Treatise on the Power and Primacy of the Pope. This title is tricky because the document is arguing against the power and primacy of the pope. The Treatise argues against three specific claims that the pope made concerning himself: (1) the pope was supreme over all pastors and bishops by divine right, (2) the pope possesses both temporal and spiritual authority, and (3) it is necessary for salvation to be subject to the pope.

The Treatise was adopted in 1537.

THE SMALL CATECHISM

In 1527, the elector of Saxony authorized a visitation of the churches. Martin Luther and a number of Wittenberg theologians visited the local parishes. Luther wrote about the conditions they found in the churches:

> The deplorable, miserable condition that I discovered recently when I, too, was a visitor, has forced and urged me to prepare this catechism, or Christian doctrine, in this small, plain, simple form. Mercy! Dear God, what great misery I beheld! The common person, especially in the villages, has no knowledge whatever of Christian doctrine. And unfortunately, many pastors are completely unable and unqualified to teach. ‹This is so much so, that one is ashamed to speak of it.› Yet, everyone says that they are Christians, have been baptized, and receive the holy Sacraments, even though they cannot even recite the Lord's Prayer or the Creed or the Ten Commandments. They live like dumb brutes and irrational hogs. Now that the Gospel has come, they have nicely learned to abuse all freedom like experts. (SC Preface 1–3)

Martin Luther, then, wrote a summary of the Bible's teaching called the Small Catechism. The Six Chief Parts of the Small Catechism are (1) the Ten Commandments, (2) the Apostles' Creed, (3) the Lord's Prayer, (4) Baptism, (5) Confession and Absolution, and (6) the Lord's Supper. The parts of the Small Catechism are divided into simple questions and answers and are meant to be taught in the home.

The Small Catechism is the chief teaching tool of the Lutheran Church, and children and adults alike are introduced to the basic teaching of the Scriptures through the Six Chief Parts. Luther also included three minor parts to the Small

Catechism: a table of daily prayers, a table of duties for various vocations, and Christian questions and answers for help in preparing for the Lord's Supper.

The Small Catechism was published in 1529.

THE LARGE CATECHISM

The Large Catechism was published in the same year as the Small, and for similar purposes—to teach the basics of the faith. While the Small Catechism was mainly a tool for parents to use in the home, the Large Catechism was to help pastors know how to teach the faith to their congregations. The Large Catechism teaches the same Six Chief Parts (with a much abbreviated part on Confession). Most of the Large Catechism is unfolding the Ten Commandments and reestablishing order in family, church, and state.

THE FORMULA OF CONCORD

After the death of Martin Luther in February 1546, a number of disputes broke out in the Lutheran churches. Philip Melanchthon moderated his positions in a number of places. Any number of teachers laid claim to the pure doctrine, but they were in conflict with one another. Finally, in 1577, a group of orthodox theologians addressed the controversies and published the Formula of Concord. The twelve articles of the Formula present the various opinions and assert and defend the Lutheran position from the Scriptures, the Augsburg Confession and other Lutheran Confessions, and the writings of Luther and other Fathers of the Church.

There are two unique documents. The Epitome is a basic statement of the twelve articles of the Formula. The Solid Declaration is a detailed explanation and defense of these twelve articles. The Formula of Concord takes up debates about original sin, righteousness, Law and Gospel, good works, election, and so on.

Together these eleven documents declare the Lutheran faith to the world. Congregations and theologians subscribe to these Confessions, thus declaring that these statements of faith are the standard by which they are to be counted as "Lutheran." To be Lutheran is to honor the Word of God. There is no other collection of documents, statements, or books that so clearly, accurately, and comfortingly presents the truths of God's Word and reveals the biblical Gospel as does the Book of Concord.